**Deloitte &
Touche**

Canadian Guide to
PERSONAL FINANCIAL
MANAGEMENT

8th Edition

0 57812 59271 1

Deloitte &
Touche

Canadian Guide to

PERSONAL FINANCIAL MANAGEMENT

8th Edition

John Budd
Claude Rinfret
Richard Daw
Danielle Brien

Prentice Hall Canada Inc., Scarborough, Ontario

Canadian Cataloguing in Publication Data

The National Library of Canada has catalogued this publication as follows:

Main entry under title:

Canadian guide to personal financial management

1986-
Annual.
Vols for 1990-   issued by: Deloitte & Touche
ISSN 1185-7854
ISBN 0-13-059271-4 (1993)

1. Finance, Personal. 2. Finance, Personal -
Canada. I. Deloitte & Touche.

HG179.C35   332.024   C92-030395-1

Prentice-Hall Inc., *Englewood Cliffs, New Jersey*
Prentice-Hall International, Inc., *London*
Prentice-Hall of Australia, Pty., Ltd., *Sydney*
Prentice-Hall of India Pvt., Ltd., *New Delhi*
Prentice-Hall of Japan, Inc., *Tokyo*
Prentice-Hall of Southeast Asia (Pte.) Ltd., *Singapore*
Editora Prentice-Hall do Brasil Ltda., *Rio de Janeiro*
Prentice-Hall Hispanoamericana, S.A., *Mexico*

Cover Design: Carol Giguère
Interior Design: Gail Ferreira Ng-A-Kien
Manufacturing Buyer: Anita Boyle
Composition: Jaytype Inc.

ISBN 0-13-059271-4

Printed and bound in Canada

1   2   3   4   5   97 96 95 94 93

Table of Contents

About the Authors

John Budd, B. Comm., FCA, is a partner in the Toronto office of Deloitte & Touche, one of Canada's "big six" accounting firms. He specializes in corporate taxation, business succession arrangements, estate planning, and personal tax planning. Mr. Budd is a frequent author and lecturer on personal tax and estate planning matters, and he has authored and instructed numerous tax courses for the Canadian Institute of Chartered Accountants. He is also the author of a new book entitled *Second Property Strategies*.

Claude Rinfret, B.Comm., C.A., is a partner in the Vancouver office of Deloitte & Touche. He specializes principally in personal and corporate income tax planning, Canada/U.S. cross-border tax planning and estate planning. He was co-author and lecturer for the B.C. Institute of Chartered Accountants' Introductory Income Tax Course. Mr. Rinfret has presented papers and seminars and authored articles on numerous personal income tax planning topics, and is a member of the committee to oversee the Graduate Diploma programme in Taxation at McGill University.

Richard Daw, C.A., is a tax partner in the St. John's, Newfoundland office of Deloitte & Touche. He practises in personal and corporate tax planning and executive compensation. A frequent lecturer to business groups, Mr. Daw writes a weekly newspaper column on tax planning and is past Chairman of the Legislation Committee of the Institute of Chartered Accountants of Newfoundland.

Danielle Brien is a tax partner in the Montreal office of Deloitte & Touche. She has extensive experience in all areas of personal financial planning, retirement counselling, and estate planning. Ms. Brien has lectured in taxation at McGill University, and for the Canadian Institute of Chartered Accountants. She is the author of numerous articles and courses on taxation matters, and she is a frequent speaker at tax conferences and seminars.

Deloitte & Touche is Canada's second largest firm of chartered accountants and management consultants, with offices coast to coast in some 65 Canadian centres. As a member of Deloitte Touche Tohmatsu International, the firm also serves clients in more than 100 countries around the world.

Acknowledgements

We wish to acknowledge the significant contribution made by Mary Turner, a former partner of Deloitte & Touche, in the preparation of the original version of this book, and the subsequent editions.

We also wish to thank the following Deloitte & Touche tax practitioners for their assistance in the preparation of this eighth edition of the book: Marian Holland, Toronto office; Anne Montgomery, Toronto office; Silvy Niquet, Montreal office; Karen Slezak, Markham office; and Bill Sherman, National office.

Disclaimer

The information and analysis contained in this book are not intended to take the place of competent professional advice. Planning your tax and financial affairs is a complex process — one that is unique to you and your family. The material that follows, and the suggestions for managing your personal finances, are provided solely as a general guide to assist you in understanding the main tax and financial issues that may be relevant in your situation. While every effort has been made to ensure accuracy, the authors cannot accept any responsibility for the financial consequences of any errors or omissions that may have been made.

Preface

In the eight years since the first edition of this book was published, much has happened in the financial world, including the worst recession since the 1930s. Major tax changes in Canada, changes in the RRSP and pension rules, high unemployment rates, drastically reduced interest rates and a near-zero rate of inflation in 1993, all make the process of achieving financial security more difficult and uncertain than ever before. In this eighth edition, we continue to include up-to-date information to help you deal with today's financial complexities.

We have often observed when counselling our clients that a salary of $75,000 or even $125,000 a year does not necessarily prevent financial worries or difficulties. Most of our executive and professional clients needed our help because they felt uneasy about their current financial situation or their financial future. Many had incomes that, after taxes, just barely covered their expenditures. As a result, few were setting money aside for investments, even though most doubted that their pensions alone would pay for the retirement lifestyle they desired. They needed to analyse their financial objectives systematically, and didn't know exactly where to begin.

With this book, we extend to you the same help that we offer the people who attend our executive workshops and those we counsel on an individual basis. Follow the step-by-step instructions and use the forms provided and you will develop a comprehensive financial plan that will make the things you want more attainable and your financial future more secure.

If you develop your own personal financial plan as outlined in this book, you could save thousands of dollars in professional fees charged by financial planners to do the same thing for you. This book should also help you minimize your income taxes, increase your investment return, improve your retirement planning and transfer your estate with less emotional and financial cost.

As you read this book, remember that it reflects applicable tax laws and regulations as of July 31, 1993. Income tax laws and other legislation relevant to personal financial management are continually changing. You should consult your professional advisors to consider the effect of any subsequent changes.

It is very easy to deal first with other "more important" or "more immediate" tasks and delay indefinitely a review of your financial situation. This can result in missed opportunities and the deferral of, or even failure to achieve, key financial objectives. By taking action on your personal financial plan now, you can improve your investment strategy and make progress in retirement planning and other areas, as well as control your current tax expenditures.

John Budd
Claude Rinfret
Richard Daw
Danielle Brien

1

PERSONAL FINANCIAL PLANNING

The objective of this book is very simple — to help you get better control of your life financially. Money should not be the central concern of your life, but the management of money is necessary in order to reach lifetime objectives — to provide funds for a home, for schooling, for travel and other leisure-time activities, for creating new employment opportunities, for retiring comfortably.

Life is exciting and challenging because it is full of opportunities and choices — a choice of what to study, what job to pursue, what hobby to take up, whom to marry, and on and on. Each choice has a *consequence*. A choice once made means a foregone opportunity, for a while or permanently. Your choice of university or college, career path, spouse, where to live, how to live, whether to have children and how to raise them, will affect what future alternatives will be available to you.

Financial planning also involves a series of choices and consequences. One of the countless examples that could be given here is that of a middle-aged couple who consulted us once late in April, after they had completed their tax returns. They complained that they paid too much in taxes and had decided they needed a tax shelter (their *choice*). We asked them whether they had ever owned a tax shelter. They said they had. "How did you do?" we asked. They replied, "We lost everything" (the *consequence*). We then asked them for specific and detailed information in order to get a complete picture of their needs and circumstances. From the data they gave us, it became quite clear to us, and also to them after subsequent discussion, that the key issue for them was an adequate retirement income. Therefore they did not need a tax shelter, which is usually risky. They needed safe investments that would give a reliable return.

The analysis of choices and consequences is the essence of decision-making. To make good financial decisions, you need good information about your financial situation and the options available to you. For example, parents wishing to fund their children's university or college education should estimate how much this will cost, plan how they will finance the expenditure, and learn about the ways available to reduce this cost through certain tax-planning strategies. In some situations, it is possible to reduce the cost by fifty percent or more. (Some ideas are discussed in Chapter 11.)

To have the financial resources you want in order to reach your goals, you also need *commitment*. You need to commit time and attention to following through on your financial choices. We have often helped clients to identify options that are financially sound. But nothing happens. They always have something else to do that seems more urgent, or they leave all financial planning and whatever actions that may entail for some vague time in the future when there may be nothing more urgent to do. Few of them realize what or how much they stand to lose, but some know it exactly.

Failure to act does not always have drastic consequences, but the time and attention devoted to planning your finances and taking the requisite action will generally result in far greater returns or savings than time spent on other, seemingly more urgent, tasks.

WHY DO IT?

All of us have read or heard about some wealthy people who pay surprisingly little in taxes. In contrast, most executives and professionals who earn between $75,000 and $125,000 a year pay a third or more of their income in taxes. After that, little is left for any investments, and those investments are often made on the strength of a sales pitch, a chance conversation at a club or a cocktail party, or some newspaper article. On the other hand, the wealthy usually make use of experienced financial advisors, who plan their clients' investments carefully and advise them on how to take advantage of tax-saving opportunities.

Maybe you can't afford the financial advisors that the more affluent can, but you can afford the time and effort to develop your plan as outlined in this book. If you do, you may be able to save between $5,000 and $8,000 in annual professional fees charged by financial planners to do the same thing for you. And if you do decide to use a financial advisor, the plan you develop by following this book will allow you to organize your financial information and communicate more effectively with your financial advisor.

People who have attended our executive seminars tell us quite often that financial planning has made a greater difference to them than a raise in salary. Whatever objectives they had — travel, cars, boats, buying or remodelling a home, a good education for their children, a comfortable retirement — they either reached or felt more confident of reaching. Once they learned the planning process and understood what was involved, they found the means to increase their net worth and their investments.

HOW TO DO IT

In our seminars, we often ask the question, "How many of you have taken a course in financial planning in university, college or high school?" Only about two percent of the participants say they have. So most people need a way to start, a structure to follow, and methods of organizing financial information, having it readily available, and keeping it up-to-date. They also need financial planning techniques and ideas for making good choices.

This book will provide both a structure for planning and managing your finances systematically and ideas and techniques to help you accumulate sufficient resources to reach your goals. The book has two basic components: its text and its forms. Between them, they will give you most of the help you need to develop a personal financial plan tailored exactly to your own particular objectives, circumstances, and obligations.

The text covers every important area of personal financial management and explains its function, showing you how to identify and evaluate alternative courses of action. It also explains and comments on each of the forms you will be asked to fill in. The forms on which you will list your financial and personal data are at the back of the book.

You may wonder whether or not to bother with the forms. If you want to make proper use of your financial resources and the financial options open to you, then fill in the forms. In that process, you will do all of the following:

- Assemble and organize all your financial data and documents.
- Calculate your present net worth.
- Analyse your present income, expenditures, and insurance coverage.
- Project your future needs, income, and expenditures.
- Identify your personal and economic objectives and their relative priorities.
- Identify the financial strategies for achieving these objectives.
- Use your projections to minimize your income tax, select your investments and plan your retirement income.

The process of financial planning we explain in this text and the forms we have included can be applied to anyone's situation. We have used the process and forms in counselling single people, married couples without children, married couples with children, divorced people, old and young people, the very wealthy and the not-so-wealthy. We may use examples in the book to clarify a point or to illustrate a form. The people in the examples may not be like you. But don't turn off at that point, because the *process* we will be explaining will be relevant to you.

You will apply the process to your situation by completing the forms with *your* data. You will be asked to make some estimates of *your* future. When you make such estimates, do not worry about precision or accuracy. Try to come up with reasonable estimates using the information available to you.

YOUR FINANCIAL PLANNER

The end result of completing the forms in this book is your "Financial Planner." It will contain all your current financial data and make them available as a reference for your future decisions, for periodic review of your goals and your progress, for updating your plan and keeping your data current, and for your survivors in the event of your death.

By preparing your Financial Planner, you may also save significant annual professional fees charged by financial planners to organize your finances for you. Once you have your Financial Planner prepared, you can use financial advisors in a much more cost-effective way and can better evaluate their advice.

Physically, your Financial Planner will be a three-ring binder holding all your filled-in forms, with dividers separating the various types of information. The top of each form specifies in which section of your Financial Planner to file the form once it has been completed. All you have to do now is to get a three-ring binder for ordinary letter-size (8½"×11") pages and eleven tabbed dividers for this binder.

HOW TO PROCEED

Every chapter that follows will tell you why and how specific forms should be completed and how to use the information you prepare. Many chapters will also suggest courses of action to be considered in light of your findings, circumstances, and objectives. We stress your action throughout the book. Any suggested course of action in the book that strikes you as desirable should be listed on the last of the forms, entitled *Action Steps*. From this list you will eventually choose the ten action steps you will try to implement this year. We have found that ten action steps are about all a person can implement in one year.

Now, are you ready to embark on the interesting process of shaping your finances so as to use, increase, and protect your resources to your own best advantage? In this book, you have all the information you need to get started.

2

FAMILY AND FINANCIAL RECORDS

Eventually, your Financial Planner will contain all the data necessary for the planning and management of your financial affairs. In the main, you will be the person who benefits from having all the relevant information in one place, where it is easy to access and easy to update. But you will not be the only one who benefits. Those who survive you will have to pick up where you left off, and you should make that as simple for them as you can. The sorrow that people feel about someone's death can be accompanied by irritation when the survivors have to overcome countless difficulties that could easily have been avoided by some advance planning and better record keeping.

What we kept in mind when we designed the three forms you will now be asked to complete was that those who will someday have to take over from you will need all sorts of basic information that you may carry in your head but that they may not carry in theirs.

FORM 1 — PERSONAL AND FAMILY DATA

This form is an easy one — so easy we call it a warm-up. Some of the information to be listed is of the bothersome variety that you frequently look up to complete loan applications and tax returns and to update wills. Once you have set it all down in this form, you will know where to find it and never have to go hunting for it again.

If you use advisors, information about your family situation is important. For example, knowing that you have children may trigger the advisor's recommending certain educational financing techniques with significant tax advantages. Another example: If your advisors know your parents' financial situation, they will be able to coordinate estate planning among your parents, you and your children.

FORM 2 — FINANCIAL DOCUMENTS

In this paper-filled world we live in, we tend to keep important papers in a variety of "safe" places — in safety deposit boxes, in the desk at home, in the basement or the attic, and at the office. As a result, most of us have spent some anxious moments looking for various important papers, rifling through a mixture of documents, only to find that the one we were looking for was not where we thought it should be.

Save yourself such anxieties in the future by listing your documents and their locations here. You will be doing it at your leisure now, but the next time you need to locate one of these papers, you may well be in a hurry. While you are doing yourself and your survivors this favour, you might also check to see that the documents you have kept are up-to-date. If your last will was made out in 1970, you may want to challenge its relevance.

When you complete this form, use the *Description* column for the specifics of the various documents. Beside *Mortgage,* for instance, you should identify the property and the mortgagor. Beside *Life Insurance Policies*, you should identify the insurance company and the policy number.

FORM 3 — FINANCIAL ADVISORS

At one of our executive seminars, a participant looked at this form and said, "I don't have all those advisors listed here. Does that mean there is something wrong with me?" Nothing at all was wrong with this person. And there isn't anything wrong with you if you have not used all of these advisors. If you have used some of them though, and have found them helpful, it would be a good idea to list them here. You may be glad one day that you did — people have been known to forget other people's names and addresses — but the main purpose of compiling this list is to give your survivors some indication of the people who could be consulted and would be familiar with some aspects of your financial affairs.

Once you have completed Form 3, consider these points:

- Make sure your spouse has met all your advisors. A forty-two-year-old C.A. with complicated investment dealings died suddenly a few years ago. Because he was the "professional" in the family, he did all the financial planning. Besides, he was too "young" to die. But he did die young, and his widow spent needless hours unravelling what were now her financial affairs.

- Consider an annual financial checkup meeting with appropriate family members present, together with all or some of your advisors. It's a great way to educate family members on financial planning.

- You should have one advisor you and other family members would turn to in the event of a very important financial decision.

3

YOUR NET WORTH

The overall goal of financial planning is to have enough resources to reach your personal goals. The best overall measure of your financial resources is your net worth.

The process of determining your net worth consists of calculating your total assets and total liabilities and then subtracting your total liabilities from your total assets. It is a fundamental starting point for almost everything in financial planning.

Because it is so fundamental, most people have filled out a net worth statement at some point in their lives. If you are one of them, chances are that you did so in order to satisfy a lender's request for financial information. When you do it this time, on Form 4, it will be for your own benefit, to provide you with an essential tool for planning and managing your own finances. You will need to know your net worth for any of the following purposes:

- Finding out what your present net worth is.

You should be more interested in your financial health than your lender is. We recommend that once a year you check on your financial health and on your progress toward the net worth goal you will be setting yourself, such as an increase of fifteen percent.

- Making "what-if" projections.

You may, for example, want to work out what your retirement funds will be in five years' time if you presently have $10,000 to contribute to an investment programme each year and get a six percent return.

- Evaluating your assets.

Your net worth statement gives you an overall picture of how you have used your assets. It tells you whether most of them are personal assets, such as your home, car, and furnishings, or investment assets, such as savings, stocks, bonds and income-producing real estate. It shows you which of your assets you could quickly convert into cash. It shows whether your investments are diversified or concentrated in one or two investment categories.

- Analysing your liabilities.

Keeping debt under control is an integral part of good personal financial management.

- Planning or revising your life insurance.

- Estimating potential taxes at death.

Your net worth is the starting point for determining your potential tax liability at death and developing an estate plan.

Now we will briefly define total assets and total liabilities.

TOTAL ASSETS

To obtain the amount of your total assets, you add your liquid assets to the value of your investment assets and your personal assets.

Liquid Assets

Your so-called liquidity, meaning your financial ability to respond swiftly to emergencies or investment opportunities, is largely determined by the amount of your liquid assets. This amount consists of your cash accounts and short-term investments, such as Treasury bills, short-term deposits and money market funds, and the cash surrender value of your life insurance. Your need for liquidity is influenced by the predictability of your income and expenditures, by your employment security and by your investment strategy.

It is generally held that your liquid assets should roughly equal three to six months' employment income. If you are in an unstable employment situation or about to make a large investment, the amount should probably be greater. If your employment is relatively secure and you anticipate no major cash expenditures in the near future, the amount could be smaller.

Investment Assets

These are defined as long-term investments, intended to store up value for major future needs like education costs and retirement. Canada Savings Bonds, stocks, bonds and real estate (other than a personal residence or vacation property) are typical investment assets. Retirement funds, too, are classified as investment assets. These may include Registered Retirement Savings Plans, Deferred Profit Sharing Plans and registered pension plans.

Personal Assets

Items you acquire for your own or your family's long-term use or enjoyment form part of your personal assets. Typically, they include your home and vacation property as well as any cars, boats, art, antiques and furnishings that you own.

TOTAL LIABILITIES

There are two types of liabilities: short-term obligations and long-term obligations. For the average person, both should be fairly easy to compute.

Short-Term Obligations

These are defined as all sums (principal portion only) that have to be paid within the next twelve months. Thus, they include whatever amounts are due on long-term obligations within the next twelve months. Typically, these might be consumer credit payments, installment loans, personal loans, accrued income taxes, or borrowings on life insurance.

Long-Term Obligations

Most long-term obligations are incurred for one of two purposes: to finance long-term investments like real estate or mutual funds or to finance the purchase of major personal assets like your residence, your vacation property, or a home computer. Normally, the asset purchased constitutes security for the lender in case you default on the loan. Over time, the value of the investment asset you purchased with borrowed funds may increase, while the amount of your obligation usually decreases. Thus, your equity — the difference between the current value of the asset and the current balance on the loan — usually increases.

Borrowing Costs

The rates of interest you pay on the various amounts you owe are your borrowing costs. Since you will want to minimize the overall amount you pay in interest, you should analyse your interest costs periodically and try to repay the loans with the highest rates of interest first.

FORM 4 — STATEMENT OF NET WORTH

Before or while you complete Form 4, you might like to see an example of the completed form. Figure 3-1 shows you this form as it was completed for a family of five: father and mother aged forty-seven and forty-three, and their three children aged twenty, nineteen and ten.

We might here make some generalizations about the net worth of people at various age levels. People in their twenties, thirties and forties tend to accumulate personal assets — cars, furnishings, homes — and then trade up and buy a more luxurious car, a larger home and vacation property. Thus, their total personal assets rise much faster than their total investments. By the time they reach their fifties, most people slow down or stop adding to their personal assets and become more concerned with their investment assets and with their financial security. Thus, the total investment assets of people who are approaching retirement will often exceed the total personal assets.

To calculate your total assets, begin by filling in the first column, *Estimated Current Value*, for each asset you own.

With regard to retirement funds, the last item listed under *Investment Assets*, enter the current value of Registered Retirement Savings Plans, employer pension or retirement plans, Deferred Profit Sharing Plans or any other retirement funds. The current value of employee retirement plans may, however, be difficult to determine because the annual information sheets employers provide will often state only what your monthly payments are likely to be when you retire. If so, omit any current value for such programmes. It is not as important to estimate the current value of your employment retirement plan for purposes of calculating net worth as it is to know, for retirement planning purposes, what the monthly benefit will be at retirement age. You will use your employee retirement information when we cover retirement planning and your sources of retirement income in Chapter 12.

When you have added up the current value of all your assets and thus obtained the dollar amount of your total assets, compute what percentage of the total each asset represents by dividing the dollar value of the asset by the dollar value of total assets and multiplying by 100, and list that percentage beside the item's current value.

In listing what you owe, any installment loans that extend beyond one year should be divided so that you list the amount due within the next twelve months under *Short-Term Obligations* and the remainder under *Long-Term Obligations*.

List the interest rate you pay for each debt beside its current value.

FIGURE 3-1

File under FINANCIAL PROFILE   Date: *February 15*

FORM 4   STATEMENT OF NET WORTH

WHAT YOU OWN	ESTIMATED CURRENT VALUE	% OF TOTAL ASSET VALUE
1. LIQUID ASSETS		
Cash (chequing, savings accounts):	$2,100	1%
Short-Term Investments		
Treasury Bills:		
Short-Term Deposits:		
Money Market Funds:	24,400	3%
Cash Surrender Value of Life Insurance	7,000	1%
TOTAL Liquid Assets	$33,500	5%
2. INVESTMENT ASSETS		
Canada Savings Bonds	$39,800	5%
Term Deposits		
Marketable Securities		
Stocks:	57,400	8%
Bonds:	3,200	1%
Mutual Funds:		
Real Estate (investment)	90,000	12%
Tax Incentive Investments	20,000	3%
Other Investment Assets (describe below)		
a. *XYZ Closely Held Business*	27,000	4%
b.		
c.		
d.		
Retirement Funds		
RRSPs	25,400	4%
Employer Pension Plan		
DPSPs		
Other		
TOTAL Investment Assets	$262,800	37%

FIGURE 3-1 Cont'd

3. PERSONAL ASSETS

Residence	$275,000	39%
Vacation Property	73,500	11%
Art, Antiques		
Furnishings	56,000	8%
Vehicles		
Boats		
Other		
TOTAL Personal Assets	$404,500	58%
TOTAL ASSETS	$700,800	100%

WHAT YOU OWE	ESTIMATED CURRENT VALUE	INTEREST RATE	INTEREST DEDUCTIBLE
4. SHORT-TERM OBLIGATIONS			
Consumer Credit Obligations			
Personal Loans			
Installment Loans			
Borrowings on Life Insurance	$6,300	6%	YES
Accrued Income Taxes			
Other Obligations (describe below)			
a. _____			
b. _____			
c. _____			
d. _____			
TOTAL Short-Term Obligations	$6,300	6%	
5. LONG-TERM OBLIGATIONS			
Mortgage on personal residences	$90,000	10.5%	NO
Loans to purchase investment assets	$16,000	8%	YES
Loans to purchase personal assets	$11,000	9%	NO
TOTAL Long-Term Obligations	$117,000		
TOTAL LIABILITIES	$123,300		
TOTAL ASSETS	$700,800		
– TOTAL LIABILITIES	$123,300		
= NET WORTH	$577,500		

When you have calculated your total liabilities by adding the current values of all your debts, subtract this from your total assets in order to arrive at your present net worth.

FORM 5 — ANALYSIS OF NET WORTH

Use your figures from Form 4 to complete this form.

- On line 1, enter your total liquid assets.

- On line 2, enter your total short-term obligations.

- On line 3, calculate the excess or deficiency of your liquid assets by subtracting the amount on line 2 from the amount on line 1. The amount on line 3 should be positive. If it is negative, you ought to start building up liquid assets and should definitely stop borrowing short-term.

- Obtain the percentage of your liquid assets excess or deficiency by dividing the amount on line 1 by the amount on line 2 and multiplying by 100. Your target should be a positive figure between 150 and 200 percent. Your liquid assets would thus be one-and-a-half to two times greater than your short-term obligations.

- On line 4, enter your total investment assets.

- On line 5, enter your total long-term investment loans.

- On line 6, calculate the amount of equity you have in your investments by subtracting the amount on line 5 from the amount on line 4. To compute the percentage of this equity, divide the amount on line 6 by the amount on line 4 and multiply by 100. If your percentage is less than twenty, it is low, and you are significantly borrowing against your investments. If your percentage is greater than fifty, it is high, and you may want to consider getting some of your equity out by increasing your borrowings. On the other hand, you may wish to be debt-free and would therefore be aiming at an equity of 100 percent.

- On line 7, enter your total personal assets.

- On line 8, enter the amount of the loans you have taken for the purchase of personal assets, including personal residences.

- On line 9, calculate the amount of equity you have in your personal assets by subtracting the amount on line 8 from the amount on line 7. Compute the percentage of this equity by dividing the amount on line 9 by the amount on line 7 and multiplying by 100. Many people have a much higher equity in personal assets than in investment assets. If your percentage is less than twenty, it is low, and you are leveraging your personal assets. If your percentage is greater than fifty, it is high, and you may want to consider borrowing on your equity. But if your goal is to be debt-free, you should aim for an equity of 100 percent.

- On line 10, check your computations by adding the amounts on lines 3, 6 and 9 and entering the total. The amount on line 10 should agree with your total net worth as shown at the bottom of Form 4.

USE OF DEBT

One way to increase your assets is to borrow funds. Borrowed funds may be used to purchase personal assets such as furnishings, automobiles and appliances. Such loans are often called consumer loans and have short repayment periods. Managing consumer debt requires a knowledge of some basic techniques.

Know the safety limit suggested by specialists in consumer debt. They suggest that the average consumer's debt payments (excluding mortgage payments) should not exceed twenty percent of take-home income (after taxes and other payroll deductions).

Specialists say a smaller percentage — say ten percent to fifteen percent — is a comfortable debt level; twenty percent gets near the debt overload position for many people.

Another use of debt is to purchase investment assets such as securities and income-producing real estate. In a financial context the use of borrowed money to acquire investment assets is sometimes called *leverage*.

Leverage is used extensively, particularly in real estate transactions. In periods of rising inflation, leverage can be very beneficial. Let us say that in the early 1970s you borrowed $50,000 at eight percent to purchase a house for rental to others. That borrowing rate was probably based on an inflation rate of four percent, giving the lender a real rate of return of four percent. Assuming that all your interest expense was tax-deductible, your after-tax cost was four percent, if you were in a fifty percent tax bracket. Although inflation went up during the 1970s, your borrowing costs would have remained steady at eight percent, but your monthly net rental income would have gone up if you, like all other landlords, increased your tenants' rents. You would therefore have had more than enough to pay back your loan, and even after paying other costs of being a landlord, such as property taxes and repairs, you might still have put some cash in your pocket. In addition, the value of your rental house would have risen as inflation went up. That shows why, during the 1970s, the real estate game was the hottest game in town — in every town.

In the meantime, what was known as creative leverage in the 1970s became creative foreclosure in the early 1980s, and again in the 1990s. Why? Some people who entered the real estate game late in the inflationary spiral didn't borrow at eight percent but at much higher rates. At these rates, their rental income could not cover their high debt payments, property taxes and repairs. In addition, as inflation decreased, property values decreased.

Many financial institutions and investment promoters suggest the use of debt to implement certain investment choices. For example, some suggest reducing equity in your personal residence through refinancing and investing the proceeds elsewhere. When you are considering the use of debt, keep these questions in mind:

1. What will the borrowing cost you annually in after-tax dollars?

    Assume, for example, that the bank sends you a notice saying it would be happy to refinance your home at ten percent. If you are in a tax bracket of forty percent, your after-tax cost would be sixty percent of ten percent, or six percent, assuming that the borrowed funds were used to make an investment. Obviously, the lower your tax bracket, the higher your after-tax cost. Interest expenses that can be deducted from your taxable income are discussed in Chapter 8.

2. What is your after-tax return likely to be on the investment you make with the money obtained through borrowing?

    A good rule of thumb is that any investment you make should have the potential to return you twice your after-tax cost. For example, if your after-tax cost on the borrowed money is six percent, the investment you make should have the potential for a return of twelve percent after taxes. In other words, since you are taking a risk with borrowed money, you should have the potential of being amply rewarded.

3. What funds will you use to pay off the debt you incur?

    If you choose to invest in something that has great growth potential but little or no cash flow, you need to have other funds to make the monthly payments on the new debt you have incurred. Say you borrow $50,000 at ten percent for twenty years to purchase a rental property; your debt repayments will be almost $5,800 a year, or $483 per month. Granted, you save taxes because of the additional interest deductions, but you still have to come up with $483 per month.

So when you are considering borrowing to make an investment, be sure you have a satisfactory answer to each of the three questions above before you take the plunge.

CHOICES AND YOUR NET WORTH

Your net worth is a snapshot of your financial condition at a particular point in time. It is the end result of choices you have made in the past. For example, if you chose to acquire an expensive home and several automobiles, you may have little in the way of investment assets. If you chose to borrow significantly to finance consumer purchases and vacations, you may not have a significant net worth because your debts will be almost as great as your assets.

Look back to understand why your present net worth is what it is, but, more importantly, evaluate choices you can make at present that will have an impact on your net worth in the future. If you want your net worth to increase, here are some choices you can make:

- Make your investments grow by getting a greater rate of return on your investments. You can improve your rate of return by acquiring more knowledge of investment alternatives, by spending more time in managing your investments or by selecting an investment advisor to help you manage your investments.

- Increase your investments by putting aside more each year from your current employment income. This can be done by spending less for your current lifestyle or by decreasing your taxes through tax planning.

- Reduce your debt. If you are making monthly payments on your mortgage or other obligations you have, your debt is decreasing and your net worth is growing. Consider accelerating your debt payments; if you do, you will also save significant amounts of interest.

4

YOUR INCOME AND EXPENDITURES

Unless you have inherited assets or married someone with substantial assets, you usually start your adult earning years with little or no net worth. In this situation, there is no magic formula for achieving financial security. What you must do is save. Save some portion of your job income on a systematic basis, invest your savings wisely and in time your investment assets will be significant. By reinvesting your investment assets so that compounding takes over, you should eventually achieve financial security.

COMPOUNDING

You can easily make calculations involving compound rates of return when you have the required compound interest tables. They let you see how much your assets will grow at various rates of return in a given number of years. The same tables can also be used to predict what income you will need in a given year if you are to stay even with whatever rate of inflation you anticipate.

With the following condensed table, you can project the future worth of an investment you make today. Assume, for instance, that you had $100,000 to invest and could get a return of eight percent on it. To what sum would an eight percent compound rate of return increase this investment in ten years?

In Table 4-1, looking at ten years from now in the eight percent column, you find the factor 2.16. Multiplying $100,000 by 2.16 will then show you that the original investment will grow to $216,000 in ten years at eight percent compound interest. Similarly, $100,000 invested at ten percent for ten years has a compounding factor of 2.59, and thus would grow to $259,000 in ten years.

The same table can be used to project the effect that various rates of inflation would have on your expenditures. For example, how much after-tax income will you need in some future year in order to be as well off as you are now? Assume that your present after-tax income is $30,000 and that the annual inflation rate is six percent. In six years, you will need an income of $42,600 after taxes merely to stay at your present standard of living. Or take some specific item like university or college costs. If at present one year at university or college costs $10,000 for tuition, books, room and board and other living expenses, and costs rise at an annual rate of six percent, how much will one year in university or college cost three years from now? As you can work out, it would cost $11,900.

If you decide that you will take some specific amount from your income each year and add it to your investment capital, Table 4-2 can show you the rewards of regular saving combined with compound interest. Suppose, for example, that you will put $4,000 in a Registered Retirement Savings Plan every year at an annual compound interest rate of eight percent. How much do you think you would have in that account after ten years? How much after twenty years?

TABLE 4-1
COMPOUND INTEREST

| Years From Now | Future Worth of One Dollar with Amount of Return Compounded Annually | | | | |
| | Annual Rate of Return | | | | |
	6%	8%	10%	12%	15%
1	1.06	1.08	1.10	1.12	1.15
2	1.12	1.17	1.21	1.25	1.32
3	1.19	1.26	1.33	1.40	1.52
4	1.26	1.36	1.46	1.57	1.75
5	1.34	1.47	1.61	1.76	2.01
6	1.42	1.59	1.77	1.97	2.31
7	1.50	1.71	1.95	2.21	2.66
8	1.59	1.85	2.14	2.48	3.06
9	1.69	2.00	2.36	2.77	3.52
10	1.79	2.16	2.59	3.10	4.05
15	2.40	3.17	4.18	5.47	8.14
20	3.21	4.67	6.73	9.65	16.37
25	4.29	6.85	10.83	17.00	32.92

TABLE 4-2
GROWTH OF ASSETS FROM SETTING A CONSTANT SUM ASIDE EVERY YEAR

| Years From Now | Annual Rate of Return | | | | |
	6%	8%	10%	12%	15%
1	1.00	1.00	1.00	1.00	1.00
2	2.06	2.08	2.10	2.12	2.15
3	3.18	3.25	3.31	3.37	3.47
4	4.37	4.50	4.64	4.78	4.99
5	5.64	5.87	6.10	6.35	6.74
6	6.98	7.33	7.71	8.11	8.75
7	8.39	8.92	9.49	10.09	11.07
8	9.90	10.64	11.43	12.30	13.73
9	11.49	12.49	13.58	14.77	16.78
10	13.18	14.49	15.94	17.55	20.30
15	23.27	27.15	31.77	37.28	47.58
20	36.78	45.76	57.27	72.05	102.44
25	54.86	73.10	98.35	133.33	212.79

As you can see from Table 4-2, you would have $57,960 after ten years. After twenty years, you would have a whopping $183,040.

More complete compound interest tables are included in Appendix I.

FORM 6 — INCOME SOURCES

All of us are familiar with earned income, and most of us would agree that it has two somewhat unromantic characteristics. The first is that you must actually work in order to receive it. The second, and this may be worse than the first, is that it is taxed to the hilt — as much as sixty percent in some cases.

In contrast to that, look at the charms of a sound investment. It generates income for you all day and every day, even if you never get out of bed or if you spend all your waking hours playing tennis or bridge. Furthermore, the income it produces may be taxed at a much lower rate and the gain on selling your whole investment may even be tax-free!

Investment income is the key to financial security and independence for most people. When your investment income becomes significant, you can reduce the time you spend working for your money and turn to whatever other activities may be important to you.

To complete Form 6, use figures from the last full year for which all data are available. Your best sources of information will be your tax return, pay stubs and monthly statements from banking and investment institutions.

To complete what percentage of your total income you derived from your investment income, divide your investment income by your total income and multiply by 100.

FORM 7 — BASIC LIFESTYLE EXPENDITURES

Your basic lifestyle expenditures are those that are difficult to avoid without changing your basic standard of living. This form lists the categories that make up most people's basic lifestyle expenditures. The first four — housing, food, clothing and transportation — account for the largest portion of basic lifestyle expenditures for many Canadians.

Your own ideas on which expenditures are basic to your lifestyle and which are discretionary may not entirely coincide with the listings you find on Forms 7 and 8. You should therefore transfer from one form to the other any item that strikes you as wrongly categorized. Contributions to church or charities, for instance, have been listed as basic here, while you may regard them as discretionary expenditures. Conversely, education costs and the support of relatives have here been listed as discretionary, though you may well regard them as basic expenditures.

To complete this form, use figures from the last full year for which all data are available. You can use either monthly or annual amounts, whichever is easier.

You might like to use Table 4-3 to compare your own expenditure patterns with the four predominant spending patterns of families in Canada.

FORM 8 — DISCRETIONARY EXPENDITURES

Discretionary expenditures are those over which you can exercise a good deal of control. You decide whether you will dine at home or eat out in style and spend a small fortune. You can choose to throw either a *canard à l'orange* dinner for fifty or a wine and cheese party. You are not strictly obligated to take your family skiing in the Rockies or the Alps; you could take them backpacking or camping in the nearby countryside.

TABLE 4-3
SUMMARY OF FAMILY EXPENDITURE FOR FOUR FAMILY INCOME LEVELS — 1990

	Lower Budget		Intermediate Budgets				Higher Budget	
	Amount	%	Amount	%	Amount	%	Amount	%
Family income	**$20,000-$24,999**		**$40,000-$49,999**		**$60,000-$69,999**		**$85,000 and over**	
Family expenditure								
Food	$4,103	17.0	$5,873	13.2	$7,874	12.4	$9,680	9.8
Shelter	5,840	24.2	7,681	17.2	10,606	16.6	13,022	13.1
Household operation, furniture and equipment	2,103	8.7	2,996	6.7	4,064	6.4	6,667	6.7
Clothing	1,359	5.6	2,357	5.3	3,523	5.5	5,522	5.6
Transportation	2,285	11.8	5,714	12.8	7,561	11.9	10,565	10.6
Health care	529	2.2	869	2.0	991	1.5	1,415	1.4
Personal care	601	2.5	852	1.9	1,126	1.8	1,410	1.4
Recreation, reading materials and education	1,318	5.5	2,919	6.6	4,062	6.4	6,664	6.7
Tobacco and alcohol	862	3.6	1,449	3.3	1,701	2.7	1,826	1.9
Miscellaneous	547	2.3	1,534	3.4	1,816	2.8	2,367	2.4
Total current consumption	20,114	83.4	32,244	72.4	43,324	68.0	59,138	59.6
Personal taxes	2,651	11.0	8,691	19.5	14,324	22.5	31,299	31.5
Security	647	2.7	1,999	4.5	3,160	5.0	4,818	4.9
Gifts and contributions	704	2.9	1,594	3.6	2,841	4.5	3,964	4.0
Total expenditure	$24,116	100.0	$44,528	100.0	$63,649	100.0	$99,219	100.0

Note: Because of rounding, sums of individual items may not equal totals.

Source: Statistics Canada, "Family Expenditure in Canada." (1990.)

Even though you have quite a lot of control over the amounts you spend on entertainment, vacations, hobbies and gifts, you will presumably be spending some amount on each of them every year. However, some discretionary expenditures are more discretionary and less regular than others. Most of us would not buy a new car or a new boat every year, nor would we subject ourselves and our budgets to home improvements with such frequency.

Form 8 lists discretionary expenditures you will likely incur every year, like hobbies and regular vacations, as well as others, like the purchase of a car, that you will only face every few years. With the latter kind of expense, you should include an annual average cost each year as if the cost were spread over several years. For example, if you expect to buy a new car for $18,000 every three years, include $6,000 each year on line 9 of Form 8.

When you complete this form, use figures from the last full year for which all data are available. You can use either monthly or annual amounts, whichever is easier.

FORM 9 — INCOME TAXES AND OTHER DEDUCTIONS

After the giddy delights of discretionary expenditures, we have now arrived at the bane of modern existence. Please use your most recent tax returns to complete this form.

FORM 10 — ANALYSIS OF EARNED INCOME AND EXPENDITURES

A few centuries ago, if you were anybody at all, you did not have to make money, you had money. The nobles and gentry had it and spent it with abandon. More of this unearned income was sure to come their way soon, either in frequent tax payments from the villages they owned or in a long-awaited lump sum after the demise of their parents or their rich but childless uncle or aunt. Not only was it possible and acceptable for aristocrats to live entirely on unearned income but also it would have been downright vulgar to do anything else.

It is amazing what a difference a few centuries make, isn't it? You probably don't own a single village, let alone several; and your expectations of a huge inheritance, too, are probably dim. If that is the case, we strongly advise you to live on your earned income now if you possibly can, and to use all your unearned income as investment capital. We therefore ask you in this form to balance your expenditures only against your earned income, not your total income.

- For line 1, enter your total employment income as shown at the top of Form 6.

- For line 2, use Forms 7, 8 and 9 to obtain the necessary figures.

- For line 3, list the sum total of your three types of expenditures.

- For line 4, subtract your total expenditures from your employment income. Any positive figure that results should be used to help you reach your financial goals.

Next, calculate and list what percentage of your total employment income you have been spending on (a) basic lifestyle expenditures, (b) discretionary expenditures, and (c) taxes. To do so, divide each expenditure by your total employment income and multiply by 100. Then arrive at the percentage of excess by dividing the dollar amount on line 4 by the dollar amount on line 1, and multiplying the result by 100.

INTERPRETING THE RESULTS

Now that you have analysed your income and expenditures, let's interpret the results and look at the choices you have.

1. How much of your earned income is left for future goals and for investment? In their employment years, people should try to set aside no less than five — preferably ten — percent of their employment income and invest it. You can increase the amount available for investment either by increasing your income or by spending less, or both.

2. Can you earn more? Maybe you can make yourself more valuable in the job market by increasing your skills through continuing education courses, or by using your time more effectively, or by focusing on job results rather than the details of the job. The best investment you will ever make is in yourself.

   Can someone else in your family earn more? Perhaps your spouse can work part-time. If your spouse is already working, perhaps he or she can expand the scope of the job. Maybe the answer is career counselling and a new job that will let you use your skills more effectively.

3. Does the amount of income tax paid seem unacceptably high? If so, perhaps something can be done to reduce the tax drain. Chapters 6, 7 and 8 will offer you various suggestions.

4. Do the combined percentages of your basic lifestyle expenditures and your discretionary expenditures come to more than sixty to sixty-five percent? If they

do and your earned income is more than $60,000 a year, then it is likely that you could reduce your expenditures without seriously reducing the quality of your life; and then you could use the difference for making investments.

Maybe it would make sense to start to simplify your life; to emphasize quality versus quantity; to evaluate your needs versus your wants; and to examine the "instant gratification" lifestyle that usually leads to significant consumer debt, resulting in the need to earn more and more with less and less time to use what we thought we couldn't live without.

If you need a system to monitor and control your expenditures, here are some useful techniques:

- Segregate your income and expenditures to assist in record-keeping and control.

- Deposit all your employment income in an interest-bearing savings account. We call this your "income account."

- Deposit all your investment income in another interest-bearing savings account, which we will call your "investment account." By doing so, you ensure that all your investment income is reinvested and is compounding.

- Monthly or semi-monthly, transfer from your "income account" to a chequing account sufficient funds to handle all planned lifestyle expenditures, taxes and discretionary expenditures for the period.

- Through the use of this chequing account, you have a running total of your expenditures for each period and an indication of what is left to cover the period's remaining expenditures. Make a commitment that the balance can never go below zero in this account before the next transfer from the "income account."

- Pay for most of your expenditures by cheque. The use of a chequebook provides a written record of your expenditures for later analysis for tax purposes and an indication of the current balance for control purposes. If you make some payments in cash, save your receipts or write the amount in a pocket diary to collect information for summarizing your expenditures.

- Be cautious with the use of credit cards. Although they provide you with a written record of your expenditures, it is easy to let charge account spending get out of control.

5. If you are contemplating major expenditures like university or college, extended travel, or home improvements over the next few years, your figures on Form 10 will show you how feasible such plans are under your present circumstances.

6. If you are toying with the idea of taking a cut in employment income in order to gain greater independence or a more stimulating professional environment, these figures will give you some guide to the impact that such a career move might have on your lifestyle.

You should analyse your income and expenditure patterns periodically because it helps you to be in control of your finances and highlights the areas in which action ought to be taken.

5

ANALYSING YOUR TAX SITUATION

For many of us, taxes are the fastest rising category of expenditures, and the largest. Taxes influence every phase of personal financial management, from producing and investing your income, to your retirement and your estate planning. Much of financial planning is therefore centred on maximizing your after-tax income, after-tax income being the dollars from your earned income and investments that are left after paying taxes and that can actually be spent by you. Most people want to reduce their personal taxes but have not taken the time to obtain the necessary knowledge. Knowing how the tax system works and what tax-planning techniques you can legally use to reduce your taxes will allow you to salvage a great many dollars to spend or invest that would otherwise be swallowed by taxes.

THE CRAZY APRIL GAME

For many Canadians, the game commences on April 15, builds to a frenzied rush on April 28, and comes to an abrupt finish at about 11:45 P.M. on April 30, when the tax return is hand-carried to the local post office. There is much yelling and screaming and frothing at the mouth during the latter stages of the game; even some mad dashes to the local bank to arrange financing to pay for the taxes due.

We're not making this up. It's the normal pattern of behaviour for too many taxpayers. What makes it worse is that once the tax return is completed, nothing is done to look ahead at the current year's tax situation to see what tax-saving ideas can be implemented. That is, not until about December 15, when time is again running out and there's all too often a frenetic scramble to save taxes by making quick decisions.

There is a better way, a much better way. Start right after you have completed last year's return, with projections of your estimated total income, deductions and taxable income for the current year. Next, set yourself a taxable income target — in other words, what you would like your taxable income to be. Your target should not be zero but some realistic level that can be achieved through implementing legitimate tax-saving ideas without undue risk on your part.

By starting with an estimate of your current year's taxable income and targeting a desired taxable income, you will be active in your tax-saving research and have the time to seek out good tax-saving investments. You will be managing your taxes rather than letting your taxes manage you. Again, it's your choice. Do you want to control your tax expenditures or do you prefer to watch your taxes increase year after year, always constituting one of your largest annual expenditures?

FORM 11 — TAX-PLANNING WORKSHEET

Before or while you complete this form, it might be helpful to look at Figure 5-1, which is an example of the completed form.

Last Year

The starting point will be your last tax return, form T1 and form TP1 for Quebec residents. Use the information to complete the *Last Year* column of this form. You will notice that this form follows the format of your 1992 tax return fairly closely, though it combines some of the items and gives some of them different captions in order to help you with your analysis and estimates.

When you have transferred all the relevant figures to the *Last Year* column and have entered last year's taxable income on line 5(a), look that amount up in the appropriate tax schedule in Appendix II and find out the percentage at which your top dollars were taxed. This percentage is called your *marginal tax rate*. Then list that percentage on line 5(b).

For federal tax purposes there are only three tax brackets for individuals, which are partially indexed for inflation. The federal 5% surtax was reduced to 4%, effective July 1, 1992, and again further reduced to 3% effective January 1, 1993. As well, there is a further surtax on high income taxpayers (income greater than approximately $70,000) of 5% of federal tax in excess of $12,500.

1993 Taxable Income Brackets	Federal Tax Rate	Combined Federal and Provincial* Tax Rates, including Federal Surtax
$29,590 or less	17%	29.0%
29,591 to 59,180	26	42.3
59,181 to 62,194	29	48.7
62,195 and over	29	49.0

*Assumes a fifty-eight percent provincial tax rate.

A worksheet is included in Appendix III to help you calculate taxes payable on the taxable income you will determine on Form 11 later in this chapter.

Estimate For Current Year

The next step in analysing your tax situation is to estimate your taxable income for the current year by performing the following steps.

1. **Estimate total income**
   - On line 1(a)(i), estimate income from employment including commissions and taxable benefits for this year. In our example, we assumed an increase of 6.9% over last year in estimating employment income. You may have a different assumption on which to base your estimate. Subtract any allowable deductions, like expenses to earn commission income, to determine net employment earnings on line 1(a)(iii).
   - On line 1(b)(i) and (ii) respectively, estimate Old Age Security and Canada or Quebec Pension Plan benefits, and any other pension income expected for the year.

     As of 1989, higher-income individuals were required to repay Old Age Security payments to the extent of fifteen percent of their net income over $50,000, partially indexed over time for inflation ($53,215 in 1993). Repayments are calculated on the individual's income tax return. This measure was phased in over three years. Any amount repaid is deductible in determining taxable income.
   - Section 1(c) contains income from other sources, including Family Allowance payments, line 1(c)(i), and Unemployment Insurance benefits, line 1(c)(ii). Family Allowance payments were to be reported by the spouse with the higher income and for 1992 higher-income individuals were required to repay Family Allowance payments to the extent of fifteen percent of their net income over $50,000. Any amount repaid was deductible in determining taxable income. For 1993 Family Allowance payments and both the refundable and non-refundable Child Tax Credits were replaced by the new non-taxable Child Tax Benefit. The Child Tax Benefit is discussed later in Chapter 6.
   - On lines 1(c)(iii) and (iv), estimate your taxable dividends, interest and other investment income for this year. As outlined in Chapter 6, you must include in your taxable income 1.25 times the amount of dividends actually received from Canadian companies. Refer to your net worth statement (Form 4) for your present dividend and interest-paying investments and make some assumptions about the amount they will produce. In our example, we have assumed dividends and interest will not increase based on the assumption that interest rates will remain constant during the next year.
   - On line 1(c)(v), estimate your net rental income or loss. Such income or loss will come from rental assets you presently own or plan to own during the next year. The amount is your total rental income less expenses paid on the properties and capital cost allowance. Capital cost allowance is the deduction permitted by *The Income Tax Act* over time for the capital cost of a rental building. Note that capital cost allowance cannot be claimed to create a rental loss, except for a special class of rental properties commonly called "MURBs" which are discussed in Chapter 7. In our example, we have included rental income. Our assumption is that net rental income will increase by approximately four percent during the next year.
   - On line 1(c)(vi), estimate taxable capital gains or allowable capital losses. These estimates should be based on your assumptions about sales of capital assets (such as shares, bonds, real estate, etc.) during the next year.

     Prior to 1988, only one-half of any capital gain (known as a "taxable capital gain") was included in income. Similarly, one-half of any capital loss (known as an "allowable capital loss") could be deducted from taxable capital gains. You cannot deduct allowable capital losses realized in years after 1985 from income other than taxable capital gains. The portion of a capital gain included in your taxable income increased from one-half to two-thirds in 1988 and increased further to three-quarters after 1989. The calculation of allowable capital losses has changed in the same way as taxable capital gains, and will continue to be deductible only against taxable capital gains.

- On line 1(d)(i), estimate your net business income. Most people who work for a company do not have business income. In our example, we have shown no business income.
- On lines 1(d)(ii), (iii) and (iv) respectively, estimate net self-employment income from a profession, from commissions and from farming or fishing. In our example, we have not included any such income.
- On line 1(e), determine the estimated total income for the year. In our example, the estimated total income is $89,500.

2. Estimate net income

- On lines 2(a) through 2(f), estimate any deductions from total income and record the sum of these deductions on line 2(g). If you are unsure whether a deduction qualifies, refer to the discussion of deductions in Chapter 6. Some deductions available before 1988 were converted into tax credits. These are discussed in more detail in Chapter 6.
- On line 3, enter the result of subtracting your total estimated deductions for next year, line 2(g), from your estimated total income, line 1(e). This is your net income. In our example, the net income estimate is $76,000.

3. Estimate other deductions from net income

- Non-capital and net capital losses of other years not previously deducted are claimed on lines 4(a) and (b) respectively. Net capital losses can only be claimed to the extent of $2,000 (where the loss arose before May 23, 1985) plus the excess of any taxable capital gains over any allowable capital losses in the current year.
- Estimate the amount of taxable capital gains exemption claimed for the year on line 4(c). See Chapter 6 for a discussion of this exemption.
- On line 4(d), enter the total of the amounts from lines 4(a) to 4(c).

4.   Estimate taxable income

- On line 5(a), enter the result of subtracting line 4(d) from line 3.
- Determine the top tax bracket (marginal tax rate) for your estimated taxable income from the appropriate tax rate schedule in Appendix II. In our example, the estimated taxable income is $74,000; the tax bracket is 52.4%, assuming our taxpayer is an Ontario resident.

Target Taxable Income

You have now estimated your taxable income for the next year. For those of you still in your working years, your estimated taxable income is probably higher than it was last year. This is because your employment earnings probably will increase.

Now you are ready to start tax planning. It begins with your setting a target taxable income. If you have never set a target for taxable income, don't worry. It is like setting any other target. The target should be realistic. You should feel good when you achieve the target (remember, you are saving taxes and that's a good feeling). You should keep the following points in mind as you set the target.

- *Feasibility*   Set a target that you are able to reach. To reduce your taxable income to a substantially lower target level will require you to find good tax-saving ideas and cash to implement them.

- *Risk*   Substantial reductions of taxable income usually require tax-shelter investments, and such investments are usually risky.

- *Tax bracket*   To target your taxable income at a level substantially below the maximum tax bracket is often self-defeating, since many tax-saving strategies are tax-deferral programmes. Reducing taxable income now in order to be taxed at lower rates usually results in your being taxed at higher rates in later years. Substantial reduction of taxable income usually involves substantial risk. It is not a good idea to deal in risky investments in order to save taxes at marginal rates much below the top tax rates.

- *Income deferral*   Defer income to years when your tax bracket may be low. You may be planning to take a sabbatical, for example, that would mean a substantial decrease of your employment income for that year. By deferring income, such as sale of property, to a year when your taxable income will be low, you may not only defer taxes but actually reduce them.

With these various observations in mind, enter your targeted taxable income and tax bracket on lines 6(a) and 6(b) of Form 11. You will, of course, need to take action if you are to reduce your taxable income to the targeted amount. The means you can use to achieve this will be discussed in the next chapters.

FIGURE 5-1

File under TAX PLANNING   Date: *May 19*

FORM 11   INCOME TAX PLANNING WORKSHEET

	LAST YEAR	CURRENT YEAR
1. TOTAL INCOME		
(a) (i) Income from employment	$72,000	$77,000
(ii) Less allowable expenses		
(iii) Net employment earnings	$72,000	$77,000
(b) Pension Income		
(i) Old Age Security and Canada or Quebec Pension Plan benefits		
(ii) Other pension income		
(c) Income from other sources		
(i) Family Allowance payments		
(ii) Unemployment Insurance benefits		
(iii) Taxable amount of dividends from Canadian companies	3,800	3,800
(iv) Interest and other investment income	1,900	1,500
(v) Rental income (loss)	5,000	5,200
(vi) Taxable capital gains	5,000	2,000

FIGURE 5-1 Cont'd.

	LAST YEAR	CURRENT YEAR
(d) Self-employed income		
(i) Business income		
(ii) Professional income		
(iii) Commission income		
(iv) Farming or fishing income		
(e) Total income	$87,700	$89,500
2. DEDUCTIONS FROM TOTAL INCOME		
(a) Registered pension plan contributions		
(b) Registered Retirement Savings Plan contributions	12,500	13,500
(c) Union and professional dues		
(d) Child care expenses		
(e) Allowable business investment losses		
(f) Other deductions		
(g) Total deductions	12,500	13,500
3. NET INCOME	$75,200	$76,000
4. OTHER DEDUCTIONS FROM NET INCOME		
(a) Non-capital losses of other years		
(b) Net capital losses of other years (1972 - 1985)		
(c) Taxable capital gains exemption	5,000	2,000
(d) Total other deductions	5,000	2,000
5. (a) TAXABLE INCOME	70,200	74,000
(b) Tax bracket	48.7	52.4
6. (a) TARGETED TAXABLE INCOME		$66,000
(b) Targeted Tax Bracket		51.0

6

WHERE AND HOW TAXES ARE SAVED

The question that people ask us most frequently is, "How can I save on my income taxes?" The answer to that is, "You can save on your taxes by knowing how various types of income are taxed and what tax-planning techniques you can use to reduce your taxes, and then by taking the appropriate action."

Governments provide certain economic incentives by taxing different types of income at different rates. Some income is tax-free; some income is given tax-favoured treatment; some income gets tax-deferred treatment, meaning that it is not taxed until several years later. Some investments, called tax shelters, enable investors to make deductions that require no additional cash outlay, such as capital cost allowance on real estate. If you want to lower your taxes, you should know which types of income are taxed at low rates or not taxed at all.

This chapter will give you a lot of tax ideas in a general sense, but bear in mind that the tax laws are complex. *The Income Tax Act* and its *Regulations* consist of hundreds of closely printed pages. A good tax practice has knowledgeable professionals and a library of case law books and loose-leaf tax services to support their research. In this one chapter, the best thing we can do is to sketch an outline of tax-saving ideas for you, with some brief explanations of these ideas. Applied to your own situation, with some additional research on your part or on the part of a tax professional, these ideas should help you to cut your taxes. Needless to say, the ideas by themselves will not do it. When you have found an idea that fits your situation, you'll have to put it into practice. All too often, taxes are not saved because people procrastinate and don't follow through on their tax-saving ideas.

TAX-SAVING IDEAS

Generally speaking, the following six means can be used to effect long-term tax savings:
1. Tax-free income.
2. Tax-favoured income.
3. Tax-deferred income.

4. Shifting income to a family member whose tax bracket is lower than yours in order to achieve such family goals as education.
5. Expenditures that result in tax deductions or in credits against your tax liability.
6. Tax-sheltered investments, which combine some tax-saving aspects of the means mentioned above with certain non-cash deductions (discussed in Chapter 7).

TAX-FREE INCOME

For tax purposes, your tax-free income is entirely excluded from your income. Tax-free income falls into one or more of the following categories:

- Gain on the sale of your principal residence. Note that a married couple and, after 1992, a common-law couple can only have one principal residence for tax purposes in any given year, and thus it is no longer possible to realize completely tax-free gains on both the family home and the family vacation property, except by using up your capital gains exemption. (However, it is still possible to partially "double up" on the principal residence exemption if either or both properties were acquired prior to 1982.)

- Most amounts you receive through gifts or inheritances. That's why it is said that the simplest way to become financially independent is to choose your parents wisely!

- In many circumstances, proceeds you receive in the form of a lump sum from a life insurance policy of which you are the beneficiary will be tax-free. Exceptions to this are discussed in Chapter 13.

- Individual taxpayers are entitled to a cumulative lifetime exemption of $100,000 for capital gains realized after 1984. In certain circumstances, individual taxpayers may qualify for an additional exemption of up to $400,000 for gains on the sale of farm property or shares of a small business corporation. The present exemption for gains realized on the sale of principal residences is in addition to, and does not affect, this lifetime entitlement.

Because of the importance of the capital gains exemption, it is discussed separately in more detail below.

Capital Gains Exemption

Under tax reform, the basic capital gains exemption was capped at $100,000. Exceptions are provided for qualified farm property which continues to be eligible for the full $500,000 exemption, and for shares of a small business corporation, which became eligible for an additional $400,000 exemption (over and above the $100,000 exemption).

A small business corporation is generally defined as a Canadian-controlled private corporation with substantially all of its assets used in an active business in Canada or invested in shares of operating companies that qualify as small business corporations. As well, the business cannot have been owned by anyone but the individual or a related person throughout the two years before the sale in order to qualify for the exemption.

Note that this increased exemption is available only on shares of a small business corporation and not on other small business assets. Gains on these assets would be sheltered by the $100,000 exemption. If you are currently operating a business in Canada as a sole proprietor or in a partnership and you intend to sell your business, you can gain access to the additional $400,000 capital gains exemption by incorporating your business before the sale.

Despite the term *small business corporation*, shares of any Canadian-controlled private corporation, regardless of its size, can qualify for the special $400,000 capital gains exemption provided they meet the tests described above.

Qualified farm property includes farm land and buildings, shares of a family farm corporation and an interest in a family farm partnership where you, your spouse or your child were actively engaged in the farming business either in the year the farm was sold, or within at least five years during which it was owned by the family. Qualified farm property acquired after June 17, 1987 will not include farm land and buildings unless they are owned by you, your spouse or your children for at least two years immediately before their resale and:

- in at least two years, gross revenue from the farming business exceeds your net income from all other sources; or

- throughout any two-year period, the property was used by a family farm partnership or family corporation to carry on a farming business in Canada.

The $100,000 exemption is not in addition to the $500,000 exemption available on qualified farm property and small business corporation shares. Your total exemption cannot exceed $500,000. If the maximum $100,000 exemption is claimed on sales of other capital assets, only $400,000 is left to shelter qualified farm property or gains realized on the sale of small business corporation shares. Conversely, if the $500,000 exemption is used for farm property or small business shares, the $100,000 exemption is not available for other capital property.

To the extent that you have unabsorbed capital losses available to be carried forward from prior years, these may continue to be offset against capital gains realized in subsequent years, eliminating the need to claim part of your exemption for this purpose.

If you are holding capital property that has increased significantly in value since you acquired it, the capital gains deduction may provide a windfall tax saving. In other cases, your investment strategy should be reviewed to assess the opportunities offered by the changes. It may be more advantageous to invest in equities that have a high potential for growth. Remember, however, that the exemption does not have to be claimed in a particular year even though it is available. If you have realized a capital gain and it will not significantly increase your taxes payable (for example, in a year when your other income is lower than usual), you may decide not to claim part of your exemption, to save it to offset gains likely to be realized in later years.

The 1987 Tax Reform did not limit the type of property eligible for the $100,000 capital gains exemption. However, the 1992 federal budget ostensibly targeted the $100,000 lifetime capital gains exemption toward equity investment by denying its use for certain real estate acquired after February, 1992, and by restricting its use for certain real estate acquired before March, 1992.

The new rule does not apply to real estate used in an active business. Thus, if you are a shopkeeper and you sell the building that is used principally in the business, the entire capital gain realized would be eligible for your lifetime capital gains exemption. In addition, the rule does not affect the $500,000 lifetime exemption for qualified small business shares and qualified farm property, nor does it affect the capital gains exemption on your principal residence.

You may also ignore the new rule if you have already used up your lifetime exemption, but if you still have all or some of the exemption available, read on.

The typical property caught by the new rule will be the second property acquired by an individual or family — not the principal residence, but the cottage, the ski chalet, the country retreat, or the rental property. For simplicity, we'll refer to these as "vacation properties" in the paragraphs below.

If you acquire a vacation property on or after March 1, 1992, the rule prevents you from sheltering any part of a subsequent capital gain on that property under your $100,000 lifetime exemption.

If you acquired the property before March 1, 1992, and realize the capital gain on or after that date, a special transitional rule will allow a prorated portion of the gain to be sheltered under your lifetime exemption, based on the number of months the property was owned after 1971 and before March, 1992. The new rule does not use the concept of a valuation day. In fact, the market value of a property as of the day of the last federal budget is irrelevant in determining the portion of a post-February, 1992, capital gain that is eligible for the lifetime exemption. The exemption formula is arbitrary, and will produce an unfair tax result in many cases.

The availability of the capital gains exemption will also be restricted in some circumstances by the net investment rules introduced under tax reform. These rules are discussed in Chapter 7.

The above discussion of tax-free capital gains assumes that the alternative minimum tax will not increase your total taxes in the year such gains are realized. If this is not the case, the tax on these otherwise exempt gains can be increased from nil up to approximately 6% to 7%, depending on the province in which you live. The minimum tax rules are discussed more fully in Chapter 7.

Elderly taxpayers will have to consider whether realizing a capital gain — though fully offset by the capital gains deduction — may result in the repayment of all or a portion of their Old Age Security, should the gain increase their net income beyond $53,215 for 1993.

TAX-FAVOURED INCOME

The two most common types of income that are taxed in a favoured manner are capital gains and dividends paid by Canadian companies.

Capital Gains

As discussed in the previous section, capital gains can be realized entirely tax-free under the lifetime capital gains exemption (subject to the restrictions applicable to real estate and subject to the application of the minimum tax). But even capital gains which are not eligible for this exemption (for example, because the taxpayer has already used up his existing exemption limit, or chooses not to use it to exempt a gain in a particular year) are still taxed in a favoured way, because only three-quarters of a capital gain need be included in taxable income.

The portion of a capital gain included in your taxable income was increased from one-half in 1987 and prior years to two-thirds in 1988 and 1989 and to three-quarters after 1989. Despite the reduction of personal tax rates which started in 1988, the increased rate of inclusion of capital gains in income resulted in a higher tax bite on capital gains for all taxpayers after 1989.

Loss carryovers were adjusted to reflect the new inclusion rates. For example, an allowable loss of $50 realized in 1987 or prior years became an allowable loss of $67 when applied in 1988 or 1989 and $75 when applied in 1990 or thereafter. Similarly, a 1992 allowable capital loss of $75 will offset $75 of taxable gains in 1991 or 1990 but only $67 of such gains in 1989. The rules governing the timing of loss carryovers have not changed; they may be carried back three years and forward indefinitely.

Capital gain treatment will normally be given to any gain realized from the sale of capital assets like shares, bonds and real estate that you hold as an investment. A gain is realized to the extent that the selling price exceeds the sum of your adjusted cost base (ACB) plus any costs of disposition. Your ACB is generally your cost of acquiring the asset plus the cost of any capital additions or improvements in the case of real estate. There are numerous other rules which may affect the determination of the ACB, plus special rules for property owned on December 31, 1971, when tax on capital gains was first introduced. Taxation of capital gains can be quite complex in certain circumstances; if you might realize a large capital gain in the near future, you should consider consulting a tax advisor.

To illustrate how capital gains are calculated, consider the following simple example. Assume you purchased 100 shares of a company for $1,000 three years ago. They are now worth $2,500. You decide to sell them in 1994 and net $2,430 after brokerage fees. In this case, your capital gain will be $1,430 ($2,500–$1,000–$70) and the taxable capital gain you include in taxable income will be three-quarters of $1,430 or $1,073.

Dividends

Dividends received by individual taxpayers from Canadian companies are also taxed on a favoured basis as a result of the dividend tax credit system. (Dividends received from foreign companies are treated as ordinary taxable income with no special treatment.) The dividend tax credit system is designed to give credit to shareholders for all or part of the tax already paid by the corporation on its earnings distributed as dividends. There is no similar credit for interest paid by a corporation because the corporation does not pay tax on earnings paid out as interest.

The system currently operates as follows. You include in income 1.25 times the amount of the dividend actually received, but you can then claim a tax credit equal to 13 1/3% of the grossed-up (taxable) dividend against your federal tax for the year. Because this reduces the base on which your provincial tax is calculated (except in Quebec which has its own dividend tax credit provisions which are explained below), the combined result is a tax reduction approximately equal to a twenty percent tax paid by the corporation.

If you are a Quebec resident you also include 1.25 times the amount of the dividend actually received, but you can then claim a tax credit equal to 8.87% of the grossed-up (taxable) dividend against your Quebec tax for the year.

The attractiveness of this treatment can be illustrated by the following comparative example (assuming a taxpayer in the top federal tax rate bracket and subject to a five percent federal surtax and a fifty percent provincial tax rate).

Although the tax rate on Canadian dividends is substantially lower than that for interest income, this does not mean that dividends are always preferable to interest income. It may be better to pay more tax if the after-tax yield is improved as a result. To illustrate, if you were in the top tax bracket and had a choice of investing at nine percent interest or in shares paying a six percent dividend, you would realize a net after-tax return of approximately 5.0% for interest, compared to approximately 4.2% for dividend income. Therefore, even though the tax cost is higher, you would be better off receiving the nine percent interest rather than the six percent dividend.

	Dividends	Interest
Amount received	$1,000	$1,000
Gross-up (dividend only)	250	nil
	$1,250	$1,000
Federal tax at 29%	$363	$290
Dividend tax credit	(167)	nil
	196	290
Federal surtax (5%)	10	15
Provincial tax	98	145
Total tax	$304	$450
Net after-tax dollars	$696	$550

It is always important to compare the after-tax yield on potential investments in order to make an appropriate investment decision. In the lowest bracket (taxable income under $29,000), dividends are taxed much more favourably than interest (approximately seven percent vs. twenty-seven percent). If your taxable income is higher than $29,000, you will achieve the same after-tax income from the receipt of approximately $80 in Canadian dividends as from $100 in interest income. Accordingly, for middle- and upper-income Canadians, an interest-bearing investment should yield about twenty-five percent more than a comparable investment in dividend-paying Canadian shares, assuming all other factors such as risk, liquidity and so on are equal.

It is interesting to note than an interest-bearing investment had to yield approximately thirty-three percent more than a comparable dividend-paying investment in 1987, and fifty percent more than in 1986, to provide the same after-tax income for higher-income Canadians. Even though the tax rate on Canadian dividend income was lowered by Tax Reform in 1987, it was not reduced to as great a degree as the tax rate on interest. This significantly reduced the tax incentive for individuals receiving dividend income. As well, since companies can deduct interest from their taxable income, but cannot deduct dividends, financing through debt rather than preferred shares is often more tax effective for corporations and their investors.

TAX-DEFERRED INCOME

The income from certain investments is tax-free for a specified time and is therefore known as tax-deferred income. Since there is a period in which compounding income on the investment is not reduced by taxation, tax-deferred income can increase at an accelerated rate.

Deferred Income Plans

Generally, the most important method of tax deferral for the majority of taxpayers is the use of one or more of the deferred income plans described below. The main purpose of these plans is to shelter income from immediate taxation. Unlike the ideas about tax shelters discussed in Chapter 7, the deferred income plans described here not only permit an income deduction for the amounts you invest but also provide for the tax-free accumulation of income while the funds remain in the plan.

Under the current system it is intended that the amount of tax assistance available should be comparable for individuals with the same income, whether they save for retirement through an employer-sponsored pension plan or through a registered retirement savings plan. Individuals now have flexibility in timing their retirement savings contributions, so that the opportunity to build a reasonable pension need not be permanently lost because more immediate financial pressures prevent maximum contributions in a year.

Registered Pension Plans

Registered pension plans (RPPs) generally include requirements for minimum employee contributions (except where the plan is only funded by employer contributions) and restrictions on the maximum contributions an employee can make. Annual employee contributions can only be made within this range.

Your ability to make pension contributions depends on whether you belong to a money purchase plan or a defined benefit plan. These plans differ in the way pension benefits received after retirement are determined. Money purchase plan benefits are dependent on the amount of funds accumulated in the plan for the employee, while benefits under a defined benefit plan are determined by formula, usually based on salary levels and years of service. These terms are described in more detail in Chapter 12.

Employees who are members of a defined benefit RPP may deduct the full amount of the current service contribution required under the plan, provided it does not exceed the eligible contribution limits under the current rules. The allowable amount will vary, depending on how much remuneration you receive and the terms of the pension plan, particularly the retirement benefits. The current maximum benefit is $1,722 per year of service. The limit of $1,722 per year of service will be indexed after 1995 to the increase in the average wage.

Employee past service contributions which are required under a defined benefit plan are also deductible, but only to a maximum of $3,500 per year for pre-1990 service. Additional voluntary contributions (AVCs) for past years' service made before October 9, 1986 and not deducted before 1987 are not deductible in future years and must have been withdrawn before 1991 to avoid being included in income upon eventual withdrawal. (The deduction of past service AVCs was extended if they were transferred before October 9, 1986, to an annuity or a Registered Retirement Income Fund.) AVCs for past service can no longer be made after October 8, 1986.

The maximum combined employer/employee contributions to money purchase plans were initially to be fully phased in by 1995 when the maximum contribution limit was to reach $15,500.

The monetary limits on deductible money purchase contributions between 1991 and 1996 are as follows:

1991	$12,500
1992	12,500
1993	13,500
1994	14,500
1995	15,500
1996	15,500 indexed

Since 1991, money purchase plans have been required to limit combined employer and employee contributions to the lesser of the above amount and eighteen percent of that year's pensionable earnings (generally equal to T4 earnings). In determining the maximum contribution limits for money purchase plans and the maximum benefit limits under defined benefit plans, other RPPs and Deferred Profit Sharing Plans must be taken into account.

Deferred Profit Sharing Plans

In the past, Deferred Profit Sharing Plans (DPSPs) provided essentially the same tax benefits as money purchase RPPs, and were often used by small business because they are generally simpler to set up and administer than RPPs and have a broader range of allowed investments. Since 1981, the use of DPSPs to provide retirement income for a company's controlling shareholders has been restricted and the use of these plans has declined as a result.

Since 1991, employees cannot contribute to a DPSP. Employee contributions of up to $5,500 per year were permitted in 1989 and 1990. Although these contributions were not tax deductible, they will not be taxed when withdrawn from the DPSP and will earn income tax-free while they remain in the plan. The amount of deductible employer contributions is limited to one-half of the amount outlined above as deductible contributions to money purchase RPPs, or eighteen percent of the employee's compensation for the year, whichever is less. However, the employer must integrate the DPSP contributions with any RPPs provided to the employee.

Registered Retirement Savings Plan

The most advertised and perhaps the best-known type of tax deferral investment is the Registered Retirement Savings Plan (RRSP).

Up to specified limits, amounts contributed to an RRSP are deductible for tax purposes, and income earned on these funds accumulates free of tax as long as the funds remain in the plan. When funds are withdrawn from the plan, the amounts received (both capital and income) are fully taxable at that time.

The rules for determining maximum RRSP contributions changed significantly in 1991. The overall contribution limit is the lesser of eighteen percent of the previous year's earned income and the following amounts:

1991	$11,500
1992	12,500
1993	12,500
1994	13,500
1995	14,500
1996	15,500

These amounts reflect the more gradual phase-in of higher contribution limits adopted by the government. Earned income is based on the previous year's income and after 1989 no longer includes pension benefits, retiring allowances, death benefits and amounts received out of an RRSP or a DPSP. Before 1989 an individual could transfer periodic pension income to his RRSP. Since 1989, these transfers are no longer permitted. Accordingly, as a transitional measure, transfers of up to $6,000 of periodic pension income to a spousal RRSP will be allowed for the years 1989 to 1994 (inclusive).

If you save for retirement through an RRSP and have not earned any retirement benefits under a DPSP or RPP in the previous year, you will be able to make RRSP contributions equal to the above limits, provided you have sufficient earned income in the preceding year ($69,444 earned income in 1991 for 1992 contributions, $69,444 in 1992 for 1993, $75,000 in 1993 for 1994, etc.). If your earned income is lower than these amounts, your maximum available contribution is reduced by eighteen percent of the difference. If you do not make all your maximum available contribution, you can "save" the unused portion to increase your allowed contribution in any of the next seven years.

If you are earning benefits for retirement through your membership in a DPSP or an RPP, in addition to your RRSP, your maximum RRSP limit will be reduced from that otherwise available to reflect these retirement benefits. If you are a member of a money purchase RPP, this reduction or "pension adjustment" will equal the total of your and your employer's contributions made in the immediately preceeding year. Amounts allocated to a member of a money purchase RPP from plan surpluses or forfeited amounts of other members and related earnings are also included in the pension adjustment. The pension adjustment for a DPSP will be the contributions made by the employer plus any reallocation of amounts forfeited after 1989. If you are a member of a defined benefit RPP, the calculation of your pension adjustment is much more complicated, as it is based on the value of retirement benefits you earned in the preceding year. The information necessary to calculate this pension adjustment will not be available to most taxpayers. Accordingly, employers and pension plan administrators are required to report your pension adjustment information in your T4 slip.

Under the new RRSP rules, you can chose when you want to deduct your RRSP contributions. Prior to 1991, RRSP contributions could only be deducted if made in the year or within sixty days after the end of the year. Deductions for contributions made after January 1, 1991 can now be carried forward to subsequent years, irrespective of the fact that they were made during the taxation year or within sixty days thereafter. If you believe your income will be higher in the future, the new flexibility in the timing of the deduction will give you the option to wait and deduct your contribution in a subsequent year when your tax rate is higher.

If you make RRSP contributions in excess of the amount you are eligible to deduct for the year, you may be subject to a special penalty tax of one percent per month until the overcontribution is withdrawn or you have additional RRSP deduction availability. The special tax only applies when your cumulative overcontributions exceed your cumulative available deductions by more than $8,000. For instance, if your contribution limit was $5,000 for 1993 and you contributed $15,000, you would be considered to have overcontributed $10,000. Only $2,000 of the $10,000 overcontribution is subject to the special tax until the $2,000 is withdrawn or you have additional available RRSP deductions in 1994 or later years. The overcontribution can generally be withdrawn tax-free in the year the contribution is made or the following year.

It may be worthwhile to consider making a deliberate overcontribution of $8,000 to your RRSP. Even though the contribution will not be immediately deductible, it will not be subject to the penalty tax and it will allow you to generate additional tax-deferred income in your RRSP.

As an alternative to contributing to your own RRSP, you may wish to consider contributions to an RRSP for your spouse (see discussion under Shifting Income to Someone in a Lower Tax Bracket later in this chapter) provided the combined contributions to your and your spouse's RRSPs do not exceed the limits described above. (Note that if your spouse has earned income, contributions that he or she makes to an RRSP do not affect your contribution limits.)

To appreciate how much an investment of pre-tax dollars can grow while the interest it earns is not taxed, take a look at Table 6-1. Also note the large differences that result from different rates of return. Investing $2,000 a year for thirty years at eight percent will give you $226,570, while at twelve percent it will give you $482,670. That is a difference of $256,100 or about 115 percent, though the difference in rates of return is only four percent.

TABLE 6-1
INVESTMENT GROWTH IN RRSPs WITH ANNUAL COMPOUNDING

Annual contributions of $2,000

Years in Plan	Your Deposits	Principal with interest		
		8%	10%	12%
10	$20,000	$28,970	$31,870	$35,100
20	40,000	91,520	114,550	144,100
30	60,000	226,570	328,990	482,670

Annual contributions of $7,500

Years in Plan	Your Deposits	Principal with interest		
		8%	10%	12%
10	$75,000	$108,640	$119,510	$131,630
20	150,000	343,200	429,560	540,380
30	225,000	849,640	1,233,710	1,810,010

Self-administered RRSPs

If you like to make your own investment decisions, you can establish an RRSP and administer it yourself. You might contribute cash and direct the investment of these funds. Alternatively, you might transfer eligible securities to the plan (up to your contribution limit). Remember, however, that security transfers to such a plan must be made at fair market value and could trigger immediate capital gains to you. (No deduction is allowed for capital losses on such transfers, and therefore transfers of securities in a loss position should be avoided.)

Qualified investments for an RRSP include a wide range of marketable securities. (If the funds in the plan are used to acquire non-qualified investments, you may be required to take an equivalent amount into income.) In some cases, mortgages qualify as eligible investments for an RRSP, but care should be taken if you wish to have your RRSP hold a mortgage on your own home or other property:

- the mortgage must be administered by an approved lender under the *National Housing Act*;
- the mortgage must be insured under the *National Housing Act* or by a corporation offering its services to the public as an insurer of mortgages; and
- the mortgage interest rate, repayment terms, etc., must reflect normal commercial practice (i.e. it must be administered as if the property were owned by a stranger).

If it fails these tests, a mortgage held by your RRSP on your home could be considered a non-qualifying investment.

For some types of investments, the advantage of tax-free accumulation of income in an RRSP must be weighed against the loss of other tax benefits available if the income were taxed outside the plan. If, for example, shares of taxable Canadian companies are held personally, any dividends received are eligible for a dividend tax credit, and capital gains may qualify for the capital gains exemption. In contrast to this, such income earned in an RRSP will be taxed in full when the funds are eventually withdrawn from the plan. On the other hand, you should probably hold deep discount bonds, stripped bonds and bearer coupons in an RRSP, rather than directly, because no special tax advantages apply to such income and tax on amounts earned in the RRSP can effectively be deferred until payments are later made out of the plan. One final point to note is that most self-administered RRSPs have an administration cost which usually exceeds similar costs for an ordinary RRSP.

Other Types of Tax-Deferred Income

In addition to deferred income plans, there are other less commonly encountered methods of deferring income, some examples of which follow.

Capital gains reserves

Capital gains reserves, primarily used in the sale of real estate, provide a way of deferring taxes on capital asset sales. By claiming this reserve, you can defer recognition of the capital gain until payments are received from the purchaser.

A taxpayer can claim a reasonable reserve for sale proceeds not receivable until after the year of the sale. For example, if you sold a rental property for a twenty-five percent cash down payment, with the remaining seventy-five percent due the following year, you could reduce the capital gain that would otherwise be reported in the year of sale by seventy-five percent. Note that a reserve cannot be used to defer taxation of a capital gain for longer than four years after the year of sale and that at least twenty percent of the capital gain must be reported each year, regardless of the actual amount of cash received. (Special rules provide a ten-year limit, with similar terms, for sales of family farms and shares of family farm corporations.)

Since the introduction of the capital gains exemption, these reserve provisions are no longer as beneficial where the gain does not exceed the available exemption. The reserve provisions still present an opportunity for deferral of income and tax reduction when the capital gains exemption has been used up and a large gain triggers a high rate of tax as the gain is all included in one year's income.

Replacement Property

In certain circumstances, taxable income realized on the sale or involuntary conversion (for example, expropriation or loss through fire) of certain capital assets, such as land, buildings and equipment used in a business, can be deferred when the former capital property is replaced with similar property of the same or greater value. The income deferral will last until the ultimate sale of the replacement assets.

A similar deferral is available when rental properties are replaced after an involuntary conversion. This deferral is not available if a rental property is sold, and the proceeds are reinvested in another rental property.

SHIFTING INCOME TO SOMEONE IN A LOWER TAX BRACKET

The basis of several tax-planning techniques is the fact that the tax bracket of children or parents whom you support may be lower than your own tax bracket. Therefore, any given source of income will yield them more spendable after-tax dollars than it would yield you.

Opportunities for income splitting have been significantly reduced in recent years. However, there are still several effective ways to split income with other family members. The examples which follow use income transfers from parents to children but the same method will generally work for shifting income to elderly parents.

Gifts

Gifts to your spouse (effective 1993, including a common-law spouse), or to children, grandchildren, nieces, nephews, etc. under eighteen years of age are not particularly effective for income-splitting purposes. Income from the gifted property or from the reinvestment of the gift will normally be attributed back to you and taxed as part of your income. These attribution rules continue to apply, in the case of gifts to your spouse, as long as you remain married or living common-law and resident in Canada. On the other hand, the attribution of income back to you in the case of gifts to minors ceases to apply in the year in which the child reaches eighteen years of age. As well, the attribution rules do not apply to future capital gains (where the property has increased in value since the time of the gift) realized on property given to a child, regardless of age, although they do apply to gains realized by a spouse on gifted property.

For income tax purposes, gifts of capital property (such as shares or real estate) are generally considered to have been made at fair market value, resulting in an immediate capital gain for the person making the gift. The exception to this is that, in the case of a gift to your spouse, you may choose either to treat the transfer as having been made at the property's adjusted cost base, thereby deferring any resulting capital gain until your spouse later disposes of the property, or to transfer it at fair market value.

If you transfer the property to your spouse at its adjusted cost base, the eventual gain will be attributed back to you, as will any income your spouse earns on the property in the meantime.

Transfers at Fair Market Value

Where property is sold to your spouse or children and fair market value consideration is received, neither the income nor capital gains attribution rules will apply. If you take back a loan, interest must be charged at commercial rates (and must be paid within 30 days after the end of the year). For this rule to apply to transfers to your spouse, you must transfer the property at fair market value and recognize any resulting gain. You cannot elect to treat the transfer as having been made at adjusted cost base for tax purposes.

The fair market value transfer to your spouse is particularly advantageous where the transfer does not result in a capital gain or results in a gain which is offset by the capital gains exemption or unused capital losses. Your spouse will be taxed on any future additional gain which can be sheltered by his or her capital gains exemption. As a result, you will have effectively doubled-up on the capital gains exemption. If your spouse is indebted to you because of the transfer, you will have to report the interest earned until the debt is paid off, but you will no longer have to report the income from the transferred property.

Loans

Before the 1985 federal budget, it was possible to loan funds interest-free to your spouse or children and have the income earned on the property acquired with the borrowed funds taxed in the hands of the borrower.

The existing income attribution rules were amended in 1985 to apply to loans between spouses — except for loans made before May 23, 1985 if repaid before 1988. The benefits of loans to your spouse for income splitting purposes are now limited. Income attribution will only be avoided on future loans if interest is paid on the loan at a market rate prescribed in *The Income Tax Act*. This limits income splitting to income earned with the borrowed funds in excess of this prescribed rate.

Before 1989, the amended income attribution provisions only applied to loans to other family members under age eighteen, so bona fide loans to children eighteen years of age or older were not affected by the changes. Income splitting could also be accomplished with children over fourteen by lending them money through a trust to purchase interest-bearing investments, which would not pay interest before the year the children turned eighteen. A deferral of interest income for up to three years was possible for investments made before 1990 because of the investment income deferral rules described in Chapter 8.

After 1989, loans to family members of any age are much less effective for income splitting. Any income earned using the borrowed funds (except capital gains realized by children) will usually be taxable in the hands of the lender. However, any further income earned by reinvesting this attributed income will be taxable in the hands of the borrower, which accomplishes some income splitting.

RRSP for Spouse

A better alternative to making contributions to a Registered Retirement Savings Plan in your own name may be to contribute to an RRSP for your spouse (including a common-law spouse). Such contributions are deductible by you up to the same limits as those applicable to your own plan (see *Deferred Income Plans*) but when your spouse later withdraws the funds, or starts to receive an annuity out of the plan, he or she will, in most cases, be taxed on the amounts received.

There are, however, rules to discourage the immediate collapse of a spousal RRSP. If your spouse withdraws funds from a plan to which you contributed, the withdrawal will be added to your income to the extent of any contributions to a spousal RRSP in that year and in the two immediately preceding taxation years. This means that if you contribute to your spouse's RRSP early in 1994 (for 1993) the funds should not be withdrawn before 1997. (This assumes, of course, that you will not have made further contributions to an RRSP for your spouse in the meantime; if you have, any withdrawal should be delayed to a later year if you wish to avoid tax.)

This income attribution rule does not apply if you and your spouse are legally separated and living apart when funds are withdrawn. This rule also does not apply where the particular plan "matures" and annuity payments start to be received by your spouse. Moreover, if the funds are left to accumulate in the plan until your spouse reaches age sixty-five, he or she will then qualify for the pension income credit that might not otherwise be available.

An RRSP may be converted into an annuity or a Registered Retirement Income Fund at any time but, in any event, must either be converted or the funds withdrawn by the end of the year in which the owner reaches age seventy-one. If a taxpayer is prevented from making further contributions to his own RRSP because he has reached age seventy-one, he can still contribute to an RRSP for his spouse until she also reaches age seventy-one.

There is no longer a minimum age limit of sixty for maturing an RRSP. This change is intended to assist taxpayers who retire before age sixty and who may require the additional retirement income before that time.

Registered Education Savings Plan

Registered Education Savings Plans can be an effective way of shifting income to school age children. Because these plans are intended only to provide financing for your children's (or grandchildren's) post-secondary education, they will be discussed in Chapter 11 which deals with education financing.

TAX DEDUCTIONS AND CREDITS

So far, we have discussed how you can minimize your taxable income by making use of all available exclusions from income, by shifting income, and by making tax-favoured and tax-deferred investments. These are the methods used to pare down the amount that must be included in total income in the first place. Another means by which you can reduce your taxable income is to make expenditures that result in tax deductions or credits. There are numerous opportunities for reducing taxes payable, if you know what deductions and credits Revenue Canada will accept and what you must do to obtain them. A brief description of the more common sources of deductions and credits follows.

Employment Expense Deductions

Up to 1987, there was a general employment expense deduction of twenty percent of employment income to a maximum of $500. Quebec had retained its employment expense deduction which was equal to the lesser of six percent of employment income and $750. The recent Quebec budget proposes to eliminate this deduction as of the 1993 taxation year.

An employee earning commissions can still deduct expenses paid and not reimbursed in the year (except membership fees for a dining, recreational or sporting facility) to earn employment income, up to the amount of commission income received, if all the following conditions are met:

1. the employee is employed in connection with the selling of property or negotiating of contracts for his employer;

2. the employee is required by his employment contract to pay his own expenses;

3. the employee is ordinarily required to carry on his duties away from his employer's place of business;

4. the employee is paid in whole or in part by commissions; and

5. the employee does not receive a tax-free travelling allowance (described in the following section).

Form T2200, signed by your employer, must be filed with your tax return to verify that these criteria are met.

Where the commission-remunerated employee receives a travelling allowance, he may choose to add this allowance to his income and deduct the eligible portion of his actual travelling and automobile expenses, as discussed below. (This option is not available for Quebec tax purposes.)

Automobile Expenses

If you are a self-employed person who uses your car for business purposes, you will be able to deduct the business portion of your automobile expenses, subject to certain restrictions. Expenses include gas, oil, insurance, repairs, interest costs to finance the purchase of the car, lease payments and capital cost allowance. An employee can similarly deduct a portion of his automobile expenses, but only if the following conditions apply:

1. the employee is ordinarily required to carry on his employment duties away from his employer's place of business or in different places;

2. the employee is required to pay his own travelling expenses; and

3. the employee does not receive a non-taxable travelling allowance.

Form T2200, signed by your employer, must be filed with your tax return to verify that these criteria are met. Where the salary-remunerated employee receives a travelling allowance, he or she may choose, like the commission-remunerated employee, to add this allowance to his or her income and deduct the eligible portion of his or her actual travelling and automobile expenses. (This option is not available for Quebec tax purposes.)

The 1987 Tax Reform introduced significant new restrictions on the deductibility of automobile expenses. (These new rules actually apply to all passenger vehicles, including automobiles, station wagons and passenger vans designed to carry less than ten people and intended for use primarily on highways and streets. The rules do not apply to taxis, rental cars and certain other special purpose vehicles.)

Only the first $24,000 (plus the non-refundable provincial sales tax and GST) of the cost of an automobile is eligible for deduction over time as capital cost allowance (CCA). The maximum deduction for car lease payments is the least of three amounts: the actual monthly lease payment, $650 ($600 before September 1, 1989) per month, or the ratio of $24,000 ($20,000 before September 1, 1989) to eighty-five percent of the manufacturer's list price times the actual monthly lease payment. Interest expenses to finance the purchase of a car are limited to a maximum of $300 ($250 before September 1, 1989) per month.

These restrictions apply to all passenger vehicles purchased or leased after June 17, 1987, for taxation years starting after June 17, 1987 and ending after 1987.

Operating expenses (including gasoline, oil, maintenance and repair costs) are deductible to the extent of the proportion of business miles to total miles.

Reasonable travel allowances or reimbursement of travel expense by your employer for business trips are generally tax-free to the employee. However, travel allowances in excess of thirty-one cents (twenty-seven cents before September 1, 1989) per kilometre for the first 5,000 business kilometres and twenty-five cents (twenty-one cents before September 1, 1989) per kilometre thereafter are not deductible by your employer. For the Yukon and Northwest Territories, the exempt allowances are thirty-five cents (thirty-one cents before September 1, 1989) for the first 5,000 kilometres and twenty-nine cents (twenty-five cents before September 1, 1989) thereafter. As a result, of these limits on the deductibility of automobile mileage allowances, most employers do not pay allowances in excess of these amounts.

Deductions from Total Income

These deductions include:

- Contributions to a registered pension plan. The annual contribution limits are discussed in an earlier section of this chapter.

- Contributions to Registered Retirement Savings Plans. Again the annual contribution limits are discussed in an earlier section of this chapter.

- Annual union and professional dues, but not including initiation fees, special assessments or amounts charged for any purpose other than the organization's ordinary operating costs.

- Baby-sitting fees, nursery school fees and payments for lodging at a boarding school or camp (excluding expenses which are reimbursed) may be claimed for children under 14 years of age — or older, if physically or mentally infirm — if the expenses enable you to earn employment income or to carry on a business.

  For federal tax purposes, the maximum claim is the lesser of:

  - child care expenses up to $5,000 ($4,000 in 1992) per child under 7 years of age at the end of the year or who is infirm, plus $3,000 ($2,000 in 1992) for each other child under 14 years of age.

  - two-thirds of your earned income (essentially salary or business income) less any amounts claimed by your spouse.

  The deduction is generally claimed by the supporting parent with the lower income. In certain instances, the deduction may be claimed by the higher-income spouse (e.g. where the other spouse is infirm, is in prison, is a full-time student at a designated educational institution, etc.). In these cases, the maximum claim is limited to the least of:

  - the amount calculated using the rules above,

  - $150 ($120 in 1992) times the number of children under 7 or infirm, per week, plus $90 ($60 in 1992) per week for other children.
    A separate deduction for Quebec tax purposes applies to children under 14 years of age with the following maximum claim per child:

  - for each child under 7 at the end of the year or who is infirm $4,600 ($4,400 in 1991); plus

  - for any other child aged between 7 and 14 $2,300 ($2,200 in 1991).
    The deduction may be claimed by the higher-income spouse; however, the deduction cannot exceed actual child care costs and cannot exceed 50% of the net employment income of the spouse with the lower net income in the case of one child, or 100% where there are two or more children.

- Allowable business investment losses. These are three-quarters of the losses on the disposition of:

  - shares or certain debt of a Canadian-controlled private company (CCPC) carrying on an active business in Canada sold to a person with whom you deal at "arm's length," or

  - certain debts of a CCPC carrying on an active business in Canada established to be bad debts and certain shares of a bankrupt or wound-up CCPC.

This loss is generally calculated in the same way as other allowable capital losses, in that only a portion of the loss can be claimed for tax purposes. Unlike other capital losses, however, the allowable portion of a business investment loss may be deducted without limit against income from all sources.

Allowable business investment losses claimed after 1984 will reduce your amount of available capital gains exemption. As of 1986, these losses have been treated as ordinary capital losses (not deductible against other sources of income) to the extent that a capital gains exemption has been claimed in previous years.

Other deductions from total income include:

- periodic alimony or maintenance payments pursuant to a decree, order, judgment or written agreement.

- expenses to move within Canada to a new home at least 40 kilometres closer than your previous home to your new work location (applicable to both employees and self-employed persons), but only to the extent of earnings from your new work location.

- Students may also claim expenses to move to a job (including a summer job) or to start a business, but only to the extent of earnings from the job or business. Students who incur moving expenses to attend full-time courses at a post-secondary school may also claim these expenses, but only to the extent of any scholarship, research grant or similar award income from the school.

- Interest paid on money borrowed to earn investment or business income is generally deductible. However, the investment loss rules described in Chapter 7 may reduce the capital gains exemption you can claim on capital gains you realize after 1987, if you are deducting interest expense that is higher than your investment income.

If you have outstanding debts on which the interest is non-deductible, it may be possible to convert the non-deductible interest into deductible interest in respect of investments. If, for example, you have an outstanding mortgage of $50,000 on your home and you hold $20,000 of Canada Savings Bonds, you should consider cashing in the bonds, reducing your mortgage and then, if you wish, borrowing the necessary funds (interest deductible) to reinvest in some form of income-producing securities. Even if you decide not to borrow for reinvestment, you should be ahead of the game because the rate of non-deductible interest payable on your mortgage is almost certain to be higher than the after-tax rate of return on your investments. However, caution is advised as this type of tax planning may be closely scrutinized by the tax authorities.

If you are paying a substantial amount of tax-deductible interest, you can apply to your local district taxation office to reduce the amount of tax withheld from your pay-cheque. You will have to demonstrate that the taxes being withheld by your employer will significantly exceed your total tax liability for the year, when your interest deduction is taken into account. Revenue Canada will then provide your employer with permission to reduce your tax deductions accordingly. As a result, you will have extra money each month to pay your interest charges or to use for other investments, instead of waiting until after you file your tax return the following spring to receive your tax refund. You can also apply for permission to reduce tax deducted from employment earnings where you have other large tax deductions like alimony or deductions resulting from tax shelter investments.

Other carrying charges or costs of holding investments which can be deducted include safety deposit box charges, investment counsel fees, accounting fees for recording investment income, and fees for the management or safe custody of investments.

Quebec Stock Savings Plan

The *Quebec Taxation Act* permits Quebec residents to claim a deduction from income of the cost of eligible shares contributed to a Quebec Stock Savings Plan (QSSP). A QSSP is established and administered by a registered broker or other financial institution that retains custody of share certificates contributed to the plan. Only newly-issued shares or convertible securities issued by public corporations are eligible for inclusion in a QSSP. These include common shares, non-redeemable preferred shares or debentures that are convertible into common shares.

A Quebec taxpayer can deduct up to ten percent of his "total income," a defined term for QSSP purposes, without reduction for any contributions to an RRSP or registered pension plan.

If the taxpayer does not hold the shares (or other eligible investments substituted for them) in the QSSP for at least two complete years following the year of contribution, an amount equal to the cost of the shares withdrawn from the plan will be included in income in the year of withdrawal.

The deduction to be claimed by the taxpayer varies, depending on the nature of the corporation whose shares are being contributed to the QSSP and the type of share issued. For example, if the corporation is a "growth corporation" — one with assets between $2 million and $250 million — its common shares with full voting rights contributed to a QSSP qualify for a deduction equal to 100 percent of their purchase price. In contrast, shares issued by a large corporation (assets of $1 billion to $2.5 billion) do not qualify for a QSSP deduction. Shares issued by a medium-size corporation (assets of $250 million to $1 billion) will, as a result of a proposal contained in the recent Quebec budget, no longer qualify for a QSSP deduction if issued after May 20, 1993. In addition, certain Quebec regional corporations qualify for a QSSP deduction of 150 percent of their purchase price.

As of May 20, 1993, the Quebec budget proposes to allow until December 31, 1994 only, convertible securities issued by a growth corporation to qualify for a QSSP deduction. This deduction is equal to 50 percent of the convertible security's purchase price.

Contributions to a QSSP are deductible from income for Quebec tax purposes only, and dividend income received on shares included in a QSSP is taxable to the investor. By comparison, contributions to a registered pension plan or RRSP are deductible from income for both federal and Quebec purposes, and income earned in these plans accumulates tax-free until termination of the plan. Accordingly, although shares held in a QSSP can be withdrawn without tax consequences after the required two-year period (achieving a permanent savings), Quebec taxpayers should consider the alternative of obtaining a greater immediate tax deferral (both federal and provincial) by contributing the maximum allowable amount to their registered pension plan or RRSP, as the case may be, before applying any available excess to the purchase of an investment in a QSSP.

Other Provincial Stock Savings Plans

Several provinces have introduced or are considering the introduction of stock savings plans to provide incentives for direct equity investment in a broad range of corporations. Many of the basic features of the Quebec Stock Savings Plan, in effect since 1979, have been adopted in these new plans.

The plans provide for a tax credit to be allowed against provincial taxes payable, equal to a specified percentage of the taxpayer's cost of eligible shares. The shares must be newly-issued common voting shares (or in some cases, non-redeemable preferred shares convertible to common at the holder's option) of corporations that operate through a permanent establishment in the province and pay a specified portion of their total wage and salary expense in the province.

The shares must be contributed to a special plan, administered by an approved trustee. The shares (or eligible substitutes) must be held for at least two years following the year of purchase, or the credit must be repaid. Shares qualifying for any other provincial or federal tax deduction or credit are not eligible under these programmes.

Alberta, Saskatchewan and Nova Scotia had stock savings plans through to 1989, 1991 and 1992 respectively which offered tax credits of up to thirty percent for emerging companies, decreasing to fifteen or ten percent for companies with larger revenue or asset bases. The yearly maximum tax credit was $3,000, but excess or unused credits were allowed to be carried forward.

Ontario and Nova Scotia have recently established new employee share ownership programs which provide for a tax credit of 20 percent of the investment (maximum $1,000).

Venture Capital Programmes

To stimulate the supply of venture capital for small businesses, several provinces have enacted special incentive legislation, which applies to new corporations created to provide equity capital and management expertise to small businesses.

At present, such programmes exist in British Columbia, Alberta, Saskatchewan, Quebec and Ontario. Although the specifics of the programmes vary from province to province, generally the venture capital corporation may acquire up to fifty percent of the equity shares of a small business engaged in an approved activity, such as manufacturing and processing, research and development, tourism or various service industries. To qualify, the small business must carry on all or most of its operations in the particular province. The incentive to the person investing in a venture capital corporation is that purchasing newly issued shares in the corporation results in a grant from the province (in Ontario, Saskatchewan and Alberta), a credit against provincial income taxes (in British Columbia), or a reduction from income (Quebec). The grant or credit is equal to thirty percent of the taxpayer's cost of the investment, for the programmes in British Columbia, Alberta, Saskatchewan and certain regions of northern and eastern Ontario. For other areas in Ontario, the former thirty percent rate was reduced to twenty-five percent for shares issued after October 24, 1985. The deduction available to Quebec investors is 150 percent (100 percent for shares issued prior to May 15, 1992) of the cost of the shares purchased, but not exceeding ten percent of total income.

For tax purposes, the grants or tax credits received by the investor are not taxable and will not reduce the cost base of the shares in calculating any capital gain realized on subsequent resale (but may restrict the deduction for any capital loss incurred).

The incentive for investing in a venture capital corporation is obvious, but it must be recognized that some investment risk is involved because the corporation is required to use most of its capital to invest in equity shares of small developing businesses.

Tax Credits

By subtracting the deductions outlined above from total income, you establish the amount of your taxable income. Then you use the appropriate tax rate schedule to establish the gross tax payable on your taxable income. Once the gross tax payable has been computed, tax credits are subtracted to determine net tax payable. A schedule is included in Appendix III to help you calculate your net tax payable after deducting tax credits.

Personal Tax Credits

A central feature of the 1987 Tax Reform was the conversion of personal exemptions into personal tax credits in 1988 and future years. Exemptions are deducted in calculating taxable income and are more valuable as your income and tax rate rises. Tax credits, in contrast, reduce taxes payable to the same extent for all taxpayers, regardless of their income level. With the move to tax credits, the tax value of personal exemptions has been reduced for middle- and higher-income Canadians and increased for lower-income Canadians.

Following is a table of the 1993 federal personal tax credit system:

	Income Amount	1993 Federal Tax Credit @ 17%	Approximate Federal and Provincial Value of Tax Credit, *Including 3% Federal Surtax
	($)	($)	($)
Basic	6,456	1,098	1,723
Married and equivalent-to-married	5,380	915	1,435
Dependants under 18 at the end of the year	NIL	NIL	NIL
Dependants 18 and over			
– infirm	1,583	269	423
– other	NIL	NIL	NIL
Age 65 and over (transferable)	3,482	592	929
Disability (transferable)	4,233	720	1,130

*Assumes average provincial tax rate of fifty-eight percent of basic federal tax (except Quebec).

These tax credits are indexed to the annual increases in the Consumer Price Index over three percent.

If you claim the married or equivalent-to-married federal credit, the credit is reduced by seventeen percent of your spouse's or dependant's net income over $538 in 1993.

The unused portion of any of these new credits is not refunded if you otherwise have no tax to pay. The unused portion of the age credit can be transferred to your spouse, and the disability credit to your spouse or a supporting parent or grandparent. The amount of the federal tax credits that can be transferred is reduced by seventeen percent of your net income over $6,456 in 1993.

Since 1987, there are no longer any deductions for dependent children over eighteen, unless they are infirm. Along the same lines, the availability of the equivalent-to-married credit has been tightened to exclude dependent children unless they are under nineteen or are infirm. With the introduction of the Child Tax Benefit, beginning in 1993 there no longer are deductions for dependent minor children unless they qualify for the equivalent-to-married credit.

To be eligible for the equivalent-to-married credit, you must be single, divorced, separated or widowed and must, by yourself or jointly with another, maintain a self-contained domestic establishment in which you live and support a person resident in Canada who, during the year, is wholly dependent on you for support and who is connected by blood relationship, marriage or adoption. In the case of a child, however, it is not necessary that the child reside in Canada. A dependant over eighteen will only be eligible as an equivalent-to-married if he or she is dependent due to an infirmity unless it is your parent or grandparent.

Since 1988 personal exemption claims under the Quebec tax system have also been converted into tax credits. Indexation for Quebec tax credits was introduced in 1990. The 1993 Quebec budget proposes to suspend the indexation temporarily in 1994 for one year.

Your credit for the married exemption and for dependent children is reduced by the dependant's net income. Dependent children include your children, grandchildren, sisters, brothers, nieces, nephews, under age 18 at any time in the year or 18 and over and studying full-time.

In Quebec a single parent may add the $1,300 exemption to the $2,600 available for the first dependent child. He or she may also be eligible for the $1,500 exemption for living alone or with dependants. These provisions replace the former "equivalent-to-married" exemption which is no longer available for Quebec tax purposes.

	Income Amount	1993 Quebec Credit @ 20%
	($)	($)
Basic	5,900	1,180
Person living alone or with dependent children	1,050	210
Married exemption	5,900	1,180
Dependent children		
— 1st dependant	2,600	520
— each additional dependant	2,250	450
— additional exemption where the dependant attends a post-secondary school: credit per term (maximum two terms per year)	1,650	330
Single Parent	1,300	260
Other dependants		
— general	2,250	450
— mentally or physically infirm	5,900	1,180
Age 65 and over (transferable)	2,245	449
Disability (transferable)	2,245	449

Other dependants include anyone 18 years of age or over at the beginning of the year who is related to the taxpayer by blood, marriage or adoption, is wholly dependent upon the taxpayer and normally resides with the taxpayer. The credit for a disabled dependant does not apply to anyone claimed as a dependent child or spouse or for whom the general credit of $450 has been claimed.

Other Credits

Other tax deductions that were available in 1987 and earlier years were also converted in 1988 to federal tax credits at a rate of seventeen percent, as outlined in the table below. Taxpayers at all income levels receive the same tax relief from these deductions after 1987.

If your taxable income is below approximately $29,000, the credit will equal the tax reduction you would have realized from the exemption under the old system, because your federal tax rate will be seventeen percent. However, if your taxable income is higher than $29,000, the new credit system reduces your tax savings from these deductions.

Federal Tax Credits

Pension Income	Seventeen percent of eligible pension income, maximum $170 ($200 in Quebec). Unused credit transferable to spouse.
Tuition Fees	Seventeen percent for post-secondary fees; up to $680 transferable to spouse or supporting parent or grandparent. For Quebec purposes, tuition fees are tax deductions and not tax credits. Also for Quebec purposes, fee deductions are not

transferable to parents; however, a general parental personal credit is available for dependents in full-time post secondary courses.

Education

$13 credit (seventeen percent of $80) for each month in full-time attendance; transferable as part of the $680 limit for tuition fees. This credit is not available in Quebec.

Medical Expenses

Credit of seventeen percent (twenty percent in Quebec) for uninsured medical expenses in excess of the lesser of three percent of net income and $1,614.

CPP/QPP and UI Premiums
(employee share)

Credit at seventeen percent (twenty percent in Quebec). Prior to 1993, these premiums were tax deductions for Quebec tax purposes.

For taxpayers sixty-five and over, eligible pension income includes annuity payments from a pension plan (except amounts transferred into an RRSP or RPP), as well as annuity payments out of an RRSP or a DPSP, payments under an RRIF, and amounts included in income for certain other annuities.

For individuals under sixty-five, eligible pension income includes annuity payments from a pension plan and certain other payments received as a result of the death of a spouse.

For persons under sixty, the sixty to sixty-five rules apply with one further restriction: no credit may be claimed if, for the same year, you deduct any amount for a rollover contribution of pension benefits to another pension plan or RRSP. CPP or QPP benefits and Old Age Security or guaranteed income supplement payments do not qualify, regardless of a taxpayer's age.

The tuition credit applies to tuition fees (but not books or other expenses) greater than $100 paid in the year to a post-secondary educational institution in Canada (or outside Canada, in limited circumstances). Students can claim a seventeen percent credit on eligible tuition fees without limit plus the $13 credit (seventeen percent of $80) for each month of full-time attendance.

Where a student does not owe enough tax to make full use of these credits, the unused portion is not refundable, but can be transferred to a spouse or supporting parent or grandparent to a maximum of $680 less the amount used by the student to offset taxes owing.

The seventeen percent federal credit (twenty percent for Quebec) can be claimed for medical expenses (excluding non-prescription drugs and provincial health care premiums) paid for yourself, your spouse or any dependants to the extent they exceed the lesser of three percent of your net income and $1,614 in 1993. Starting in 1993, whenever you claim medical expenses of a dependant other than your spouse, the credit is to be reduced by sixty-eight percent of the dependant's income in excess of the basic personal amount.

Political Contributions

A credit of up to $500 (seventy-five percent of first $100, fifty percent of next $450, and 33.1/3% of any excess) is available for contributions to registered federal political parties or candidates for election to the House of Commons. Depending on your province of residence, you may be eligible for a similar credit or a deduction for contributions to provincial parties or candidates in provincial elections. There is no credit or deduction available for contributions to candidates in civic elections.

Refundable Child Tax Credit

In January, 1993, the Child Tax Benefit Program replaced family allowance payments and both the refundable and non-refundable child tax credits. This new program provides for payments of $1,020 for each of two children and increased by $75 for the third and each subsequent child in a family. This child tax benefit is remitted monthly and is generally paid to the mother. Families not claiming child care expenses will receive an additional $213 for each child under seven. These benefits are gradually reduced for families with incomes above designated thresholds and then eliminated where family income exceeds $75,000.

Prior to 1993, child tax credits of up to $601 per child under eighteen were available to lower-income Canadian families. The refundable child tax credit available for children aged six and under or seven to fourteen with special needs was $213 for parents who cared for their children at home or who did not claim a deduction for child care expenses. This credit was reduced by $5 for every $100 of net income of the supporting parents over a threshold amount of $25,921 in 1992. The $213 supplement was reduced by twenty-five percent of child care expenses claimed for the child. The child tax credit was fully refundable to the extent it was not required to reduce taxes payable. Contrast this with the previously-noted credits which are not refundable and are only transferable in limited circumstances to other family members.

Foreign Tax Credit

You may claim a credit for income taxes paid to foreign countries. The credit is limited to the amount of Canadian tax due on income from the foreign country. For foreign taxes paid on investment income, you can also deduct any excess foreign taxes which do not qualify as a credit.

GST Credit

A refundable tax credit of $198 is available to eligible individuals. An eligible individual is defined as an individual resident in Canada who is married or, as of 1993, living common-law, a parent or at least 19 years old at the end of the year.

An additional credit of $198 may be claimed for an individual's spouse or for a dependant under 19 years of age in respect of whom the individual has claimed an equivalent-to-married credit. If this additional credit is available, only one individual may claim the GST credit.

Further credits of $105 are available for each other person under 19 years of age who is wholly dependent on the individual or the individual's spouse. A single individual may claim an additional credit equal to two percent of income in excess of the basic personal amount for the year ($6,458 for 1993) up to a maximum of $100. The individual's total credit is reduced by five cents for each dollar of income that the taxpayer, and the person for whom an additional $198 credit has been claimed, exceeds the indexed threshold ($25,921 in 1993). Payments are made quarterly, or as a lump sum where the credit is less than $100.

Example

GST credit for a married couple with three young children for the 1993 taxation year:

Basic credit		$198
Spousal credit		198
Three children (3 x $105)		315
		711
Net income of both spouses	$32,000	
Less: Credit threshold	25,921	
	6,079	
Subtract 5% of $6,079		(304)
GST credit for the year		$407

The spouse receiving the credit will receive it in four installments of $102 in July and October 1994 and January and April 1995.

Dividend Tax Credit

A commonly encountered credit is the dividend tax credit. As explained earlier in this chapter, a grossed-up amount of dividends received from Canadian companies is included in taxable income, but a credit is then allowed against the resulting taxes payable. As a result, the net tax rate on Canadian dividend income is lower than that on many other types of investment income.

7

WHERE AND HOW TAXES ARE SAVED: Tax-Sheltered Investments

Another traditionally important tax-saving technique involves investing in tax-sheltered investments. Simply put, a good tax shelter enables you to use dollars that you would otherwise pay in taxes (along with some of your own investment dollars) to acquire investments that will increase your net worth.

Investment in tax shelters was a very popular way of reducing tax in the 1970s. But many of these tax shelter deals turned out to be poor investments and sometimes the promised tax savings were not accepted by Revenue Canada. As a consequence, tax shelters generally have a tarnished image in Canada and they have been usually approached warily by investors since the 1980s. In addition, the *Income Tax Act* has restricted the deductibility of costs related to tax shelter investments, and has actually eliminated certain types of tax shelters. Therefore, tax-sheltered investments are not as important in personal tax planning as they once were.

Most tax shelters are a means of deferring, not eliminating, taxes. Most, if not all, tax shelters are generally high risk investments which are characterized by leverage and the availability of deductions that require no investor cash to obtain.

LEVERAGE

Leverage is a term used to describe a situation in which you control a large investment with a relatively small amount of your own money. The rest is financed with somebody else's money, and this will give you interest deductions. But leverage increases risk.

To illustrate, assume you invest in a $100,000 two-bedroom condominium for rental purposes. You make a $20,000 down payment and get a five-year loan from the seller at 10.5% a year for the remaining $80,000. The seller allows you to make payments on the loan using an amortization schedule of thirty years, but expects you to pay off the remaining balance on the loan at the end of five years. After three years, you resell this condo for $120,000 (net of selling expenses). Your annual payments on the $80,000 loan are about $8,800. After three years, you've paid off about $1,000 on the loan. Assuming that the rental income you received on the condo has covered your interest payments on the loan, then your total outlay has been $21,000 (the down payment plus the principal payments), but your gain before taxes would be about $20,000, (i.e. $120,000 less $100,000). That's a profit of almost 95 percent in only three years. If you had paid $100,000 cash down, your gain would still have been $20,000 or twenty percent. Note, however, that instead of using your rental income for interest payments, you would have received significant cash amounts each year, and these would increase your rate of return.

However, leverage also increases risk, as some real estate speculators have recently found out when real estate prices plunged. Using the same condo example, let's assume that you can't sell your condo after three years for as much as you paid for it, so to pay off the loan balance of $79,000 you sell it for $90,000. Now you have lost $10,000. Since you invested $21,000, you have realized a loss of about forty-eight percent. If you had paid the $100,000 in cash, your loss would have been a mere ten percent.

DEDUCTIONS

One attractive feature of tax shelters is that they provide you with deductions without requiring any cash contributions on your part (because assets are being purchased with borrowed funds). Tax shelters normally provide one of the following deductions:

Capital Cost Allowance

This is the deduction of the capital cost of equipment or a building over a period which may be shorter than its estimated useful life. In the case of manufacturing equipment purchased after 1987, it may be depreciated for federal tax purposes on a twenty-five percent declining balance basis (12 1/2% in the first year). Buildings acquired after 1987 may be depreciated on a four percent declining balance basis (two percent in the first year).

Natural Resources Exploration and Development Deductions

Investors in natural resources (mining and energy) exploration and development programmes are allowed various write-offs for expenditures incurred. The timing of the write-offs depends on the nature of the expenditures, which range from Canadian exploration expenses (100 percent write-off available in the first year) to Canadian development expenses (written off on a thirty percent declining balance basis) to Canadian oil and gas property expenses and foreign exploration and development expenses (ten percent declining balance basis). For Quebec purposes certain of these expenditures may be eligible for additional write-off if these were incurred to promote exploration and development in Quebec.

Scientific Research and Development Deductions

Direct investors in scientific research programmes and partnerships can deduct current or capital expenditures on qualified research undertaken in the year, except for most expenditures on building acquisitions and rental payments for buildings after 1987. To qualify for these deductions, for federal tax purposes you must be actively involved in the business which can benefit from the research. To offset this federal restriction, Quebec has expanded its research and development incentives for research and development carried out in Quebec.

In addition, interest paid on the money borrowed to finance all of the above expenditures is usually deductible.

INVESTMENT TAX CREDIT

This is a dollar-for-dollar reduction of taxes due. Tax credits are more valuable than tax deductions. A deductible dollar reduces your taxable income by one dollar. A dollar of tax credit reduces your taxes by one dollar. Say you have taxable income of $60,000 and are considering a tax-sheltered investment. You are considering one investment that provides current year deductions of $5,000 and another investment that provides current year deductions of $3,000 and tax credits of $2,000. Which investment is best from a tax standpoint in the current year? The analysis below will help answer the question.

	Investment #1	Investment #2
Taxable income before tax-sheltered investment	$60,000	$60,000
Deductions	(5,000)	(3,000)
Taxable income after investment	55,000	57,000
Tax on taxable income (using 1993 rates for an Ontario resident)	24,431	25,319
Credit against tax	—	(2,000)
Net Tax Due	$24,431	$23,319

But as a result of previous budget amendments, the previously existing rates for many types of investment tax credits, other than scientific reasearch tax credits, were phased out as of 1989.

DEFERRAL OF TAXES

Most tax shelters do not eliminate taxes; they simply defer them to a later period. The tax deferral created by claiming tax losses in earlier years and recognizing the income in later years may have varying results:

- It may be a simple deferral of tax that gives the investors the benefit of using the tax dollars for a period of years before repaying them without interest.

- The deductions may be taken when your tax rate is high (or low), and when the income is recognized your tax rate may be low (or high). Depending on your circumstances, this could be either to your advantage or to your disadvantage. You should therefore know what your tax bracket is at the time you invest in a tax shelter and what it will be at the time you plan to dispose of the investment.

- In some limited instances, the losses previously claimed by the investor may later have to be included in income, but at the favourable capital gain rates and they may also be eligible for the capital gains exemption.

UNFAVOURABLE TAX CONSEQUENCES

Tax-sheltered investments have "tax goodies." They also have some "tax gotchas." The "tax gotchas" include the at-risk rules, the alternative minimum tax, and the net investment loss rules. These are discussed in the following paragraphs.

The At-Risk Rules

In the past, many tax shelters were structured as highly leveraged limited partnerships. In some cases, a substantial portion of the investment was financed with funds for which the borrower had no personal liability (non-recourse debt), and investors claimed deductions for expenses that they might never be called on to pay.

In response to such situations, "at-risk" rules were introduced to strengthen Revenue Canada's ability to deny such deductions. Under these rules, an investor in a limited partnership tax shelter can only deduct business losses or claim investment tax credits that exceed the amount of his at-risk investment in the partnership. Generally speaking, the at-risk amount is calculated as the adjusted cost base of the partnership interest, plus the current year's income, less certain amounts owing by the investor to the partnership and less any guarantee or indemnity provided to protect the limited partner against the loss of his or her investment. As well, the at-risk amount is reduced by investment tax credits allocated to the investor.

Minimum Tax

Alternative minimum tax (AMT) addresses the government's concern that some taxpayers with large incomes are able to avoid paying part or all of their income tax. Part of this avoidance was previously accomplished legally through tax-favoured or tax-sheltered investments. The government felt that this was unfair and that no one should be permitted to avoid his or her fair share of the tax burden so in 1986 AMT was introduced.

All higher-income Canadians are potentially subject to this tax, although it actually only affects a relatively small group of taxpayers. The minimum tax is most likely to affect taxpayers who have contributed large amounts (for example, a retiring allowance) to an RRSP, those who have made substantial tax-sheltered investments or those who have realized significant capital gains in the year.

To determine whether you must pay a minimum tax over and above the taxes you would otherwise pay, you must recalculate your net income (line 3 on Form 11) for the year to include or exclude certain items which the government feels can be used to unfairly reduce taxes. Accordingly, net income is recalculated to deny tax-shelter deductions such as losses arising from Canadian exploration expenses, Canadian development expenses and depletion deductions, and capital cost allowance claims on multiple-unit residential buildings or Canadian films. Deductions for contributions to an RRSP or a registered pension plan must be added back to net income as well. Adjustments are also necessary for tax-favoured income. The untaxed quarter of net capital gains for the year is included in adjusted net income.

This adjusted net income amount is then reduced by any non-capital or capital losses of other years deducted from ordinary net income. Adjusted net income can also be reduced to delete the grossed-up portion (i.e. twenty-five percent) of any dividends received from Canadian companies, so that only the actual amount of dividends received are potentially subject to the minimum tax. (Your net income may also be adjusted for less common items than the ones just described.)

This amount is then further reduced by $40,000; the remaining amount, if any, will be subject to a federal minimum tax of seventeen percent plus a provincial tax of about nine percent (in Quebec twenty percent for 1993 and sixteen percent for 1992). The actual provincial tax rate varies depending on the province in which you live. This minimum tax amount is then reduced by the personal tax credits you are entitled to (as described in Chapter 6) plus other tax credits for charitable donations, tuition fees, and so on. You are required to pay the higher of the two taxes, so that either you pay on your unadjusted taxable income or you pay the minimum tax, calculated as above.

Where the minimum tax does apply, the extra tax paid can be carried forward for up to seven years to reduce future income taxes, to the extent that regular tax in that year exceeds the minimum tax.

The above is a simplified (believe it or not!) version of the minimum tax rules. It is not possible to briefly deal with all the circumstances in which this tax may apply. This potential additional tax cost should certainly be considered by anyone thinking of investing in a tax shelter or anyone who has already made substantial tax-sheltered investments. It will also be an important consideration for anyone with significant realized or expected capital gains, whether or not exempt under the lifetime capital gains exemption. But for the average taxpayer, whose major income source is salary or business earnings, and who does not have any large deductions, the minimum tax should not apply.

The Quebec minimum tax rules are substantially the same as those introduced by the federal government except that for Quebec minimum tax purposes, deductions for certain investments included in your "strategic economic investment account" are exempt from minimum tax, up to fifteen percent of net income. Strategic investments include certified Quebec films, investments in Quebec Stock Savings Plan, Quebec Business Investment Companies (QBIC) or SPEC, Cooperative Investment Plan (CIP) and Savings and Credit Union Permanent Share Savings Plan. Investments in scientific research and resource exploration carried out in Quebec are also considered as strategic investments.

Net Investment Loss Rules

The cumulative *net investment loss* rules may restrict your ability to claim the capital gains exemption.

Your cumulative net investment loss account represents the net of the investment expenses you deducted after 1987 minus the investment income you earned in the same period. Investment income includes interest, taxable dividends, rental income from real property and other income from property or a business in which you are not actively involved. Investment expenses include one-half of resource deductions other than earned depletion from flow-through shares or a limited partnership, rental losses from real property, business losses, including interest expenses, where you are not actively involved in the business, and investment carrying charges, including interest expense.

These rules do not match the investment expenses of a particular investment with the gain on the investment. If you realize a gain on an investment for which you have not incurred any expenses, you will not be able to claim an exemption on this gain, to the extent your cumulative investment expenses exceed your cumulative investment income. For example, if you realized a capital gain in January 1992, your capital gains exemption would have been reduced by any carrying charges incurred in 1992 even if these were incurred after the sale on other investments.

ECONOMIC SUBSTANCE

An investor needs to analyse any prospective tax shelter from an economic viewpoint. The potential profit should be commensurate with the risk involved. If an investment fails economically, you are probably going to lose money in real dollars, and consequently it does not make much sense to go into it only for tax reasons.

Unfortunately, many individuals are lured into "investments" by tax shelter promoters who promise large tax savings. Upon analysis, many shelters with promises of large tax savings may turn out to have very little economic potential and a very aggressive interpretation of tax laws. The promised deductions may be challenged and disallowed by Revenue Canada, or the tax shelter itself may even be considered a fraud, which will cause you more problems. Take care, therefore, to evaluate the economic substance of any tax shelter. Get a prospectus, read it, have your questions and concerns answered to your satisfaction. Check on the reliability, reputation and track record of the promoter, and apply the following tests, adapted from an article in *Medical Economics.**

1. Why is the tax shelter promoter contacting you? Is it based on a long-standing business relationship, or is it an unknown phone call promotion for an out-of-country orange-growing project? Perhaps the promoter has run out of close contacts who trust his projects.

2. What's the track record of the tax shelter manager? Has he or she compiled a successful track record in substantially similar projects? Tax shelters have some common characteristics, but they are worlds apart in most business aspects. A specialist in rental properties may know very little about oil-drilling ventures.

3. Can you read the prospectus without raising your eyebrows? See what the general partner in the deal is taking out. How much of your money will actually go to the proposed project rather than into the promoter's pocket through commissions and management and acquisition fees? If much less than eighty-five cents of every investment dollar is going to the project, be skeptical. The more money the promoters skim off the top in fees, commissions and promotion costs, the smaller the part of your investment that will actually be working for you.

4. Is there a clear profit motive in the deal? Revenue Canada's policy toward tax shelters can be summed up in two words: economic reality. This means that a shelter should be structured as Parliament intended — to encourage investment in a risky but potentially profitable business venture. If a venture has little chance of making a profit, Revenue Canada may say that its true purpose is only to avoid taxes.

5. What do tax advisors think? After you have done the initial research on a tax-sheltered investment possibility, get backup advice from a lawyer or tax expert whom you trust — and one whose specialty is the field you're interested in. Get advice on the economic substance of the investment and the credibility of the tax benefits. This advice may cost you several hundred dollars in fees paid to the expert, but may save you a bundle later on.

6. Is there a better way? After you have checked out the risks and rewards, and if the tax shelter still looks like a good bet, ask yourself whether there isn't some other way to shave your tax bill just as much without the risk of a tax shelter — with an RRSP, or by investing in Canadian equities to receive tax-favoured dividends or tax-free gains.

---

* "Tax Shelters — Seven Tests Any Deal Should Pass." Medical Economics. March 31, 1980.

TYPES OF TAX SHELTERS

As you study the tax shelters described below, keep in mind that each type of investment has its own range of economic risk. The following comments relate solely to the tax issues and do not deal with investment potential or provide a risk analysis.

Rental Real Estate

In the past, rental real estate, particularly multiple-unit residential buildings (MURBs) were a popular form of tax shelter. MURBs (certified as such by Canada Mortgage and Housing Corporation) were more attractive from an income tax standpoint than other rental real estate because the maximum available capital cost allowance (generally five percent of the declining balance cost of the building) could be deducted even if it created a rental loss. Capital cost allowance on other rental real estate is generally limited to an amount that will reduce net rental income to nil after first claiming all other deductible expenses such as interest, property taxes, insurance and repairs. Tax reform contained several changes that reduced the tax incentives for rental real estate after 1987. The ability to deduct rental losses created by claiming capital cost allowance on MURBs will be eliminated. If you are the owner of a MURB bought before June 18, 1987, it will be treated in the same manner as any other rental property after 1993 — that is, you will no longer be able to deduct a rental loss created by claiming capital cost allowance. If you bought an existing MURB after June 18, 1987, you have not been able to create a rental loss by claiming capital cost allowance in any year.

Tax reform also reduced the capital cost allowance rate on buildings bought after 1987 to four percent from five percent.

The deduction of so-called soft costs, including interest during the construction period, financing fees, landscaping, and rental guarantees, has also attracted investors in the past who are looking for tax shelter. The deduction of these costs has been significantly restricted in recent years. For example, most soft costs (particularly interest expense) incurred before or during the construction, renovation or alteration of a building are no longer deductible. Instead, these expenses must be added to the cost of either the land or the building, with the cost of the building then being eligible for capital cost allowance. As a result, what was once an immediate deduction has now been limited to a deduction of four percent (or five percent, for buildings bought before 1988) a year on a declining balance basis.

In addition, the maximum capital cost allowance claim permitted in the year of purchase of any assets, including rental buildings, is limited to one-half of the normal annual rate.

Hotels, Motels, Retirement Homes, Recreational Vehicles, etc.

Investments in these properties may seem to be unlikely ways to shelter income from tax, but these investments have been a popular form of tax shelter in past years for high-income tax-payers, even though the investors may have little knowledge of the particular industry.

Typically, a group of investors would buy the property with the down payment largely financed by a bank loan and the balance of the purchase price represented by a longer-term mortgage. A professional manager and staff would usually be hired to operate the business.

Until recently, these investments offered good tax shelter advantages. Capital cost allowance could be claimed at relatively high rates on the various classes of assets (even with the rule that now permits only one-half the normal allowance in the year of acquisition) so that business losses for tax purposes often resulted in the early years of operation. Each partner could then deduct his share of these losses and the resulting tax savings were often sufficient to repay the initial borrowings in a few years.

The government considered such arrangements to be abusive, with overly generous tax treatment. As a result, the *Income Tax Act* has been amended to limit the ability to shelter other income with losses created by capital cost allowance on property used in businesses that offer services combined with the use of that property. In effect, income from such property is to be treated as rental income and capital cost allowance claims will be limited to an amount that reduces net income to nil. These rules apply, unless the investors are personally active in the daily business operations.

Where available capital cost allowance is a key factor in the decision to make a tax shelter investment, investigate thoroughly to ensure that these restrictions do not apply. Such investments should be evaluated as normal business investments rather than as conventional tax shelters, as no shelter is generally provided against other income except to the extent of any actual operating losses excluding capital cost allowance.

Natural Resource Investments

There always seems to be interest in oil, gas or mining investments that offer tax shelter opportunities. One of the most common forms of such investments has been the limited partnership, where the general partner is the operator of the project and the investors are limited partners (with limited legal responsibility for partnership debts). At the end of each year, the limited partners are provided with a statement showing their share of the year's income, the amounts of exploration and development expenses incurred by the partnership during the year and any special deductions such as the amount of oil and gas property expense. This information is then included in the investor's tax return for the year.

Exploration and development as well as oil and gas property expenses will reduce the adjusted cost base of your partnership interest and hence can limit your claims for investment tax credits and business losses. This erosion in the adjusted cost base reflects the impact of the at-risk rules which were extended to most resource expenditures incurred by partnerships after June 17, 1987.

Another popular form of tax-sheltered natural resources investment is the so-called "flow-through" share. The investors purchase newly issued shares of a company which uses the funds for exploration. Instead of the company claiming the tax deduction that it would otherwise be entitled to for the exploration costs, these deductions "flow through" to the investor. The investor recoups a substantial part of his investment in the short term through current tax savings, and thus has purchased an investment in the natural resources company at a reduced cost. When he eventually sells these shares, the entire proceeds will normally be taxed as a capital gain, which may be tax-free to the extent that the investor has not used his lifetime capital gains exemption. The net investment loss rule has significantly reduced the attractions of flow-through shares for many investors. If you have invested in flow-through shares and have claimed the resource deductions after 1987, you will not be able to realize a completely tax-free gain after 1987 on their sale by claiming the capital gains exemption, unless you have other investment income to offset one-half of the resource deductions claimed.

Films

For many years, one of the main tax incentives for investing in a certified Canadian feature film or videotape was that the entire cost of the investment could be deducted as capital cost allowance over two years. The capital cost allowance could be deducted against any other income thus providing significant tax deferral opportunities. As well, as little as five percent of the purchase price could be paid in cash at the time of purchase with the balance paid within four years. For example, you could buy a $100,000 Canadian film interest for a $5,000 cash payment resulting in tax savings of approximately $50,000 over a two-year period.

However, this ability to shelter non-film income through capital cost allowance claims on certified productions has now been significantly curtailed. The capital cost allowance on such films was reduced from a two-year write-off to an annual deduction of thirty percent on a declining balance basis. Any film loss resulting from the claim of this reduced level of depreciation continues to be available as a tax shelter for income from all other sources. An additional capital cost allowance claim for the unclaimed cost of the film is available to the extent you have any film income in the year. For Quebec purposes, certain investments in Quebec certified films may allow you to reduce your income by the amount of labour production costs in respect of which the producer of the film has foregone claiming his available tax credit.

FORM 12 — YOUR TAX-SAVING IDEAS

Now that you know how taxes can be saved and you have a targeted taxable income on Form 11, which you completed before, fill in Form 12. Then take action. You may want to discuss your tax-saving ideas with a tax advisor. You will probably make best use of your advisor's time by first doing your homework on Forms 11 and 12. Figure 7-1 shows you a sample of a filled-in form related to the sample shown in Form 11 in Chapter 5.

- Many tax-saving ideas, once implemented, have a multi-year impact. For example, when you purchase real estate for rental purposes, capital cost allowance and interest deductions are predictable for many years according to a capital cost allowance schedule and a loan repayment schedule.

- You may need significant resources to implement some tax-saving ideas. For example, to purchase rental real estate you may need a substantial down payment. Other tax-saving ideas may require the sale of existing investment assets or borrowing against these assets.

- Prepayment of planned multi-year tax-deductible expenditures such as large charitable contributions is a very good idea when your top tax rate will decrease over the next few years.

- The earlier you implement your tax-saving ideas, the better. The later it is in the year, the harder it is to reduce your taxable income without making riskier investments.

FIGURE 7-1

File under TAX PLANNING   Date: *May 28*

FORM 12   TAX-SAVING IDEAS

TAX-SAVING IDEA

Tax-Free Income: *Shift $10,000 into equities (growth-oriented mutual fund) to take advantage of capital gains exemption.*

Tax-Favoured Income: *Borrow $10,000 to invest in dividend paying Canadian stock.*

Tax-Deferred Income: *Continue maximum contribution to RRSP.*

Tax-Sheltered Income:

Shifting Income to Dependants: *Set up a registered education savings plan for my two children ($3,000).*

Tax-Deductible Expenditures: *Increase amount of interest paid which is tax-deductible (i.e. investment loans) while decreasing personal loan interest.*

Action	Action Date	Funds Needed	Reduction of Taxable Income	
Tax-free Income	*June 30*	*None–use existing assets*	*($4,000)*	
Tax-favoured Income	*June 30*	*$10,000*	*—*	*gross amount of dividends will approx. equal interest expense but will generate tax credit of approx. $350.00*
Tax-deferred Income	*Feb. 28 (or earlier if possible)*	*$12,500*	*Already in Schedule 11*	
Tax-sheltered Investments				
Shift Income to Dependants	*May 15*	*None–use existing funds*	*($500)*	
Tax-deductible Expenditures	*June 30*	*None–rearrange existing debts*	*($4,500)*	
TOTALS		*$22,500*	*($9,000)*	

8

YEAR-END PLANNING

The last steps in the tax-planning process as the end of the year approaches are the computation of your current year's actual taxable income, the comparison of your actual taxable income with the targeted taxable income for the current year that you established some months ago, and the implementation of some year-end action steps to make sure you achieve your targeted taxable income.

Thus, year-end action is merely the last phase of a process that began with your formulation of your tax plan and the implementation of some tax-saving ideas some months or even years ago. Although these are the last steps in the process, they are very important, for after December 31 there is little you can do to save taxes other than contribute to an RRSP in the first sixty days of the next year. For those of you who have procrastinated, despite our discussions in Chapters 5, 6 and 7 about the importance of tax planning long before year end, year end is the only time you have to do any tax planning.

The best time to do year-end tax planning is the fall, no later than November. Fall is the proper time of year for finalizing your tax plan, for by then you have most of your financial data for the year, but there is still time to take action before the end of the financial year.

If you have capital gains or losses for the year, probably the best place to begin year-end planning is with Forms 13A and 13B. If you have no capital assets, skip Forms 13A and 13B, and begin your final tax-saving thrust by completing Form 14, *Year-End Tax Plan.*

FORMS 13A and 13B — CAPITAL GAINS AND LOSSES

Once completed, Form 13A will provide you with an estimate of the amount of taxable capital gains you must include in taxable income for the current year. Form 13B will indicate the taxable capital gains or allowable capital losses that could be triggered before the year end to adjust the amount determined in Form 13A.

The discussion of the tax treatment of capital gains and losses and of the lifetime capital gains exemption (included in Chapter 6) can be consulted to help you complete these forms. As well, a completed sample of each form is shown in Figures 8-1 and 8-2.

FIGURE 8-1

Date: *November 5*

FORM 13A   CAPITAL GAINS AND LOSSES REALIZED TO DATE

Number of Units	Investment Type	Date Acquired	Adjusted Cost Base	Date Sold	Net Proceeds	Gain (Loss)
100	Acme Stock	5/30/90	$2,400	4/10/93	$2,000	(400)
10	Best Bonds	7/1/88	7,800	10/30/93	8,200	400
300	Chance Stock	6/30/87	5,200	11/1/93	1,400	(3,800)
200	Dandy Stock	2/28/89	3,000	5/1/93	5,000	2,000
5	Early Bonds	11/30/89	4,000	7/1/93	3,200	(800)
200	Grinch Stock	6/24/90	1,200	10/30/93	1,000	(200)

Capital Gains Dividends
(received from mutual funds) — $400

Capital Loss Carry-overs*
(full amount of loss) — (—)

Total Loss — ($2,400)

Taxable Capital Gains (Allowable
Capital Losses) — three-quarters x Total — ($1,800)

Cumulative Taxable Capital Gains
exemption available (three-quarters of Cumulative
Capital Gains exemption available) — $75,000

Taxable Capital Gains (Allowable Capital
Losses) to be included in Taxable income — ($1,800)

* Capital losses realized after May 22, 1985 may not be used to reduce taxable income other than capital gains.

FIGURE 8-2

File under TAX PLANNING   Date: _November 5_

FORM 13B   UNREALIZED GAINS OR LOSSES OF CURRENT INVESTMENTS

Number of Units	Investment Type	Date Acquired	Adjusted Cost Base	Current Market Value	Unrealized Gain (Loss)
400	Dandy Stock	2/28/89	$6,000	$10,000	$4,000
5	Early Bonds	11/30/89	4,000	3,500	(500)
100	Hotshot Stock	6/24/89	2,000	1,200	(800)
Total Unrealized Capital Gains and Losses					$2,700

The appropriate year-end action plan for you depends on your specific circumstances. The following comments can, however, provide you with some general guidelines.

There are some who suggest that the capital gains exemption will not be a lasting part of the Canadian tax system. As a result, that capital gains exemption may be prudent to sell sufficient investments to use up the available capital gains exemption in the current year.

To the extent that you are currently paying tax at a lower rate than you expect to in the future, you may also wish to trigger some additional taxable capital gains to increase your current taxable income, thereby reducing future years' income. But make sure you take into account the cost of paying tax now rather than deferring it for one or more years.

On the other hand, if you are currently paying tax at a high rate and you have realized taxable capital gains in excess of your available capital gains exemption limit, you may wish to sell some investments with unrealized losses to offset these taxable gains.

Before any of these strategies are undertaken, however, you should also consider the investment implications; it makes little sense to sell a promising investment just to create a tax loss or gain.

If you do decide to sell, don't forget that for tax purposes the settlement date, not the trade date, is the effective selling date. Therefore, your sales should be done in time to permit settlement by December 31 (usually five business days before December 31 are needed). Also remember that, under the so-called superficial loss rules, you will not be allowed to deduct any loss triggered on the sale of an investment if you (or your spouse or a company you control) repurchase the same investment within thirty days.

In analysing our example situation we might recommend selling the 400 shares of Dandy Stock before year-end to offset the allowable capital loss or to use up more of your available capital gains exemption, thereby receiving the proceeds tax-free. But remember, in selecting year-end strategies, do not be guided solely by tax considerations. For example, do not sell a stock to trigger a gain (or a loss, for that matter), if you believe it is ready to take off.

FORM 14 — YEAR-END TAX PLAN

To help you analyse your tax situation for the current year and determine what year-end action is required, we have provided Form 14. The listed items on the form are similar to those on Form 11 and follow the structure of your 1993 tax return. In the first column, Actual to Date, you record your actual taxable transactions for the current year up to the date you complete Form 14. In the second column, *Estimates to Year-End*, you record your estimates of taxable transactions from now until the end of the year. In the third column, *Estimates for Total Year*, you place the total of the amounts in the first two columns.

To help you complete the form, refer to the instructions in Chapter 5 for completing Form 11 and to Figure 8-3 that shows you a filled-in sample of Form 14.

Here are some observations on the sample that may be of help to you in completing Form 14:

- The amounts shown under *Actual to Date* come from your records — pay records, information from financial institutions on dividends and interest and securities transactions, chequebook information on deductible expenditures, etc. You need to summarize this information to record it on Form 14. To summarize the data, you probably should have a lined pad and a calculator or home computer handy.

- The amounts shown under *Estimates to Year End* are your best estimates of transactions that are likely to occur, if you do not take any other action between the time you prepare Form 14 and the end of the year. In our example, the form was completed on November 7, and $13,000 is the estimate for additional salary during the remaining two months of the year. These estimates should be based on what you believe is likely to happen for each line on the form. For example, based on what you have received to date in compensation, you probably have a good idea of what you are likely to receive in compensation for the rest of the year. You may not have made your RRSP payment yet, but if you plan to, as our example family does, then put the estimated amount of the RRSP contribution under the "estimates" column.

- The amount of targeted taxable income comes from Form 11, *Tax-Planning Worksheet*, on which you targeted your taxable income for the current year. In our example, the targeted taxable income is $66,000. This amount is compared to the estimated taxable income for the year on line 5(a) of Form 14 — $72,800 in our example. If you have implemented all your tax-saving ideas on Form 12, your estimated taxable income for the year should be pretty close to your targeted taxable income. If you have procrastinated, you may be way off your target. Again, let us emphasize the need to start tax planning long before year-end, so that you are on or near your target by the time the end of the year rolls around. In our example, the difference between estimated and targeted taxable income is $6,800. If no action is taken in the remainder of the current year, the example taxpayer, who is in a 52.4% tax bracket, will have to pay an additional $3,563 in taxes over the targeted amount — $6,800 multiplied by 52.4%.

- This brings us to the point of this whole year-end exercise — to highlight year-end action required. If you want to get closer to your targeted taxable income, you have to take some additional tax-saving steps between the time you prepare *Your Year-End Tax Plan* and December 31. The rest of this chapter will focus on year-end action.

    As you read the rest of the chapter, list your action steps on Form 15, *Year-End Tax Action*. It would now be useful to complete the top of Form 15 using data from Form 14.

- At the top of Form 15 fill in your estimated taxable income from line 5(a) of your Form 14.

- On the next line of Form 15 fill in your targeted taxable income from line 6(a) of your Form 14.

- Then determine the required year-end reduction in taxable income. At the end of this chapter, we shall see if you have listed enough year-end action steps to reach the required reduction.

SHIFTING INCOME AND DEDUCTIONS

Effective year-end tax planning will generally involve the following:

- The implementation of tax-saving ideas you listed in Form 12 but have not yet carried out.

- The postponement of income to next year.

- The acceleration of deductions and credits into the current year.

You may be able to save taxes either by postponing income or by accelerating deductions and credits this year in the expectation that your tax rate next year will be lower. Even if your tax rate is the same next year, a deferral of taxable income to next year is the equivalent of an interest-free loan because it enables you to use funds that you would otherwise pay out in taxes.

Bear in mind that in some situations shifting taxable income into the *current* year may result in greater tax savings. For example, if you anticipate that your income next year will be substantially higher, or if you think you will have unusually large investment losses or other deductions this year, then you may want to accelerate income this year and defer deductions until next year to minimize your tax liability over this year and next.

Tax professionals who use computers to make "what-if" analyses can be very helpful at year-end. For example, at Deloitte & Touche we provide such year-end analyses for many clients.

DEFERRING INCOME

There are several ways of deferring income to next year, although there is little room for such manoeuvres as far as your income from salaries or wages is concerned.

FIGURE 8-3

File under TAX PLANNING   Date: *November 7*

FORM 14   YEAR-END TAX PLAN

	ACTUAL TO DATE	ESTIMATES TO YEAR-END	ESTIMATES TOTAL
1. TOTAL INCOME			
(a) (i) Income from employment	*$64,000*	*$13,000*	*$77,000*
(ii) Less allowable expenses			
(iii) Net employment earnings	*64,000*	*13,000*	*77,000*
(b) Pension income			
(i) Old Age Security and Canada or Quebec Pension plan benefits			
(ii) Other pension income			
(c) Income from other sources			
(i) Family Allowance payments			
(ii) Unemployment Insurance benefits			
(iii) Taxable amount of dividends from Canadian companies	*3,300*	*500*	*3,800*
(iv) Interest and other investment income	*1,000*	*500*	*1,500*
(v) Rental income (loss)	*3,700*	*1,500*	*5,200*
(vi) Taxable capital gains	*1,000*	*1,000*	*2,000*
(d) Self-employed income			
(i) Business income			
(ii) Professional income			

FIGURE 8-3 Cont'd.

	ACTUAL TO DATE	ESTIMATES TO YEAR-END	ESTIMATES TOTAL
(iii) Commission income			
(iv) Farming or fishing income			
(e) Total income	$73,000	$16,500	$89,500
2. DEDUCTIONS FROM TOTAL INCOME			
(a) Registered pension plan contributions			
(b) Registered Retirement Savings Plan contributions	—	$12,500	$12,500
(c) Union and professional dues			
(d) Child care expenses			
(e) Allowable business investment losses			
(f) Other deductions (including deductible interest)	$1,200	1,000	2,200
(g) Total deductions	1,200	13,500	14,700
3. NET INCOME	71,800	3,000	74,800
4. OTHER DEDUCTIONS FROM NET INCOME			
(a) Non-capital losses of other years			
(b) Net capital losses of other years (1972-1985)			
(c) Taxable capital gains exemption	1,000	1,000	2,000
(d) Total other deductions	1,000	1,000	2,000
5. (a) TAXABLE INCOME	70,800	2,000	72,800
(b) Tax bracket			52.4
6. (a) TARGETED TAXABLE INCOME			66,000
(b) Targeted Tax bracket			51.0

You are, of course, taxed on salaries or wages received in cash. But as well, you are considered to have received your salary when you have control of it or when it is set aside for you. Therefore, you cannot defer taxation of your salary to next year by not cashing year-end paycheques or by arranging with your employer to postpone issuing your regularly scheduled paycheque until after December 31.

Distributions from Pension or Profit Sharing Plans

If you are about to retire and expect a lump sum distribution from a registered pension or Deferred Profit Sharing Plan in the near future, you may wish to defer the distribution to a lower-income year. Part or all of the distribution can generally be rolled over into your RRSP. This will be discussed in more detail in Chapter 12.

Investment Income

A person has more opportunity to defer investment income, such as interest. An individual may choose to report interest income on the cash, receivable or accrued basis. On the cash basis, interest income is only reported when received. On the receivable basis, interest is included in income when you have a clear legal right to receive it. To illustrate, assume that you bought a $1,000 bond on its issue date of April 1, 1993, bearing interest of eight percent payable by semi-annual coupon on April 1 and October 1. On October 1, 1993, interest of $40 would be receivable, and would be included in your 1993 income, even if you did not cash the $40 coupon until 1994 or even later. In 1994 and subsequent years, until the year the bond becomes due, you annually will report $80 of income on the cash and/or receivable basis, if you still hold the bond. If the bond matures on April 1, 2000, income for that year would be $40.

Under the accrual method, interest is considered to be earned on a daily basis, regardless of when the interest actually becomes receivable or is received. Using the example above, under the accrual method you would report interest of $60.27 in 1993 for the 275 days in the year during which you owned the bond (275/365 x 8% x $1,000 = $60.27). The same interest income of $80 would be reported in each subsequent year up to the year of maturity. But in 2000, income of only $39.73 (90/365 x 8% x $1,000) would be reported.

Under all three methods, the same total amount of interest is reported over the bond ownership period. The only difference is the timing of inclusion in income during the period. Which method is best for you? It depends on your estimated tax position throughout the expected ownership period, although the cash method will generally be preferable if you are expecting your tax rate to stay about the same or decrease during the ownership period.

You are allowed some flexibility in choosing how to report interest income. Interest income from different sources can be reported using different methods, although all interest from the same source (i.e. same payor, on the same type of interest-yielding property) must be reported using one method. As well, Revenue Canada will generally allow a taxpayer to switch either from the cash to the receivable or accrual basis or from the receivable to the accrual basis. You will not, however, be allowed to change from one method to another which delays the recognition of interest income (i.e. from accrual to receivable or cash basis).

There are additional rules in the *Income Tax Act* which are designed to limit the opportunity to defer interest income. Before these rules were introduced in 1981, an individual could purchase, for example, a five-year compound-interest term deposit and report no income until the fifth year when all the interest was received (assuming he could choose the cash method for his investment). This is no longer possible. There are comprehensive (and complicated!) rules which essentially prevent you from delaying recognition of interest earned but not yet received for more than three years. And for investments acquired after 1989, or where terms of an investment have been extended or materially extended or changed after 1989, accrued income must be reported annually on each anniversary date of the investment. These rules are important to consider before buying any investment which does not pay interest at least annually (long-term deposits, deferred annuities, long-term stripped bonds, and compound interest Canada Savings Bonds). If you're not careful, you could end up paying tax currently on income you aren't entitled to receive until a future year.

Now that you have ideas about how to defer income to next year, note them on Form 15, *Year-End Tax Action*.

USING DEDUCTIONS

Another tax-planning strategy is to increase or accelerate your deductions and credits. If any of the following deductions apply in your situation, note them on Form 15, *Year-End Tax Action*.

Expenses of The Office In The Home

If you are an employee, you must meet all of the following requirements in order to claim a deduction for home office expenses:

1. You must be required by your employment contract to pay these expenses, and will not be reimbursed by your employer;
2. The expenses are incurred solely for the purpose of earning employment income;
3. The home office is used exclusively for business purposes — it cannot double as a part-time spare bedroom or den;
4. Your employer cannot have an office within a reasonable distance from your home; and
5. After 1990, your home office must be your principal place of employment, or be used on a regular basis for meeting customers or other persons in the ordinary course of employment.

If you are a self-employed person, you can deduct expenses of a home office used to earn business, professional or commission income provided certain tests are met. Again the office must be used exclusively for business purposes and should be separate from the family living quarters. It should be necessary for the operation of your business, profession or sales activities and not merely a convenience. It should be used regularly and not just occasionally. As well, for fiscal periods commencing after 1987, home office expenses will only be allowed if your home office is either your principal place of business, or is used on a regular basis for meeting clients, customers or patients.

Home office expenses are deductible only up to your income for the year from the business; therefore, you cannot create a deductible loss from a part-time business run out of your home by claiming home office expenses. You can, however, carry forward expenses, disallowed because of this limitation, and deduct them against business income of a subsequent year. This rule will also apply after 1990 to home office expenses claimed by employees.

Revenue Canada will be more likely to accept the deduction of your home office expenses if there are indications of business activities such as a separate business telephone line, or a sign on your home indicating the presence of a business office.

If you qualify to deduct home office expenses, add up all the allowed costs of maintaining your home discussed below, and deduct a reasonable portion related to your office. For example, let's say you live in a home with 2,500 square feet of space and you devote 250 square feet to a home office. Ten percent (250 of a total of 2,500 square feet) of the allowed costs could be deducted from your income.

An employee who rents his home may claim a portion of the rent paid. Where an employee owns his own home, a reasonable portion of the costs of maintaining the home (such as fuel, electricity and other utilities, minor repairs, etc.) may be deducted. A commission remunerated employee may also deduct a portion of property taxes and insurance paid on the home.

In addition to the home office expenses that can be deducted by an employee, a self-employed person may also claim capital cost allowance on the business portion of the home, and on any furniture or equipment used for business purposes. A self-employed person may also be able to deduct a portion of the mortgage interest paid to finance the purchase of the home.

Note that if you claim certain expenses for a home office, Revenue Canada may treat that part of your home as being converted to a business property, unless you make a special election available under Section 45 of the *Income Tax Act*. If you do not make this election, a portion of any gain ultimately realized on the sale of your home could be taxable. If you do make this election, you will not be able to claim capital cost allowance on the portion of your home used for your home office. It is almost certainly better to make this election if you claim home office expenses, assuming the value of your home will increase over time.

Other Business Expenses

Taking some action now to avoid trouble later should be part of your tax planning. So be sure to document all your travel, entertainment and other business expenses carefully. Court decisions have continually supported the disallowance of numerous types of expenses because they were not adequately substantiated. All these cases have shown the importance of maintaining a current record of expenses. Spending a little time now could save a lot of dollars later.

Receipts for your expenses do not need to be filed with your tax return, but should be retained in an orderly fashion for presentation on a subsequent review of your return by the tax authorities.

Deloitte & Touche has prepared a Business Expense Log to assist taxpayers in recording and organizing their business expenses, particularly automobile expenses. This log may also be used by employees who are eligible to deduct automobile expenses (see Chapter 6) or who wish to reduce their taxable benefit from an employer-provided car by demonstrating business use. Contact the nearest Deloitte & Touche office if you are interested in obtaining the Business Expense Log.

Registered Retirement Savings Plans

You may deduct contributions to an RRSP each year up to certain limits which have been discussed in Chapter 6. These contributions can be made at any time in the year or during the first sixty days of the following year. Although you can delay your contribution, consider contributing to your RRSP in the early part of each year, so that you may maximize the deferral on the income earned by the RRSP. Generally, it is not worthwhile to borrow to make early contributions because interest paid on the borrowed money is not deductible.

Interest Expense

In general, interest paid on money borrowed to earn business or investment income is deductible. Interest paid on money borrowed for personal use (such as buying your home) is not deductible.

Interest on business or investment loans may be deducted even if the business or investment does not immediately generate profits in excess of the interest paid. However, there must be a reasonable expectation of such a profit in the long term. For example, Revenue Canada would not let you deduct all of your interest expense if you borrowed at nine percent to invest in a term deposit which had a fixed yield of seven percent, since it would never be possible for you to make a profit on this transaction.

Currently, interest may only be deducted during the period you own the investment. If you sell the investment, you may not deduct any future interest, even if the sale proceeds were not enough to pay off all the loan. However, after 1993, new rules have been proposed to ensure that interest on such borrowings will continue to be deductible in certain circumstances.

Because Canada's personal tax rates reach a fairly high level even for middle-income earners (see Appendix II — not just the rich pay high rates of tax, as we're sure you're already well aware), structuring your borrowings to maximize your interest deduction can result in very significant tax savings. If at all possible, borrow to finance your investments and use your excess cash to pay off personal debt or contribute to an RRSP. If you have substantial equity in your investments yet still have a mortgage on your home, consider selling your investments, using the proceeds to reduce your mortgage, and borrowing to repurchase similar investments. However, before you proceed to do this, you should seek professional advice since recent jurisprudence has cast certain doubts as to the acceptability of this type of planning. Also you should consider the tax and other effects of this transaction.

If you buy the same investments within thirty days of selling them, any loss triggered by the sale will not be deductible under the superficial loss rules. If, on the other hand, the investments have significant accrued gains, their sale may trigger capital gains tax to the extent they exceed your available capital gains exemption. You may have to pay brokerage or other fees to sell and repurchase your investments. There may also be a risk that you cannot repurchase investments of the same quality as those you sell.

The rewards of converting non-deductible interest to deductible are potentially so significant that you should always look for opportunities to do so. This is one of the most effective tax-planning strategies available.

OTHER DEDUCTIONS, EXEMPTIONS AND CREDITS

Charitable Donations

The deduction available in 1987 and prior years for charitable donations was converted to a two-tier non-refundable tax credit in 1988. A seventeen percent federal tax credit is available for the first $250 of charitable donations paid in the year, with a twenty-nine percent credit for any additional gifts.

Only charitable donations up to twenty percent of net income can be claimed in a year, except for gifts to the Crown or gifts of cultural property, for which there is no limit. Unclaimed gifts can be carried forward for credit for up to five years.

Apart from the first $250 of donations, the credit system provides all taxpayers with the tax relief calculated at the maximum federal rate (an approximate combined federal and provincial tax rate of 45%). This tax credit system provides a greater tax incentive to lower- and middle-income Canadians for charitable giving compared to the previous income deduction system.

You may also wish to donate investments or other property to a charity. You will generally be able to claim a credit calculated on the current value of the donated property (subject to the twenty percent net income limit), but will be considered to have sold the property for the same amount. This may trigger a taxable capital gain for property that has increased in value since you acquired it. You may be able to shelter this gain with your available capital gains exemption, but will only pay tax on three-quarters of any unsheltered gain, while being able to claim a credit on all of the value of the gift.

If this does not produce desirable tax results, you may choose to contribute your property by transferring it at your adjusted cost base. Your credit will be calculated on this lower amount, but no gain will be triggered by your donation.

Review the other deductions and credits described in Chapters 5 and 6 for any other opportunities to reduce your taxable income or taxes payable.

OTHER YEAR-END TAX-PLANNING STRATEGIES

Tax Shelters

Late autumn is traditionally the most active time for marketing tax shelters — the largest range of products is available at this time. Tax shelters can allow you to reduce your current taxable income, as discussed in Chapter 7. But always remember to examine the investment quality of any tax shelter deal — don't just buy in for the tax savings.

Electing Capital Gains Treatment

If you frequently buy and sell investments, there is some concern that Revenue Canada will treat you as a trader (i.e. tax you on the full amount of your net gains) rather than as an investor realizing capital gains and losses. This can be a particularly harsh treatment if it prevents you from using your available capital gains exemption.

If your investment activities are sufficiently frequent that this is a concern, consider making an election to ensure your future transactions in Canadian securities will be given capital gain or loss treatment. This election will only apply, however, to Canadian shares, trust units and certain debt instruments. It has no effect on the tax treatment of real estate transactions or the sale of foreign securities. As well, once made, the election cannot be revoked and therefore should not be made without carefully considering the potential consequences, preferably with the help of a qualified tax advisor.

Salary and Dividend Mix

If you own an incorporated business, there is considerable opportunity for tax savings by choosing the right mix of salaries and dividends for your total compensation package. This can be a complicated calculation, influenced by many factors, and is best done with the help of your tax advisor.

FORM 15 — YEAR-END TAX ACTION

Year-end is the last time you have available to do anything about this year's tax situation. You should already have completed the top of Form 15 to determine the required reduction of taxable income by year-end. Also, we hope you have listed action steps on Form 15 as you read this chapter. If not, spend some time now listing those steps you want to take between now and year-end to reduce your taxable income.

Some of the action steps on your list may require no cash expenditures on your part, but others will. Work out and list how much cash is required for each of the tax-reducing steps you have proposed. Eliminate the steps for which the necessary funds are not available either from your capital or from borrowing. Then work out and list how much each of the remaining steps will reduce your taxable income. Total the reductions. Compare that figure with the required reduction you computed at the top of the form to see whether your year-end action steps result in the reduction in taxable income you require. Then put the feasible, desirable tax-saving steps into action as soon as you can. After all the work and thought involved in analysing your tax situation and targeting the taxable income you desire, you don't want to end up with a lot of splendid ideas but no results.

9

SETTING FINANCIAL OBJECTIVES

The setting of objectives may be the single most important part of financial planning. We tend to live from day to day — "muddling through" or "operating in mediocrity" — with only the haziest notion of where we are going or what we really want out of life. Living in this way, we may never have the sense of fulfillment or the variety of experiences we vaguely hoped for, and we may never be in control of our lives or achieve financial security. The effort to focus on what we really want to achieve and do with our lives propels us toward those goals and we also gain a sense of purpose and direction.

As you set your financial objectives, you will evaluate the trade-offs between your short-term and your long-term goals, you will investigate the various alternatives you have for using your financial resources, and then you will decide which alternatives are best for you.

Keep in mind that researchers who have studied peak performance in individuals — executives, professionals, athletes, teachers — have observed that the successful ones have one common characteristic: They set goals for themselves. So give these next four forms on your objectives — Forms 16, 17, 18 and 19 — some careful thought and set goals you can live by, goals you can achieve with knowledge, effort, commitment and persistence.

FORM 16 — FINANCIAL SECURITY

Item 1 asks you to define financial security, which has different meanings to different people. Some might say, "It is not having to depend on a salary," or "Financial security is $80,000 a year before taxes." Some express it in terms of debt: "I'll feel financially secure when I have no more debts." To others, financial security is a way of life: "Being able to do what I want when I want," or "Not having to worry about meeting income needs."

First, write your own definition of financial security. Then try to express it in quantitative, measurable terms that will give you specific targets to reach for.

- What specific annual income would give you financial security? Would you feel financially secure with earned income of $60,000 or $80,000 or more than $100,000? Maybe you would rather express financial security in terms of annual investment income — having your money work for you so you would be free to pursue your avocational interests more frequently or for longer periods of time. As you will see below, you can determine the amount of investment assets required to provide your desired investment income level.

- What specific net worth are you seeking in order to gain financial security? If your goal is $60,000 of annual investment income, then you will need a certain level of investment assets. For example, if you believe you can realize an eight percent before-tax return on your investments, you will need investment assets of $750,000 to achieve financial security.

- What specific debt level do you want to accept in order to achieve financial security? Most people we counsel still believe in having relatively little debt when discussing financial security. They may have relatively high debt levels at some stage of their lives in order to finance investments and personal assets but when they get around to financial security, they are really worried about keeping debt at high levels. For most people, high debt levels mean anxiety and stress that they would rather do without at some point.

Item 2 on Form 16 asks you to determine when you want to achieve financial security, based on your present financial position, earning power, expenditure patterns and investment strategy. This question may be less difficult to answer than most people initially believe if you use the information you prepared in the first part of this book. For example, if you believe you need $750,000 of investment assets to achieve financial security and your net worth statement, Form 4, currently shows investments of $500,000, you may be able to achieve that goal in the next few years. If, on the other hand, you currently have investment assets of $1.23 and a pack of chewing gum, you may take a long time to achieve your goals without marrying for money or becoming the favourite niece or nephew of that aging, rich uncle.

Item 3, asking what you perceive as the chief obstacles to your financial security, commonly receives one of the following answers: *taxes, inflation, my boss, lack of knowledge, lack of time.* Most of the obstacles people perceive, though, are self-imposed and therefore can usually be removed by self-management. There is something you can do about your taxes, your inflation rate, your lack of knowledge. You can choose to spend time on financial planning instead of some other activity.

To determine whether your timetable for achieving financial security is realistic or a pipe dream, do some overall analysis.

- Use the Rule of Seventy-two to determine how many years it will take to double your money. Merely divide seventy-two by the expected annual after-tax rate of return on your investments. For example, if your expected annual after-tax rate of return is four percent, your investments will double in eighteen years (72 ÷ 4 = 18). For your investments to double in ten years, you will need an annual after-tax rate of return of 7.2% (72 ÷ 10 = 7.2).

- Use compound tables such as Tables 9-1, 9-2, 9-3 and 9-4, and the more complete tables in Appendix I.

Table 9-1 lets you see how much a lump sum investment will grow in various years at varying rates of return. Merely multiply the amount listed for the rate of return and number of years involved by your investment assets divided by 10,000. For example, if you have $100,000 to invest and you want to know what such a lump sum will grow to in fifteen years at eight percent, you find the amount $31,721 in Table 9-1 and multiply it by ten ($100,000 ÷ $10,000) to get your answer — $317,210.

Table 9-2 lets you determine what lump sum investment you need in order to accumulate a targeted investment amount by the end of a specified period. Let's say you want to have $500,000 of investment assets in ten years and believe you could invest your present assets to return ten percent per year. You would need to invest $192,770 today ($38,554 x $500,000/100,000).

Tables 9-3 and 9-4 show you how much an invested amount will grow at varying rates for varying periods. For example, if you have $1,200 per year to invest (approximately $100 per month), such an investment programme will produce $87,727 in twenty-five years if your investment funds return eight percent per year. If you were able to invest $2,400 per year ($200 per month) at eight percent, your investments would grow to $109,828 at the end of twenty years, according to Table 9-3.

Table 9-4 shows how much you have to invest each year for how many years and at what rate in order to get $100,000. For example, if you wanted $100,000 in five years and thought you could get a ten percent return each year, you would need to invest $14,890 per year.

Obviously, these tables can also be used to see what your investments might be at the end of an expected number of years with an expected rate of return, assuming you either invested a lump sum (your present investment assets) or an annual amount of both. For example, if you have $50,000 of investment assets today and can invest another $5,000 per year, your investment assets would be approximately $507,615 at the end of twenty years at a rate of eight percent. The computation is shown below:

- From Table 9-1 (Investment of $50,000 @ 8% for 20 years):
  $50,000/10,000 × 46,609 = $233,045

- From Table 9-3 (Investment of $5,000 per year @ 8% for 20 years):
  $5,000/1,200 × 54,914 = $274,570
  $233,045 + $274,570 = $507,615

As well as the Rule of Seventy-two and compound tables, you can use an inexpensive financial analysis calculator to do the calculations. For less than $40 you can buy some makes of hand-held calculators programmed to do financial analysis. Such calculators have keys for each of the five financial variables we have used in the calculations with the compound tables. These five keys are:

1. **PV**, or the present value or amount of your investment assets;

2. **PMT**, or the annual amount or payment you can make in your investment programme;

3. **N**, or the number of periods (years, months) you expect to invest your money;

4. **i**, or the rate of interest or return you expect to get on your investments; and

5. **FV**, or the future value or amount of your investment assets (i.e. *the value to which your assets will grow* over a specified number of years at a specified rate of interest).

Using the calculator with these five function keys, you can determine, in a matter of seconds, the answer to investment questions such as:

- If I have $20,000 (PV) in my present investment fund and can put aside $2,400 (PMT) per year to invest, what rate of return (i) do I need to have $500,000 (FV) in ten years (N)? Answer: 32.88%.

- If financial security for me is $1,000,000 (FV), how long will it take to reach that objective if my present assets are $300,000 and I can set aside $15,000 a year for investment and can get a fifteen percent return on my investment? Answer: a little more than seven years.

TABLE 9-1

$10,000 LUMP-SUM INVESTMENT COMPOUNDED ANNUALLY END OF YEAR VALUES

End of Year	6%	8%	10%	12%	15%
5	13,382	14,693	16,105	17,623	20,113
6	14,185	15,868	17,715	19,738	23,130
7	15,036	17,138	19,478	22,016	26,600
8	15,938	18,509	21,435	24,759	30,590
9	16,894	19,990	23,579	27,730	35,178
10	17,908	21,589	25,937	31,058	40,455
15	23,965	31,721	41,772	54,735	81,370
20	32,071	46,609	67,274	96,462	163,665
25	42,918	68,484	108,347	170,000	329,189

TABLE 9-2

RATES OF RETURN AND THE INVESTMENT AMOUNTS REQUIRED TO HAVE $100,000 AVAILABLE AT END OF SPECIFIED PERIOD

Rate of Return	End of Year				
	5	10	15	20	25
6%	74,726	55,839	41,727	31,180	23,300
8%	68,058	46,319	31,524	21,455	14,602
10%	62,092	38,554	23,940	14,864	9,230
12%	56,743	32,197	18,270	10,367	5,882
15%	49,718	24,718	12,289	6,110	3,040

TABLE 9-3

FUTURE WORTH OF $1,200 INVESTED EACH YEAR AT VARYING RATES COMPOUNDED EACH YEAR

Rate of Return	End of Year				
	5	10	15	20	25
6%	6,764	15,817	27,931	44,143	65,837
8%	7,040	17,384	32,583	54,914	87,727
10%	7,326	19,125	38,127	68,730	118,016
12%	7,623	21,058	44,736	86,463	160,001
15%	8,091	24,364	57,096	122,932	255,352

TABLE 9-4

APPROXIMATE ANNUAL INVESTMENT REQUIRED TO EQUAL $100,000 AT VARYING RATES

Rate of Return	End of Year				
	5	10	15	20	25
6%	16,736	7,157	4,053	2,565	1,720
8%	15,783	6,392	3,410	2,024	1,267
10%	14,890	5,704	2,861	1,587	924
12%	14,055	5,088	2,395	1,239	670
15%	12,898	4,283	1,828	849	409

FORM 17 — INCOME AND EXPENDITURE OBJECTIVES

For most people, what is left of their employment income after paying current expenses is the primary means of accumulating net worth and achieving financial security. Therefore, any increase in employment income without a similar increase in expenditures, or any reduction in expenditures without a similar reduction in employment income, will provide you with that much more money to invest — money that could be working for you to help you reach future goals.

When answering the questions in this form, refer to Form 10, Analysis of Earned Income and Expenditures, for your current total employment income and expenditures.

To answer item 2, refer to Form 7, *Basic Lifestyle Expenditures.*

To answer item 3, refer to Form 8, *Discretionary Expenditures.*

- When estimating your and your spouse's employment income for the next three years, start with an estimate of an annual percentage increase. For example, maybe you think employment income will increase by ten percent per year for each of the next three years. Maybe you think next year your income will be the same as last year, but will increase by ten percent per year for years two and three. Once you have estimated a rate of increase, estimate the amount of employment income for each of the next three years.

- Questions 2 and 3 ask you to evaluate how much you could reduce your present expenditure levels. Such evaluation is important in order to do the following:

  - Determine whether your expenditures are resulting in the quality of life you expect.

  - Determine whether your present lifestyle expenditures are using up dollars that are important for future goals.

  - Remind you that the best way, from a tax standpoint, to increase amounts available for investment is to reduce your expenditures.

Every expenditure dollar saved means one whole dollar available for investment. Every additional dollar of employment earnings produces only 50 cents for investing if you are in a fifty percent tax bracket, or 67 cents if you are in a thirty-three percent tax bracket.

- Question 4 gets at your "wish" list. Everybody has one. The items on the list are your dreams — the sleek sports car, the sailboat cutting sharply through the dashing waves, the cobblestone streets of a European village, the entertainment room in your home. If you are married, sit down with your family and discuss a family wish list. Determine what you would like. If you are single, talk to a close friend or advisor about your dreams and get some feedback on your list.

In developing your list, determine not only what you want but by when. Keep in mind that some goals can be achieved in the near future, while others can only be achieved in the long term.

You will use your estimates of income and expenditures in building a summary financial plan in Chapter 15.

FORM 18 — EDUCATION AND OTHER SUPPORT OF CHILDREN

Inflation has had a noticeable impact on family expenditures, including education costs and living expenses of young adults after leaving high school. As a result, most of them now require assistance from their parents to pay for their university or college tuition and living expenses. Some families also incur, or plan to incur, considerable expenses by sending their children to private elementary or secondary schools.

- If you are planning to send your children to private elementary or secondary schools, be aware that it is expensive and that financial plans should be made well in advance. Good private elementary day schools may cost anywhere from $3,000 to $7,000 or more per year. Secondary schools run higher. Of course, boarding schools are even more expensive because they also cover room and board.

  Question 1 asks you to estimate for each child the total cost of private education in today's dollars. For example, if your children are aged nine and seven and you plan to send them to private secondary schools in six and eight years, respectively, and you estimate the cost for each year to be $5,000 (in today's dollars), the total estimated cost for each child will be $20,000; the total for both children will be $40,000.

- If you are planning to send your children to a college or university, you should begin well in advance to evaluate the potential costs. University or college education may cost anywhere between $2,000 and $10,000 or more per year, including room and board, books and incidentals.

  Question 2 asks you to estimate the amount you will provide for each child in today's dollars. For example, if you have two children and plan to help each of them with eighty percent of their university or college costs for each of the four years, you will have to pay $16,000 for each child if each year of university costs $5,000 in today's dollars ($5,000 x 80% x four years); a total of $32,000. Depending on the rate of inflation, the amounts required for university costs could, and probably will, be significantly higher in future years.

- Obviously, with many families facing the possibility of significant educational expenditures, plans should be made to set aside funds before the schooling begins. A good idea may be to start an educational fund for your children when they are very young. Let the power of compounding work over a period of years so that significant funds are available when your children go off to college or university.

  Question 3 asks you to indicate what funds have been set aside for your children's education. Some families start a savings programme for their children; some make annual money gifts to the children and invest the money in high-yielding securities; others set up a trust with a lump sum fund and let the earnings on the fund accumulate in the trust until the children's education begins. In Chapter 11 we will discuss educational financing techniques and how to get the most after-tax dollars for your children's education.

- Question 4 asks you to estimate what support your children may need apart from education. Some families have a disabled child who needs support. Others are supporting unemployed children or helping their children finance the purchase of a home.

Again, you will use the information on your objectives for the education and support of your children to build your summary plan in Chapter 15.

FORM 19 — RETIREMENT PLANNING

The retirement years are generally referred to as "the golden years" — a time for leisure activities and relaxation after many years of work. They are not likely to be golden, however, unless you have planned how you will use your time, where you will live, and how you will finance your expenses.

Few people prepare adequately for retirement, particularly from the financial point of view. Twelve percent of men aged sixty-five to sixty-nine were still in the labour force in 1987. Certainly not all of these people were working purely for job satisfaction, but rather needed to supplement their retirement income. As well, a major source of income reported by Canada's elderly is government transfer payments, such as Old Age Security and Canada or Quebec Pension Plan. Given the amount of these payments, it seems safe to assume that many of Canada's elderly cannot look forward to a financially secure future.

We strongly believe a retirement programme should be started early in your life — at least ten to fifteen years before you plan to retire. This form asks you some questions about the financial aspects of retirement, such as the age at which you plan to retire, your financial requirements at retirement, and the financial sources available to meet your needs.

You will use the information on Form 19 in Chapter 12, when we ask you to analyse the feasibility of your retirement objectives.

SUMMARY

In this chapter, we have discussed the importance of financial objectives and have asked you to determine your objectives for financial security, income and expenditures, education and support of your children, and retirement.

In setting objectives, you have to weigh the trade-offs between short-term and long-term goals (Do I take an expensive vacation this year or set aside some funds for my child's university or college education five years from now?) and identify the steps involved in reaching your goals. (To reach my financial security goal, I need to set aside more each year for investment and get a higher return on my assets. I should probably reduce my tax expenditures, learn more about investment alternatives, and monitor my investments more closely.)

Once your objectives have been established, you need to take some action. In the chapters that follow, we will discuss investments, educational financing and retirement, and you will identify what action you can take.

10

INVESTMENTS

As you must surely realize by now, the road to financial independence is paved with good investments. You, too, should be able to obtain investment results that are above the average, once you know your investment objectives and take the time to evaluate and monitor your investments.

Broadly speaking, your investments consist of all the means by which you store up assets for the future. These would include your home and your retirement programme, which should form a part of your overall investment programme and should relate to such other investments as stocks, bonds and income-producing real estate.

This chapter will guide you to formulate an investment programme of your own that is specifically geared to your age, responsibilities and objectives, as well as your expendable income and your tax position.

INVESTMENT OBJECTIVES

What are the important factors in making an investment decision? Most people answer this very quickly by saying, "I want my investments to give me a good return." Then we say, "Okay, but what kind of return are you looking for?" Some reply, "A steady return." Some say, "The kind I don't have to watch and worry about." Others say, "The highest return I can get for the risk I am willing to take." or "I need an annual income." or "I want capital appreciation."

When you analyse these and other answers, you find the following concerns:

- Safety of principal
- Hedge against inflation
- Future income
- Current income
- Tax consequences
- Liquidity of the investment
- Ease of management

We will now investigate these objectives and, inasmuch as some are contrary to others, we will consider them in pairs.

Safety of Principal Versus Hedge Against Inflation

If your overriding concern is to keep a sum of money intact for a specific purpose, such as a down payment on a house, you might invest in a regular savings account, Treasury bills, Canada Savings Bonds, or a money market fund, since these will pretty much guarantee that you can get your principal back when you need it. Liquidity and safety of principal are usually the main considerations when you invest in such funds. You should be aware, however, that in inflationary periods the longer you hold an investment that provides the safety of principal you get with something like a savings account, the more you will lose in purchasing power. As the inflation rate goes up, so the purchasing power of your funds goes down. Thus, investments that are safe with regard to return of principal are not always a good hedge against inflation.

For those who want a return that will keep up with inflation, the primary objective should be safety of purchasing power, not safety of principal. In past years of high inflation, safety of purchasing power has usually been achieved with investments such as common stocks and real estate.

Current Income Versus Future Appreciation and Tax Consequences

Some people, particularly those who have retired or are widowed, may regard current income as their primary investment objective. Such current income could take the form of interest on savings accounts or Canada Savings Bonds, or dividends from common or preferred stock, or rent from income-producing real estate. In assessing current income from investments, the two terms commonly used are *current return* and *current yield*. Current return is usually expressed in dollars; yield is expressed as a percentage. Thus, the current return on a $1,000 savings account with a yield of five percent is $50. With common stock, the current return is the dollar amount of your dividend per share, while the current yield shows the dividend received as a percentage of the current price of the stock. So with a dividend of $1 per share and a stock price of $15, the current yield would be one divided by fifteen, or 6.67%.

Some investors have both safety of principal and current income as their investment objectives. They are the investors who need this investment income to cover their living expenses and cannot risk the loss of their principal. As a rule, this would apply to people who are unemployed or fear unemployment in the future, those about to take a substantial reduction in employment income, and those in or near retirement.

For people whose employment income covers their lifestyle expenditures and people of substantial net worth, the *future return* or *appreciation* of their investments will be their main concern. Though they may not need further current income, they may want to add to their capital base through appreciation in order to meet future expenditures such as the costs of education or retirement. Known as *growth investments* or *capital gain investments*, these investments with a potential for appreciation will usually provide little or no current income.

When considering your return on investment, there are three points to keep in mind. The first is *total return*. Investments — stocks and income-producing real estate, for instance — may result in appreciation as well as current income. Their total return is the sum you get from adding their current yield to their appreciation yield. Thus, a stock that had a six percent dividend yield and an appreciation of five percent in the last year had a total return of eleven percent for the year.

The second point to bear in mind is the investment's *after-tax return*. Capital gains eligible for the lifetime capital gains exemption can be exempt from tax if you can claim a capital gains exemption. Furthermore, only three-quarters of capital gains (not eligible for the exemption or in excess of the exemption limit) realized from the sale of investments are subject to tax. Dividends from Canadian companies are subject to tax at approximately two-thirds of the marginal tax rate otherwise applicable, as a result of the dividend tax credit system. Other investment income, such as dividends from foreign companies, interest and royalties, etc., are taxed like ordinary earned income. Therefore, different types of investment income can be taxed very differently. Thus, total after-tax return is an important measure of investments.

The third point to consider is the *certainty of return* on your investment. With investments that solely or primarily provide current income, you can usually be quite certain of receiving this current income. Bonds, for instance, carry contractual agreements to pay their interest when due. Dividends are not contractually fixed, but are decided upon by the company's board of directors, who increase or decrease them according to the company's financial situation. The future capital appreciation of an investment is not a certainty. For that type of investment, the potential total return should therefore be much higher than for investments made to generate current income. The higher the potential of losing all or some portion of your invested capital, the higher should be the potential return. The greater the risk, the greater the potential return should be.

Liquidity

Liquidity refers to the ease with which you can convert an investment into cash. If you might need the money you invested to take care of emergencies or to take advantage of some other investment opportunities, liquidity can be very important.

Regular savings accounts, Canada Savings Bonds and money market investments provide great liquidity, and so do most common stocks and the bonds of large companies. When you invest in smaller companies, you have less liquidity or marketability, because there are fewer shares of such stocks or bonds and fewer people interested in such investments.

Real estate is another example of a non-liquid investment. You may have to wait for months before you find a buyer who is willing to buy the property at your asking price, and then it will take additional time to close the transaction and get your cash out. Furthermore, your purchaser may not be able to give you the entire amount in a lump sum payment, but only in installments payable over several years.

Typically, a higher liquidity is tied to a lower return. If you want high returns, be prepared to accept low liquidity and generally more risk.

Ease of Management

There are a lot of people who say, "Investments and financial matters are not the most important things in my life, and I don't want to spend much time watching or worrying over them." For such people, ease of management is an important investment objective. If they don't want to spend much time managing their investments, they should either pay someone like an investment advisor or a trust company to manage their investments, or they should choose the kind of investments that demand little involvement or judgement: savings accounts, Canada Savings Bonds, term deposits, mutual funds and bonds held to maturity. What they need to avoid are investments that are subject to large and rapid price fluctuations.

Table 10-1 summarizes the general investment characteristics we have been discussing.

RISK AND RETURN

Risk and *return* occur in tandem. In Table 10-1, you can see how expected risk increases with investments which offer a higher expected return. Risk can be defined as the probability of loss in the future. Loss usually means partial loss of your invested capital, not total loss, although some investments may result in total loss. For example, if you are investing in an exploratory oil well and the drillers do not find oil, your investment is a

TABLE 10-1
INVESTMENT OBJECTIVES

Type of Investement	Safety Principal in Constant Dollars	Hedge Against Inflation	Current Income	Future Appreciation	Liquidity	Ease of Management
Regular savings accounts/ Canada Savings Bonds	Excellent	Not very good	Fixed; very steady but low rate	None	Excellent	Very easy
Money market investments (Treasury bills, money market funds)	Good to excellent	Not very good	Fixed; very steady; rate near inflation	Generally none	Very good	Easy
Common stocks Income stocks	Fair	Fair	Relatively fixed; rate near inflation rate	Some	Good	Easy
Growth stocks	Moderate to poor	Generally good	Variable; low rate	Moderate to great	Good	Difficult
Bonds (high-quality corporate and government issues)	Good to excellent	Not very good	Fixed; very steady; rate near inflation rate	Generally none except discounted bonds	Good	Fairly easy
Mutual funds (common stocks)	Fair to poor	Variable but generally good	Variable	Moderate to great	Good	Easy
Real estate (income producing, other than residence)	Generally good	Generally good	Variable	Moderate to great	Relatively poor	Moderate to difficult
Precious metals (gold, silver)	Fair to poor	Generally good	None	Moderate to great	Good	Difficult

total loss except for the value of the tax write-offs. A totally new company with unproven products has a much higher probability of going bankrupt in the near future than a company with a proven record of profitability in a stable industry.

With most investments, the probability of losing all of your investment capital in the foreseeable future is relatively low. However, the probability of losing some portion of your investment — say twenty percent — may be very high with such investments as common stock in a company in a volatile industry, or with real estate in a depressed market.

If you are prepared to accept greater risks, you have the chance of getting higher returns. The only way to attract investors to an enterprise with a high probability of loss is to offer them the possibility of a high return. Conversely, a low-risk enterprise attracts investors readily and therefore does not have to offer investors a chance of high return. Figure 10-1 is an Investment Vehicle Pyramid that shows many types of investments and

FIGURE 10-1
INVESTMENT VEHICLE PYRAMID

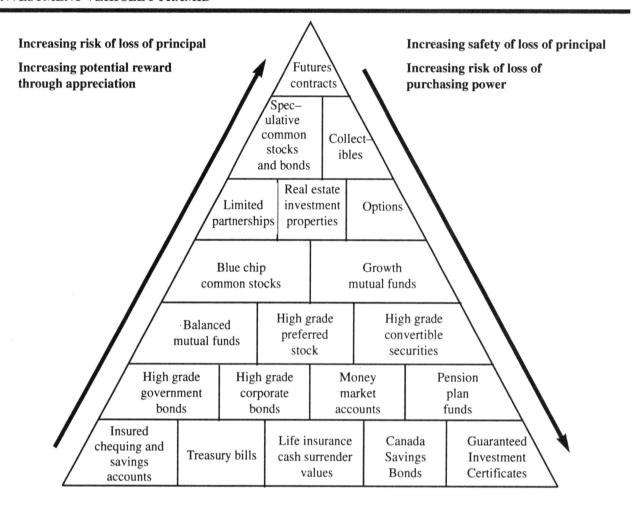

FIGURE 10-2
RISK AND RETURN TRADE-OFF

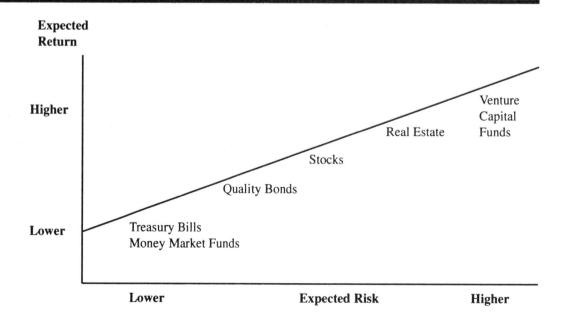

the relative risk and return. Figure 10-2 shows the expected risk/reward for selected investments as measured by the incremental return above what most would call a risk-free investment — Treasury bills. Note that as you go up the risk/return line, you have a higher probability (known as the standard deviation) that you will earn more or less than the expected return.

Risk of Purchasing Power

As you know to your sorrow, high inflation results in the reduced purchasing power of your dollar. In consequence, if you buy a four-year term deposit and inflation increases significantly, the principal and interest that are returned to you will have less purchasing power than the dollars you paid for it four years ago. Even though such investments are good with regard to safety of principal, they are not good with regard to maintaining your purchasing power.

During the early 1980s and late 1970s, years of high inflation, fixed-return investments that were tied up early in the inflationary cycle in savings accounts, term deposits, insurance policies, and bonds resulted in a substantial loss of purchasing power for those who invested in them.

Investments with growth potential will usually offer better protection in periods of inflation. If you refer to Table 10-1 once again, you will see that real estate and growth stocks generally do relatively well in periods of inflation. During periods of declining prices and severe recession, fixed-return investments become profitable, while variable-return investments lose in value. During the 1930s, a period of economic depression, people who owned real estate and common stocks watched the value of their investments decline steeply as rents, corporate profits and dividends declined. In recent years we have witnessed a sharp decline in inflation (and a corresponding reduction in interest rates). Loss of purchasing power will be less of a concern.

Financial Risk

Financial risk, also called business risk, is the possibility that unfavourable business conditions may reduce the expected returns from an investment. This might happen if the company you have invested in has a competitor who starts to produce a better product or finds a cheaper method of producing the same product, thereby reducing the earning potential of the company in which you have invested. It could happen if new rent control legislation applies to an apartment building you own, making it less attractive for potential purchasers. It could also be brought about by environmental protection laws that increase the operating costs of a company whose shares you hold.

Interest Rate Risk

This risk is usually associated with fixed-return investments such as bonds. What you risk here is a decline in the market value of your investment due to a higher rate of return on comparable new investments.

As an example, take some Government of Canada bonds that were issued in October 1968 at 6.50% annual interest or $65 per $1,000 bond. In August 1991 these bonds, which mature in the year 1995, were selling for about $900. The Canadian government is financially sound, so why did the price of these high-quality bonds go down by 10%? The reason is that between 1968 and 1991 the interest rates for bonds of similar quality and maturity had risen from 6.5% to more than nine percent.

If you had purchased those Government of Canada bonds in 1968 and sold them in August 1991, you would have suffered a capital loss of $100 for every $1,000 bond you held. You would have suffered the adverse effects of interest rate risk, because investors will not pay $1,000 for a bond that earns $65 a year when they can buy another bond of comparable quality and maturity date that pays them over $90 a year. By the same token, when interest rates have fallen, the bonds you bought before the fall will have risen in market value. It is interesting to note that in September 1992 these bonds were selling in excess of $1,000 because interest rates had fallen back to less than 6.5% for similar quality bonds. If you had purchased the bonds in August 1991 and sold them in September 1992, you could have realized a capital gain in excess of $100 per $1,000 bond.

Real estate, too, is affected by interest levels. For example, when interest rates rose dramatically in the early 1980s, it became much more difficult for buyers to obtain financing at a rate they could afford. As a result, the housing market declined, and many a seller had to offer his house on contract at a lower interest rate or had to reduce the price of the house in order to make a sale. Fortunately this is not the case currently. Low inflation has produced low interest rates.

Market Risk

Volatility in investment prices that is due to changes in "market psychology" or investors' attitudes is known as market risk. Such price fluctuations may affect the whole securities market — as was the case in the Depression, again in 1974, and the "market crash" in October 1987, when stock prices, as measured by widely used indexes, dropped by one-third to fifty percent. Price fluctuations may affect a particular industry or a particular security regardless of the financial ability of a particular company to pay the promised or expected investment returns. As an example, several small Canadian financial institutions experienced a drop in their share prices as a result of the failure of two regional banks in western Canada in 1985, although their own financial situation had not changed.

Price fluctuations give rise to buying and selling opportunities. For example, when the stock market is depressed because investors' attitudes are sour, buying opportunities in general for stocks may be very good. Also, when an individual stock is depressed but its fundamentals are still strong, the buying opportunity may be very good. On the other hand, when the market in general has experienced a significant increase in prices and investor attitudes are favourable, look around, evaluate the price increases in the securities you hold, and contemplate selling.

Leverage and Risk

Leverage denotes the borrowed money you invest together with your own funds in order to get a higher return on your money. When leverage works in your favour, it is great; but when leverage works against you, it can be disastrous.

To illustrate how leverage works, let's use a common leverage investment like real estate. Assume you buy a condominium for $60,000 and finance it with a $15,000 down payment and a $45,000 mortgage. You pay the annual expenses and mortgage payments with your rental income. After three years, you decide to sell the condominium and get $65,000 for it. You now have a gain of roughly thirty-three percent — a $5,000 gain on your $15,000 investment. If the $60,000 you invested had all been your own money, your gain on the sale would only be about eight percent — $5,000 on your investment of $60,000.

Conversely, with leverage you can lose money faster than without it when prices decline. Assume, for example, that after three years your leveraged $60,000 had dropped in price to $55,000. By selling it now, you would suffer a loss of thirty-three percent — a $5,000 loss on your $15,000 investment. Without leverage, your loss would be only eight percent — a $5,000 loss on your $60,000 investment.

You can use leverage in buying stocks or bonds by "buying on margin." When you buy on margin, you pay only a portion of the total cost, and your broker extends credit to you on the balance — and charges interest monthly. The word margin refers to the difference between the market value of the stock bought and the loan which the broker will make against it.

The reason for buying on margin is capital appreciation. If you choose a stock that you think will increase in price fairly rapidly (and more than your interest charges), you may make more profit by buying a greater number of shares on margin than by buying a smaller number for cash — if the stock goes up in price. Table 10-2 shows the rate of return (or loss) you will reap, with and without using margin, when the stock price increases (or decreases). In our example, we assume the stock was held for one year and we ignore brokerage commissions and the effect of taxes. The example shows that by trading on margin, an investor would realize forty percent more return than would be realized through a cash transaction (without margin). But leverage works both ways. If the stock declines to $40 per share, as shown in the example, an investor would have incurred 160 percent more loss using margin.

The general rules regarding margin trading are established by the various provincial exchanges where the stock is being traded and are binding on all brokers. Although the exchanges set the *minimum* amount the investor has to put up when buying stock on margin, brokers may and often do set their margin requirements substantially higher. The prescribed margin requirements vary with a security's selling price. For example, the Toronto Stock Exchange requires the investor to put up at least fifty percent of the purchase price of securities selling at $2.00 and over. A higher percentage is required for securities selling for less than $2.00.

One of the potential drawbacks of buying stocks on margin is that if a stock price subsequently declines, an investor may become "undermargined" (meaning that the investor's margin — down payment — plus the maximum margin loan his broker may credit to the investor on the current value of the stock falls under the original price of the stock). If this occurs, the broker would make a margin call to the investor requiring him to make up the deficiency in cash or to sell his stock.

Using our example in Table 10-2, the account of the investor who buys 200 shares at $50, putting down only the minimum fifty percent margin, and then subsequently sees the shares fall to $40, would receive a margin call for another $1,000 computed as follows:

MARGIN CALL

Total purchase (original price $50 × 200 shares)		$10,000
Less:	Maximum margin loan from broker	(4,000)
	(50% × $40 × 200 shares)	
	Investor's original deposit	(5,000)
	(50% × $50 × 200 shares)	
Margin deficiency for which a margin call would be issued		
	($10,000 − $9,000 = $1,000)	$1,000

MINIMIZING RISK

Eventually, you will have to choose between the various investment alternatives available to you and judge the risk inherent in each type of investment. You will have to decide what investment risks you are willing to take. If you are in your twenties, for example, and trying to save enough money for a down payment on a house, you will probably want to avoid investments with high financial and market risks. If, on the other hand, you have already bought your own house and are earning more than your current expenditures, and you have money put away for emergencies, then you may be quite willing to accept high financial and market risks in hopes of getting a high return.

As your needs and economic status change, so will your investment objectives and the risks you are ready to take. Regardless of such changes, however, good investment strategy will dictate that you minimize overall risks through knowledge and diversification.

TABLE 10-2
INVESTMENT RETURNS (OR LOSSES) BUYING ON MARGIN

	With Margin	Without Margin
Dollars Invested		
Your funds	$5,000	$5,000
Broker's funds	5,000	0
Total purchases (per share price $50)	$10,000 (200 shares)	$5,000 (100 shares)
1. Sale of stock for $60 per share		
Gross proceeds	$12,000	$6,000
Less repayment of borrowed funds	(5,000)	0
Less interest on borrowed funds at 12%	(600)	0
Net proceeds after repayment of borrowed funds	$6,400	$6,000
Return of original dollars invested	(5,000)	(5,000)
Net profit (or loss)	$1,400	$1,000
Return on your investment	$1,400 ÷ $5,000 = 28%	$1,000 ÷ $5,000 = 20%
2. Sale of stock for $40 per share		
Gross proceeds	$8,000	$4,000
Less repayment of borrowed funds	(5,000)	0
Less interest on borrowed funds at 12%	(600)	0
Net proceeds after repayment of borrowed funds	$2,400	$4,000
Return of original dollars invested	(5,000)	(5,000)
Net profit (or loss)	$(2,600)	$(1,000)
Return on your investment	$(2,600) ÷ $5,000 = (52%)	$(1,000) ÷ $5,000 = (20%)

As a rule, the people who are successful investors know more than the average person about specific investments, about particular types of industries, about economic cycles, and about diverse factors of the economy. If you understand an investment opportunity and study its future potential, you should be able to reduce your risks substantially.

You will minimize risk by diversifying your investments so that they will not all be open to the same risks. Then, for example, if rising inflation and high interest rates decrease the value of your bonds, they will also increase the returns on your money market funds. You spread your risk by having various types of investments.

FORM 20 — INVESTMENT OBJECTIVES

Now that you have an overview of the various types of investment objectives and risks, you can evaluate the relative importance that each of the listed investment objectives has for you. Once you have forced yourself to become clear about your priorities, you will have a sound basis for your investment decisions. On Form 20 the objectives we discussed earlier in the chapter are listed.

Figure 10-3 is an example of a couple in their mid-forties with significant employment income. They are primarily concerned about investments with growth potential and tax advantages that do not require a lot of time and effort to manage. They are also interested in using leverage and having diversification in their investment programme. They are not very concerned about safety, liquidity and current income.

FORM 21 — REVIEW OF YOUR PRESENT INVESTMENTS

The next step in your investment analysis is to review your present investments using Form 21. Before you complete this form, it might be helpful to look at the example in Figure 10-4 of the couple whose investment objectives are shown in Figure 10-3. Once you have completed Form 21, you can evaluate your present investments in terms of your objectives and see what changes should be considered.

- In the first column, list all the types of investments that make up the total of your liquid and other investment assets on your net worth statement (Form 4).

- In the second column, enter the current value of each investment. The totals should agree with the amounts shown on your net worth statement (Form 4). In our example, total liquid assets are $33,500; other investments are $262,800; total investments are $296,300.

- In the third column, determine how diversified your present investment programme is by dividing the amount of each investment by the total amount of your investments. In our example, real estate of $90,000 is thirty percent of the total investments of $296,300.

- In the fourth column, list the investment objectives shown on Form 20 that each of your investments is to accomplish.

- Next, compute each investment's current yield before taxes as a percentage by dividing the income you received from it in the last year by the current value as listed in column 2.

- For those investments that had either a growth or a loss in value, enter the estimated annual percentage of gain or loss in column 6 using the following simple formula: [Current value (in column 2) minus purchase price] ÷ [the number of years you have owned the asset times the purchase price] times 100. This formula is a simple way to approximate annual gain or loss. There are other more sophisticated ways to compute the annual gain or loss in value, and if you know one, by all means use it .

- To compute the total annual return for each investment, add the percentages in columns 5 and 6.

Now that you have completed Form 21, you are in a position to evaluate your present investments in light of your objectives. The data on your form should tell you a lot about your present investment behaviour and is the starting point for making any changes in your investments.

1. How important is diversification? Look at the percentages in column 3. If a particular investment is thirty percent or more of the total, you might want to consider further diversification. In our example in Figure 10-4, one of the seven investment categories is thirty percent of the total.

2. How important is liquidity? Look at the total of your liquid assets and compare it to your employment income. If the total is more than fifty percent of your employment income, you probably have too much liquidity.

3. How important are safety and current income? These two objectives are closely related. Add up the current values of those investments for which you listed safety and current income as objectives under column 4. If these objectives are very important, the current value of investments providing safety and current income should exceed seventy percent of the total investment assets.

4. How important is growth? Add up the current values of those investments for which you listed future appreciation (inflation hedge) as an objective. If appre-

ciation is very important to you, the current value of investments providing appreciation should exceed seventy percent of the total investment assets. In our example in Figure 10-4, those investments for which appreciation is listed as one of the objectives comprise seventy-four percent of the total.

5. What about tax shelters? Often an investor interested in appreciation is also interested in tax-saving investments. If tax shelter is important, evaluate those investments in which tax advantage is a factor — real estate, oil and gas and mining shares, Canadian securities and retirement funds. If saving tax is important to you, probably at least thirty to forty percent of your investment funds should be invested in tax-advantaged investments. In our example in Figure 10-4, those investments for which tax advantage is an objective comprise forty-four percent of the total.

6. What about leverage? Are you interested in using borrowed money to make money? If so, analyse your investments to see to what extent you are using borrowed funds. Leverage is frequently used in investing in real estate, stocks, and bonds, where growth is a primary objective.

FIGURE 10-3

File under INVESTMENT STRATEGY   Date: *May 5*

FORM 20   INVESTMENT OBJECTIVES

Indicate the relative importance you attribute to the following considerations by placing the appropriate number after each statement.

NOT IMPORTANT — 1
MARGINALLY IMPORTANT — 2
REASONABLY IMPORTANT — 3
DEFINITELY IMPORTANT — 4
MOST IMPORTANT — 5

Diversification	How important is it for you to hedge against big losses by spreading your risks?	*3*
Liquidity	How important is it that you have cash available for emergencies or investment opportunities?	*2*
Safety	If we went into a deep economic depression, how important would it be for you to sell your investments at about the price you paid for them?	*2*
Current Income	How important is it that you get maximum income from your investments this year and next?	*1*
Future Appreciation	How important is it that your investment dollars keep pace with inflation or do better than inflation?	*5*
Tax Advantage	How important is it that you get all the tax relief that may be available to you?	*4*
Leverage	How important is it for you to use borrowed money in hopes of reaping a higher return on your investment?	*3*
Ease of Management	How important is it for you to have investments you do not have to watch or worry about?	*4*

7. What about ease of management? If you believe it is important for professionals to assist you in selecting and managing your investments, then many of your investments should be made with the advice of investment counsellors or purchased through mutual funds. If you want to spend your time managing your own investments or if you are interested primarily in safety and current income and can easily find investments providing such objectives, then select and manage your investments yourself.

Rate of Return Analysis

In column 7 of Form 21, you should have entered the total annual rate of return before taxes that you achieved on each of your investments. How have you done? One measure of performance is inflation. Did you stay ahead of last year's increase in the Consumer Price Index (a widely used measure of inflation) in each of your investments? If not, which ones lagged behind inflation? Does it concern you to have some investments not keeping up with inflation?

Another measure of performance is the index in Table 10-1. How well did your stocks, bonds, real estate and other investments compare with the average rate of return for similar investments listed in Table 10-1?

FIGURE 10-4

File under INVESTMENT STRATEGY   Date: *May 6*

FORM 21   REVIEW OF YOUR PRESENT INVESTMENTS

TYPE OF ASSET	CURRENT VALUE	% OF TOTAL	INVESTMENT OBJECTIVES	CURRENT INCOME	APPR'N (LOSS)	ANNUAL RATE OF RETURN
Savings Account	$9,100	3%	Liquidity & Safety	8%	—	8%
Money Market Funds	24,400	8%	Liquidity & Safety	10.5%	—	10.5%
Shares in Cdn. Public Companies	84,400	28%	Growth, Tax Savings	5%	10%	15%
Bonds	43,000	15%	Current Income	10%	(0.1%)	9.9%
Real Estate	90,000	30%	Growth	5%	10.3%	15.3%
Flow-through Shares	20,000	7%	Growth, Tax Savings	—	Too Early to tell	—
RRSP	25,400	9%	Tax Deferred Growth	12%	—	12%
TOTAL	**$296,300**	**100%**				

You should evaluate your total rate of return against some commonly used measures of performance to see how your present investment programme stacks up.

After you have completed the analysis of your present investments, you are ready to evaluate investment alternatives and consider changes in your present investment strategy.

ALLOCATION OF INVESTMENT DOLLARS

There are many investments to which you can allocate your investment funds, but the best way is to allocate your funds according to investment objectives appropriate for you. What is appropriate is related to your stage in life. Normally, safety, liquidity and current income are important when you are young and interested in acquiring a car, furnishings, a home. As your employment income increases and you have additional funds for investment, growth and tax savings become of primary importance. As you approach retirement, safety and current income along with some inflation hedge usually become the important investment objectives.

Because of the large number of variables involved, such as health, employment stability, divorce and inheritances, it is important to individualize an investment strategy, usually with the help of someone who can take an informed, unbiased view of your financial situation and objectives. With the information on Form 21, the independent advisor can review your present programme and help you allocate your investment funds to meet your objectives.

The following guidelines can help you develop an investment plan that is appropriate for your particular stage in life.

Before Marriage

As a financial stage in your life, this period begins with the first paycheque you receive in your first full-time job, and it lasts until you acquire family responsibilities. You may have a student loan to repay, but apart from that, you can probably do as you please with what is left after you've paid for your living expenses.

One of the best investments at this stage is in additional education or self-improvement programmes that will raise your professional prospects and your earning potential. This calls for some extra effort, of course, and takes up some of your previous spare time, but it pays off very handsomely, as a rule.

It is also sensible at this stage to establish a cash reserve in a savings account. This should be primarily for emergencies; but it can also help one over the common discomfort of being high and dry on Thursday and standing in a huge line at the bank on Friday.

It is probably not necessary to buy life insurance at this stage in your life. You do not need it unless you are supporting someone other than yourself.

If, like many young people nowadays, you are making quite a lot of money, and if you can keep your expenditures fairly low, you may be able to save substantial amounts that you can put into long-term investments. Given a reasonable housing market, you might use them to start acquiring a home of your own. In recent years such an investment has been an excellent hedge against inflation, and generally any gain realized on its eventual sale will be tax-free.

In addition to this, or as an alternative, you could look for investments with a potential for growth. A growth-oriented mutual fund might be your best investment of this type, since it allows you to diversify even when you do not have a lot of capital to invest. It is, moreover, managed for you, which is important to you at this stage in your life, when you should be spending your time and energy promoting your career prospects.

Before You Have Children

In our current social environment, it has become quite common for young couples to wait several years before they have children, or to decide not to have any children at all. With both spouses working, you have the income and opportunity to build up your net worth before you start to assume financial responsibility for children. Insurance is not a big factor yet, since there is little need for such protection when both spouses are working and the survivor can continue to work after the death of his or her spouse.

If the couple can keep their committed expenses at a reasonable level, then significant sums may be available for an investment programme. Of course, in the early years of marriage, there may be tremendous pressure to spend money on furnishings for a house or apartment, to have two cars if both spouses are working, and to buy labour-saving appliances because both spouses go out to work. Nonetheless, one should start on some careful budgeting during this period in order to ensure that funds are set aside for investment.

Before Your Children Are In University Or College

From the time that your first child arrives to the time that your youngest child has become self-supporting, financial considerations will have a high order of importance. The first and most compelling aspect of financial planning then will be the protection of the spouse and children in case the primary wage earner should die, and this protection will have to be increased as the size of the family increases. Your need for life insurance should be analysed carefully during this period, to determine the length of time for which insurance will be needed and how to obtain that coverage in the most economical way.

Aside from that, this is a time for living — a time when spending money may be the best way of using it. There are the obvious needs for additional clothing, housing and food, which raise your basic committed expenses. There is also a need for vacations and travel, and maybe for private school fees as well.

Fortunately, your income, too, is likely to go up quite a lot in this period, and therefore tax planning will become a critical aspect of your overall financial planning. And if your spouse is also working, tax planning will be much more critical. If your spouse has been primarily a homemaker, he or she may decide to enter or return to the job market when the children begin school. But before you become a two-income family, there may be some education expenditures if the non-working spouse needs to prepare for a career change.

The financing of children's university or college costs is something that parents should start to consider a great many years ahead of time. No matter how you finance these costs (the options that have some tax advantages will be discussed in Chapter 11), you will need to have fairly substantial funds available as your children reach university or college age.

When Your Children No Longer Require Support

The time when your earning power is at its highest will usually start when your children's education has been completed and you and your spouse are in your late forties or early fifties (maybe even the sixties for couples who delayed having children). That time should be used to establish your retirement income. Once the children need little or no financial support, your committed expenses decline, and you will have funds to invest in income-producing assets. You may also be able to spend more time managing your investments, which usually means that you can accept higher risks.

At this stage, you should review your life insurance. Taking your total resources into consideration, you may find that your need for insurance has become minimal. If so, the money you save by reducing or even eliminating insurance premiums can be used to build up your retirement fund.

As you get close to retirement, your investment strategy can still be aimed at building capital, but risk should be viewed as a more negative factor than it was in the earlier stages of your life. You may now want to start shifting your capital to investments that will provide income during retirement and will also provide a hedge against inflation. At this point, it will probably be advisable to get financial counselling to help you develop an effective investment strategy and assess the tax aspects of the various ways you might be paid your retirement funds.

Retirement

A comfortable income during retirement is one of the primary goals of financial planning and investment decisions. Financial independence during retirement is the result of planning and self-discipline in the earlier stages in one's life. For most people, it requires an early start, investments suitable to the various stages in one's life, an intelligent compromise between too much and too little insurance, and a great deal of determination.

It would be correct to conclude from the foregoing discussion that your investment objectives will and should change as your life situation changes. One thing that will not change is the need to keep your objectives clearly in mind as you formulate your investment strategies and make your investment decisions.

INVESTMENT MIX

An investment programme has to be related to the major periods of a planner's lifetime. In Table 10-3 we have provided some guidance as to how one might allocate investment funds in different periods of a lifetime to reflect changing investment objectives. As the table indicates, the need for safety and current income is usually greater in one's twenties and sixties than in one's thirties and forties. Also, the table reflects only selected investments — four traditional ones, and precious metals, which became more important in the past when Canada experienced high levels of inflation.

TABLE 10-3
SUGGESTED INVESTMENT MIX AMONG SELECTED INVESTMENTS

	Allocation in Percentages			
Age	Liquidity (Savings and Money Market Investments)	Current Income (Bonds, Low-Leverage Real Estate)	Growth (Common Stocks, Leveraged Real Estate)	Purchasing Power Hedge (Precious Metals)
20s	40-50%	20-30%	20-35%	5-10%
30s	10-20	10-20	60-80	10-15
40s	5-10	10-15	70-90	10-15
50s	5-10	15-20	55-70	10-15
60s	20-30	20-30	25-40	5-10

ASSESSING YOUR INVESTMENT STRATEGY

Just as the different stages in your life should be reflected in your investment strategies, so there are some specific events — a new child, a higher-paying job, a large bonus, an inheritance, a large capital gain, a higher tax bracket, a change in the tax laws — that may call for modification of your investment strategy. Given such specific events as well as the overall changes, it is imperative that once, or better twice, a year you reassess your status, your investment objectives, and your investment strategy. We also recommend a minor review monthly or quarterly, or whenever there has been some change that will have financial consequences.

FORM 22 — YOUR INVESTMENT STRATEGY

We strongly believe that you will achieve the best investment results by setting specific investment goals and then following an investment programme that is designed to accomplish your goals.

On Form 20, you assessed your current investment objectives. You then completed Form 21, *Review of Your Present Investments*. Now it is time for you to select from among your objectives those that will be the most important to you over the next three years. When that is clear to you, determine what changes you want to make in your present investment position.

- The first step in formulating your investment strategy is to review Form 20, *Investment Objectives*, and enter those objectives most important to you during the next three years under question 1 on Form 22.

- Next, enter your estimation of the inflation rate during the next three years. One of the measures of performance you should consider in targeting an overall return on your investments is the inflation rate.

- In light of your estimation of inflation and your past investment performance, enter your target overall annual return for the next three years under question 3 on Form 22. Be realistic in setting this target return; take into consideration your objectives and the time and effort you will devote to your investments.

- Under question 4, list the specific changes, if any, you want to make in your present investments. If you desire a higher return than you are presently achieving, you may have to reallocate some investment funds presently in safe, liquid investments to investments with greater growth potential.

- Another important factor in your investment programme is to determine what annual amount you can set aside from your current employment income during each of the next three years. For example, you and your spouse may plan to set aside $4,000 a year for investment in an RRSP. Or you may be planning to set aside $5,000 a year for an investment in a mutual fund. Try to set a goal for investing some amount of your employment income each year and enter that amount under question 5.

- Under question 6, list those investments you will make with the funds you have identified under question 5. These investments should be related to your objectives as well.

Figure 10-5 illustrates a completed Form 22 for the mid-life couple we used as an example in Figures 10-3 and 10-4.

MUTUAL FUNDS

Before we leave the general topic of investments, let's look briefly at the subject of mutual funds, a type of investment which has become increasingly popular in recent years. Mutual funds are professionally managed pools of investments which provide an individual investor with an opportunity to invest in the stock market or other areas without the responsibility of making specific investments. Mutual funds also allow individuals with limited funds to invest their money, together with a large number of other individuals, in many different investments, thereby "spreading the risk." When you buy units of a mutual fund, you own a share of all of the investments made by the fund, and as income is earned by the fund (dividends, interest, or capital gains), your portion can be reinvested in additional units of the fund or be paid to you in cash if current income is important.

Mutual funds are sold by trust companies, banks, brokerage houses, insurance companies and by mutual fund managers. There are many different funds available. You can choose a fund that invests in the Canadian, U.S. or other countries' stock markets, Treasury bills and other money market instruments, corporate or government bonds, mortgages, precious metals, other commodities, or a combination of some or all of these. Some funds invest primarily to achieve capital appreciation, while others concentrate on earning current income. Many funds, often called "balanced funds," aim for both moderate capital appreciation and current income. Depending on the types of investments made by the mutual fund, a fund can qualify as an investment for your RRSP. You should be able to determine the type of fund that is best for you by matching the kind of investments it makes with your investment objectives identified earlier in this chapter.

Mutual funds are best for investors who want an easily managed investment with the potential for a higher return than other such investments, like Canada Savings Bonds. The reliability of the return from a mutual fund is, of course, dependent on its underlying investments — funds which invest in precious metals or other commodities will be more risky investments than those which invest in preferred shares or government bonds. Your mutual fund investment is also not covered by Canadian deposit insurance, unlike investments such as guaranteed investment certificates.

If you are interested in investing in a mutual fund, there are several factors you should consider in choosing among the various funds which match your investment objectives. The single most important criterion for choosing a fund is the quality of its investment counsel, and this is usually but not always measured by past performance. Compare the fund's performance in the last year and over the previous five to ten years. Look for sustained performance. A fund with a tremendous gain in the last year, but mediocre performance over the last five years, may not be able to repeat its recent success. You can get information about a fund's performance directly from the fund manager or from regular surveys of registered fund performance in the financial press. Some funds do better during a down turn in the economy while others do better during periods of high inflation. Past performance may not be relevant if financial conditions have substantially changed. See Chapter 15, *Keeping Up with Current Financial Information*, for some sources.

FIGURE 10-5

File under INVESTMENT STRATEGY   Date: *May 7*

FORM 22   YOUR INVESTMENT STRATEGY

1. What investment objectives (see Form 20) will be most important for you during the next three years?

    Growth, Tax Shelter

2. What do you assume the inflation rate will be during the next three years?   *3-5%*

3. What overall annual pre-tax return on your investments do you want to achieve in the next three years?

    9-11%

4. What specific changes do you have to make in your present investments to achieve your objectives and overall rate of return in the next three years?

    Decrease real estate investments to less than 30% of total investments

5. What annual amount do you believe you can set aside for investment during the next three years?

    Very little except through tax savings and investment income of approximately $10,000

6. What investments will you make with your additional investment dollars? *Growth stocks, mutual funds*

You should also consider the costs of investing in the various funds. Many funds charge substantial commissions (from one to nine percent) when you purchase units — these are often referred to as "front-end load" funds. All funds charge an annual management and administration fee, usually between one-half and two percent of the current value of the fund's assets. There may also be fees to withdraw money from the fund or to transfer to another fund. These fees will reduce the growth in value of your investment, but in the long term (five to ten years or more) a well-managed fund should realize a better rate of return, even after deduction of fees, than most people could achieve on their own.

11

EDUCATIONAL FINANCING

Education is a very special investment. It can introduce you to an entirely new way of looking at things. It can open up new directions and options in life. It can be a rare period of unencumbered time to pursue ideas for their own sake, to reflect, and to philosophize; and like many other special investments, it requires significant financial resources.

Although the most important considerations in choosing a school programme are educational, there are financial considerations also, and these have become a matter of concern for a great many families. Educational expenditures are no longer confined to four years of university. Many families have children attending private pre-schools, elementary schools, and secondary schools, where tuition and fees may approach or exceed $6,500 a year per child. On the other side of undergraduate school, there may also be masters' and doctoral programmes that require additional years of funding.

In this chapter, we will discuss the costs of education and how to meet them. We will focus on university costs, but much of this discussion will also be applicable to the costs of graduate schools and colleges.

HOW MUCH WILL UNIVERSITY OR COLLEGE COST?

Typically, university or college costs consist of the following major items:

- Tuition fees
- Books and supplies
- Room and board
- Transportation
- Personal expenses

University or college fees are a major, although not necessarily the largest, component of educational cost. Although costs vary among provinces, you can expect to pay approximately $2,000 per year. With increasing pressure on all levels of government to cut spending and balance their budgets, it seems reasonable to assume that students in future will be required to pay more towards their education.

The costs of books and supplies do not vary much from one university or college to the next. However, certain fields of study, such as engineering and the physical sciences, will generally require more expensive books and supplies than other fields of study. You should anticipate spending at least $600 to $700 on books and supplies.

Room and board costs vary considerably. For students who live at home and commute to school, room and board will be considerably less than for students who live on or near campus. For students who do not live at home, the costs vary with the type of residence chosen, which might be a dormitory on campus, or a privately-owned apartment or rooming house. But, in general, you should expect to pay $3,000 to $5,000 per year for basic room and board on campus. Costs can go much higher when living off campus.

Transportation expenses for students who attend school a great distance from home are often considerable at the beginning and end of an academic year or term and during holiday breaks, while students who commute will have small daily transportation expenses.

Personal expenses include such items as laundry, toiletries, recreation, clothes, and furnishings for the student's "home away from home."

More accurate information about the cost of a particular school can be obtained from the school's admissions office.

FORM 23 — UNIVERSITY, GRADUATE SCHOOL AND COLLEGE COSTS

University or college costs can be very high. It is therefore a good idea to do some planning ahead of time, and the first step in that process is to estimate what those costs are likely to be. Before or while you are filling in this form, it might be helpful to look at Figure 11-1, which shows you an example of the filled-in form.

- On line 1, list your children's first names.

- On line 2, list your children's present ages.

- On line 3, list how many years from now each child will be starting university or college. If a child is already in university or college, put a zero on line 3.

- On line 4, enter the estimated number of years each child will attend university or college and graduate school. If a child is presently in university, college or graduate school, enter the number of years required to complete his or her education.

- On line 5, compute the number of years to be used in an inflation adjustment. This number is determined by adding the years on line 3 to fifty percent of the years on line 4.

- On line 6, estimate the average annual inflation rate between now and the end of the child's educational programme.

- On line 7, enter the compound factor from Table 1 in Appendix I for the number of years on line 5 and for the estimated inflation rate on line 6.

- On line 8, enter for each of your children the present cost of one year's attendance at university or college. Obtain the approximate figures from the relevant institution's catalogue or use the approximate amounts discussed above.

- On line 9, estimate the inflation-adjusted annual university or college costs for each child by multiplying the amount on line 8 by the factor on line 7.

- On line 10, calculate the total estimated university or college costs for each child by multiplying the amount on line 9 by the number of years on line 4.

- On line 11, estimate the annual after-tax rate of return on educational funds invested.

- On line 12, enter the compound factor from Table 1 in Appendix I for the number of years on line 5 and for the estimated rate of return on line 11.

- On line 13, enter the amount of funds presently set aside for the education of each child.

- On line 14, calculate the estimated future value of the present educational funds by multiplying the amount on line 13 by the factor on line 12.

- On line 15, calculate the annual amount to be invested for each child's education.

    (a) First subtract the amount on line 14 from the amount on line 10.

    (b) Divide the result in 15(a) by the compound factor from Table 2 in Appendix I for the estimated rate of return on line 11 and the number of years on line 5. The result is the annual amount to be invested for each child, to be entered on line 15(c).

Now that you have picked yourself up off the floor after the fainting spell induced by the grand total of your children's estimated university or college costs and the annual amount to be invested.

WHO PAYS?

Most universities, colleges and grantors of financial aid have developed guidelines for determining how much a student's family can pay for education and how much financial aid may be needed. They start with the premise that the responsibility of paying university or college costs falls on the student's parents and the student to the extent of their ability to pay them.

Financial Aid

The provincial governments have programmes which provide students with financial assistance in the form of loans and grants. Qualification for these programmes is based on a means test and examines the financial resources of both the student and the parents. Details of the programmes and applications are available through universities, high schools or by contacting the Ministry of Education.

There are many scholarships available through both the universities and colleges and private foundations. Again you should contact the universities, colleges or high schools for information. Many companies have educational assistance programmes for children of their employees. The personnel office should be able to assist you in this matter.

If you or your children do not qualify for financial assistance, you should investigate other ways of reducing your costs such as the Registered Education Savings Plan, loans or gifts.

Reducing the Cost of an Education

The benefits of a Registered Education Savings Plan and other income splitting methods result from tax-planning techniques discussed in Chapter 6. Shifting income from the parent who is in a high tax bracket to the student who is in a low tax bracket will reduce the taxes paid by the family as a whole, thereby providing the same kind of financial relief as a scholarship grant.

Now let us see how income shifting might work for you if your child is attending a university away from home and his or her education costs are, say, $7,000 a year. We

FIGURE 11-1

Date: *June 11*

FORM 23 UNIVERSITY, GRADUATE SCHOOL AND COLLEGE COSTS

		Sue	John	Elizabeth
1.	Children's Names	*Sue*	*John*	*Elizabeth*
2.	Ages of Children	20	19	10
3.	Number of Years until University	*in university*	*in university*	8
4.	Estimated Number of Years in University and Graduate School	4	5	6
5.	Number of Years for Inflation Adjustment	2	2.5	11
6.	Estimated Annual Inflation Rate between Now and End of Education	3	3	4
7.	Inflation Factor	1.06	1.075	1.54
8.	Estimated Annual University Costs in Today's Dollars	$7,000	$7,000	$7,000
9.	Estimated Annual Costs Adjusted	$7,420	$7,525	$10,780
10.	Estimated TOTAL Costs Adjusted	$29,680	$37,625	$64,680
11.	Estimated After-Tax Rate of Return on Educational Funds	5%	5%	5%
12.	Compound Factor for Rate of Return on Line 11	1.10	1.13	1.71
13.	Present Value of Funds Set Aside for Education	$10,000	$8,000	0
14.	Future Value of Funds Set Aside	$11,000	$9,040	0
15.	Annual Amount to be Invested for Education *a) Total Req'd*	$18,680	$28,585	$64,680
	b) Compound Factor	2.05	2.60	14.21
	c) Annual Amount Req'd	$9,112	$10,994	$4,552

will assume that your child has agreed to earn and pay $2,000 of that cost and you have agreed to pay the remaining $5,000. If you are in the fifty percent tax bracket, you would have to earn $10,000 to have $5,000 left after taxes, and that is a very expensive way to go.

Now let us look at the child's tax bracket. With an income of $2,000 for the year, the child will not be taxable. Even if the child had income that amounted to $5,000, the child would pay no tax. But you would have paid $5,000 in taxes to generate the same $5,000 after-tax income. Therefore, if you can manage to transfer sufficient income to your child to finance education costs, significant tax savings can result.

Registered Educational Savings Plans

A Registered Educational Savings Plan (RESP) can be a useful tool for parents or grand-parents who wish to set aside funds to help their children finance their post-secondary education.

A parent or grandparent sets up the RESP by making a contribution and designating a child or grandchild as beneficiary. Depending on the plan, contributions may be made in lump sums or as a series of regular payments. There are limits on the amount that can be contributed to a plan. The 1990 federal budget limited total contributions to RESPs to $1,500 per beneficiary a year, to a cumulative maximum of $31,500. The contributions are not tax-deductible but income earned on the contribution accumulates tax-free in the plan. The contributions may be refunded tax-free to the contributor. The timing of such refunds depends on the terms of the particular RESP.

The major restriction with RESPs is that the accumulated income must be used to finance the beneficiary's post-secondary education. Therefore, if the child chooses not to continue his or her education after high school, the income in the plan cannot be paid to the child or the contributing parent. For this reason, it is preferable to choose a plan which will allow you to change the beneficiary so that the income can be used by another child instead. Plans with flexibility in the choice of beneficiaries are available through several major investment dealers, mutual fund managers and life insurance companies.

Education costs are very broadly defined and include room and board as well as tuition and books. As long as the child is attending school full-time, income can be distributed from the plan to finance some or all of the child's reasonable education costs. The child will pay tax on such income received in the year only if it, plus any other income earned in the year, generates taxes payable which exceed the child's tuition and education tax credit, basic tax credit and any other credits the child is entitled to.

In summary, the advantages of RESPs are that:

1. they allow income to accumulate tax-free; and

2. the income is ultimately taxed in the hands of the child who should pay tax at a lower rate than the parent and should have available substantial credits that could not otherwise be claimed by the parent.

There have been very few RESPs offered in the past and these have been very restrictive. However, plans are offered now which are more flexible with respect to investments held by the plan, subsequent changing of beneficiaries, refunds of contributions, academic requirements and eligible schools. But, before you invest in one of these plans, you should be aware of all of its terms and how they may affect you.

Loans or Gifts

As discussed in Chapter 6, opportunities for income splitting with spouses and children have been severely restricted in recent years. However, as most post-secondary age students are eighteen years or over, income splitting is still possible. The student may be loaned or given funds for investment. All income generated by gifted funds and capital gains earned on loaned funds will be taxed in the hands of the student who usually has a lower marginal tax rate than his or her parents. The result is that from the same income, more after-tax dollars will be available for financing the child's education.

Family Allowance and Child Tax Benefit

Prior to 1993 family allowance was taxed in the hands of the person who claimed the children as dependants. Provided that the payments were deposited in a separate account and invested for the child's benefit, the income earned on the funds deposited was attributed to the child rather than to the parent. Beginning January 1993, the family allowance payment, the tax credit for dependent children and the refundable child tax credit was replaced by a unified tax benefit of $1,020 per child. However, the benefit will begin to be reduced when family income exceeds $20,000 and will be totally phased out for incomes between $60,000 and $75,000. Families with income exceeding $75,000 will not receive any payments. The child tax benefit is not taxable to the parent receiving the payment. In addition, if the benefit payment is deposited in a separate account or invested for the child for whom the benefit was paid, the income earned on the funds deposited or invested will be attributed to the child rather than to the parents. "High income" families that previously split income by investing the family allowance payments in their children's names will no longer be able to do so.

12

RETIREMENT PLANNING

Until they retire, people who have been working most of their adult years are usually unaware of how much their jobs and their work environments mean to them. Unprepared, many of them experience a tremendous sense of loss, emptiness and uselessness. Some companies now hold pre-retirement clinics to help their employees make the transition from organizational life to private life. Essentially, such clinics tell the impending retirees to do the following:

- Evaluate your accomplishments; assess your strengths and weaknesses, your likes and dislikes; and envisage your activities during your retirement years.

- Widen your personal interests. Explore pursuits from which you would derive great satisfaction — a hobby, a service project, an autobiography.

- Analyse your financial requirements and the sources of your retirement income.

There are regrettably few retirees whose financial provisions for retirement prove to be adequate. Retirement planning is essential if you are to reach the goals you have set for that period of your life. To do this effectively, you should start to work on your retirement programme at least ten to fifteen years before you expect to retire.

You will have to work out what your financial requirements will be at retirement and then plan to have the necessary financial resources available.

FORM 24 — ESTIMATED BASIC LIFESTYLE EXPENDITURES AT RETIREMENT

Before you can estimate your financial needs and resources at retirement, you must set a time frame for your projections by deciding at what age you want to retire. Most people think of sixty-five as retirement age, but you may want to retire earlier or later than that, or maybe plan on partial retirement instead of complete retirement.

The simplest way of estimating your financial needs at retirement is to begin with your present pattern of expenditures, and then to visualize in what respects the pattern will be different once you have retired.

- Begin by completing the first column, *Current Year*, with the figures you listed on Form 7, Basic Lifestyle Expenditures, filed under *Financial Profile*.

- In the second column, *At Retirement*, complete lines 1 through 18 by putting your estimated expenditures in terms of today's dollars (present-day prices). In some categories, such as medical care, it may be wise to allow for greater expenses than those you have at present. In other categories, such as housing, clothing and transportation, you are likely to have smaller expenses than at present. Your home mortgage, for example, may be completely paid off by the time you retire. In fact, it had better be paid off by the time you retire; otherwise you haven't been doing a good job with your personal financial planning!

- On line 19, enter the total of your estimated annual expenditures in retirement. This will not be your final forecast, because so far it has not taken inflation into account.

- On line 20, list in how many years you plan to retire.

- On line 21, estimate the average annual rate of inflation for the years before you retire.

- On line 22, select the right figure from Table 1 in Appendix I. Choose the column with the same percentage as the one you listed on line 21. Then go down that column until you get to the number of years you listed on line 20, and there you have your compound factor.

- For line 23, multiply the total on line 19 by the inflation factor on line 21.

FORM 25 — ESTIMATED DISCRETIONARY EXPENDITURES AT RETIREMENT

In completing this form, you will essentially do the same things you did to complete the previous form.

- Begin by completing the first column, *Current Year*, with the figures you listed on Form 8, D*iscretionary Expenditures*, filed under *Financial Profile*.

- In the second column, *At Retirement*, use today's dollars (present-day prices) for your estimates on lines 1 through 12.

In some categories, such as vacations or hobbies, you may want to spend more in retirement than you do now; but in others, such as support of relatives or contributions to retirement plans, you might be spending much less or nothing at all.

- On line 13, add up the amounts on lines 1 through 12 in the second column.

- On line 14, list the same inflation factor you listed on line 22 of Form 24.

- For line 15, multiply the total on line 13 by the factor on line 14.

FORM 26 — ESTIMATED RETIREMENT NEEDS, INCLUDING TAXES

- On line 1, list your total from line 23 of Form 24, *Estimated Basic Lifestyle Expenditures at Retirement*.

- On line 2, list your total from line 15 of Form 25, *Estimated Discretionary Expenditures at Retirement*.

- On line 3, put the sum of lines 1 and 2.

The Impact of Taxes

So far, none of your estimates have taken income taxes into account. Therefore, the next and last step in estimating your financial needs at retirement will be to calculate the impact of income taxes on your retirement needs. It is likely that some, if not most, of the income you will receive during retirement will be taxable. The federal and provincial governments expect their share of your retirement income. Due to inflation, you may actually find yourself in quite a high tax bracket after you retire. A "rule of thumb" that can be used to estimate your tax requirements during retirement is to assume that taxes will constitute thirty-five percent of your estimated needs. Although this may seem lower than the average tax rate you are currently paying, remember that some of your income during retirement may not be taxable or may be taxed in a favoured way.

- To estimate retirement expenditures including taxes using an estimated average tax rate of thirty-five percent, put a tax factor of sixty-five percent on line 4 of Form 26.

- Then, on line 5, compute your total estimated retirement needs including taxes by dividing the amount on line 3 by the tax factor of sixty-five percent.

If you would like a more accurate estimate of taxes payable on your retirement income, fill out Form 11 assuming you were already retired. Include all your expected sources of income as listed in Form 19 and any expected deductions. Use the resulting taxable income figure calculated on Form 11 to estimate your total taxes payable by referring to Appendix III. Your total retirement needs including taxes will then be the sum of your estimated basic and discretionary lifestyle expenditures on retirement (lines 1 and 2 on Form 26) plus this estimated tax amount.

RETIREMENT INCOME

To have sufficient income to meet one's retirement needs requires some long-term planning. Although most people have an employee retirement plan, these plans are not necessarily designed to provide all your needs at retirement. All too often, the remainder of a person's needs is not adequately covered by Old Age Security or the Canada or Quebec Pension Plan. So it will be up to you to have sufficient investment income to make up any deficiency.

We have counselled some people who did not realize the importance of investment income to their retirement dreams until they were just a few years away from retirement. They were then faced with the need either to continue working or else to scale back their retirement lifestyle. The need to start serious retirement planning at least ten to fifteen years before you wish to retire cannot be emphasized enough. Ten to fifteen years before retirement, you have probably completed the children's education, settled comfortably into your dream house, and stopped your "accumulating phase." You have completed phases of your life that require heavy expenditures, so you will probably have more funds available for investment and should concentrate on funding your retirement.

Allocate your funds to investments with a solid growth potential. You should now avoid investments with a high risk because you do not have much time to recover from substantial losses. As you near retirement, you should continue to invest primarily in quality, growth-oriented investments; but start to look for quality income-oriented investments as well. You should, however, also be concerned about the impact of inflation during retirement, so investments that provide a hedge against inflation should be a substantial part of your investment programme.

Below is a brief description of the more common sources of retirement income.

COMPANY RETIREMENT PLANS

The most common type of retirement plan offered by companies in Canada is the registered pension plan. In addition, some companies have established Deferred Profit Sharing Plans (DPSPs) for their employees, but they are not widely used. A registered pension plan can be either benefit-oriented or contribution-oriented. A pension plan is registered if it complies with certain conditions and limits and has been accepted for registration by the Minister of National Revenue. Virtually all pension plans in Canada are registered because only registered pension plans qualify for the special tax advantages described below.

With a *defined benefit plan*, the amount of the benefits you will be paid at retirement has been set in advance, and the company's contributions to the plan are actuarially determined to give the plan the assets necessary for paying these predetermined benefits. Often, retirement benefits are set according to a formula related to your earnings (for example, for each year's service, you might be paid a percentage of your highest five years' earnings, as an annual pension).

With a *defined contribution* or *money purchase plan*, the company's contribution on behalf of its employee is either a flat dollar amount or a percentage of the employee's compensation. Here, the amount of the employee's retirement benefits will depend on how much capital has been contributed on the employee's behalf, on how much this capital has earned, and on how large an annuity can be purchased with the accumulated funds, given prevailing interest rates at the time of retirement.

As a result of recent changes to rules and regulations that govern pension plans, individual pension plans (IPPs) are becoming a popular executive perk. IPPs provide a means by which an enhanced pension can be paid to executives and business owners.

Deferred Profit Sharing Plans, which are contribution-oriented, are funded by the company according to a formula based on a percentage of the company's profits. The level of these contributions varies with the company's profits, and if there are no profits, there are no contributions. As is the case with pension plans, a Deferred Profit Sharing Plan must also be registered as complying with certain terms and conditions, in order to qualify for the special tax advantages described below. Deferred Profit Sharing Plans tend to be used much less than registered pension plans as retirement plan vehicles by Canadian companies.

Tax Advantages

The money you have in a company's Deferred Profit Sharing Plan (DPSP) or registered pension plan (RPP) does not become taxable until you receive it upon retiring or leaving the company for some other reason. It can therefore accumulate and gather a compound rate of return untaxed, and this is a tremendous advantage. A given sum of money invested at eight percent untaxed will double itself in nine years; but it will take about sixteen years for that sum to double itself if your eight percent return is taxable every year and you are in the forty percent tax bracket.

Let's look at these two tax situations further by comparing two people, Joe and Fred. Each sets aside $3,000 a year from current compensation for a retirement plan. Let's say that in Joe's case, this is done by his employer contributing $3,000 on his behalf to the company's RPP. Because the pension plan is registered, Joe does not have to pay tax currently on this $3,000. Fred, however, operates on a do-it-yourself basis; he has to include his $3,000 of compensation in taxable income, then takes what is left of it after taxes and invests it. If both Joe and Fred are in the thirty percent tax bracket, Joe's $3,000 can all be invested (in the company's RPP) because he has paid no tax on that portion of his compensation. Fred has only $2,100 to invest, because thirty percent of his $3,000 has to be paid to Revenue Canada. Further, the income on Joe's annual $3,000 pension contribution is tax-deferred because it is in an RPP; the income on Fred's investment will be taxable. Assume that the RPP holding Joe's pension contributions gets ten percent on its investments and that Fred finds a similar type of investment that yields ten percent before taxes. Joe's funds compound tax-free: Fred's compound annual rate will only be seven percent because of his thirty percent tax bracket. After the first year, Joe's $3,000 has earned $300 in the RPP. Fred's $2,100 has earned $210, but after he pays his tax, only $147 is left for reinvestment. After one year, Joe has $1,053 more than Fred. If they continue on the same basis, after a period of thirty years, the difference is even more impressive.

If you use a calculator and punch in the data for the annual amount invested ($3,000 versus $2,100) and rate of return (ten percent versus seven percent), the results after thirty years of steady investing will be:

Joe	$493,500
Fred	$198,400

The difference between the retirement funds of Joe and Fred, about $295,000, is due to the tax-free compounding of $3,000 per year at ten percent on Joe's behalf in his employer's RPP versus the after tax compounding of $2,100 per year at seven percent in Fred's account. Well, you say, that's not a fair comparison because Joe's funds will be taxed when he receives them during retirement. That's right — your retirement benefits are taxed when received, at your applicable marginal tax rate of up to approximately forty-five percent or higher. Fred would not be taxed on any of his $198,400 at the end of thirty years, since he has already been taxed on the capital he invested and on the earnings of this invested capital. However, there are tax-favoured ways of receiving your retirement payments that we will discuss in a few pages, which allow you to spread the tax impact throughout your retirement years, and minimize the total tax paid.

And even if Joe took all his pension funds out in a lump sum and paid tax at a rate of forty-five percent, he would still have about $271,400 after tax, or over $73,000 more than Fred.

This example assumed Joe accumulated his retirement funds in an RPP; the same tax advantages would have resulted if his employer's contributions had instead been invested in the company's DPSP.

This example also assumed only the employer contributed to the RPP. If the terms of the RPP also required contributions by employees, Joe's contributions would have enjoyed special tax treatment. Joe's contributions would have been deductible from his taxable income (subject to certain limits already discussed in Chapter 6) and income on these contributions would also accumulate tax-free, giving the same special tax treatment as provided for employer contributions.

Retirement Plan Terms and Conditions

Retirement plans (RPPs, DPSPs and other unregistered plans) are generally administered by a trustee or several trustees, such as a trust company or the employer (usually represented by a group of the company's executives resident in Canada). As already discussed, most companies have retirement plans that comply with terms and conditions required for registration by the Department of National Revenue, in order to take advantage of the tax benefits described above. As well, there are provincial or federal standards under applicable *Pension Benefits Acts* which must be met.

The standards for all pension plans governed by federal legislation were significantly changed in 1986, effective January 1, 1987. Similar changes have been enacted for pension plans governed by legislation in Ontario, Alberta, Nova Scotia, New Brunswick, Saskatchewan, Manitoba, British Columbia and Quebec. These changes have improved employee pension benefit entitlements by providing for earlier entitlement for membership in employer pension plans, earlier vesting of pension benefits, minimum rates of return on employee contributions and greater transferability of pension benefits on ceasing employment. The equal division on marriage breakdown of pension benefits which accrued during the marriage is also provided for.

The present reform of pension benefits standards has been underway for several years, and will probably take several more years to complete. But given the significant action taken by the federal government plus the five provinces mentioned above, similar legislation will likely apply to all public and private pension plans in Canada in the near future.

If you are covered by a company retirement plan, make sure you understand the details of the plan and know your rights and benefits. Ask for an annual update on the details of your retirement accounts; in particular, find out what monthly benefit you will receive at retirement and what vested benefits you have.

To assist you in better understanding your retirement plan and the potential effect of pension reform, the more important and common terms in such plans are discussed below.

Eligibility Requirements

Normally, there is a waiting period before a new employee is eligible for coverage under a plan. You should find out how long this waiting period is with your company.

Following pension reform, full-time employees and some part-time employees (if they have sufficiently high earnings) are generally eligible for membership in the company pension plan after two years' service.

Contributions to the Plan

Contributions to finance a pension plan can be made in several ways:

- The company contributes all the funds.

- The company and the employees share in the contributions on some predetermined basis.

- The employees can make voluntary contributions in addition to their regular contributions. The ability to make tax-deductible additional voluntary contributions was severely restricted as a result of tax changes introduced in October 1986. Refer to Chapter 6 for details.

One of the major changes introduced in the current round of pension reform is the so-called "fifty percent rule." Under this rule, the employer must pay for fifty percent of the employee's accrued benefits on termination, death or retirement. Any excess payment by the employee to the time of his termination may be refunded, used to fund increased pension benefits or transferred to the pension plan of his new employer, depending on which legislation applies. This rule is waived under the federal Pension Benefits Standards Act if the pension plan provides sufficient inflation protection.

Retirement Date

Most pension plans specify a retirement age for their employees, such as the first day of the month after which the employee reaches the age of sixty-five. An employee may be able to retire earlier, but that will usually reduce the employee's benefit according to a formula outlined in the plan.

In Ontario, the pension plan must specify a normal retirement age, which cannot be later than one year following age 65. In Quebec, the normal retirement age cannot be more than the beginning of the month after the month when the member attains age 65. In other jurisdictions, the rules vary.

Under most pension legislation, an employee can retire early within ten years of normal retirement.

Vesting Rules

Whether an employee will receive some part of the company's contributions upon dismissal or resignation is determined by the vesting rules set out in the company's benefit package. Under these rules, the percentage of the company's contributions to which the employee is entitled will increase with the number of years of employment. A company might have a vesting schedule that fully vests its employees after ten years with the company. In that case, upon retiring or leaving for other reasons after ten years, the employee is entitled to 100 percent of the contributions made on his or her behalf. Pension plans have a deliberate bias in favour of employees who stay with the company for a long time.

The changes introduced in the latest round of pension reform have significantly reduced the time period necessary for vesting. Under the federal, Nova Scotia, Ontario, British Columbia, Saskatchewan, Manitoba and Quebec legislation, full vesting for post-reform service must occur after only two years of membership in the pension plan. Full vesting occurs after five years of employment under the Alberta and New Brunswick legislation. Legislation in other provinces varies.

Death Benefits Prior to Retirement

Your retirement plan will outline what benefits, if any, will be available to your survivors, should you die before retirement age.

Death benefits prior to retirement have been significantly increased under pension reform, to reflect the value of vested pension benefits rather than just employee contributions. Under federal legislation, your surviving spouse will be entitled to the commuted value of the amount accrued since 1986, including any additional value resulting from the fifty percent rule. Under Quebec and Ontario legislation, your spouse or your estate will receive 100% of the commuted value of your vested benefits. Under Nova Scotia, Alberta and New Brunswick legislation, the mandatory pre-retirement death benefit will be at least sixty percent of the commuted value of the deferred pension, rather than the 100% Ontario requires.

Retirement Payments

Retirement benefits from an RPP are paid out in the form of an annuity for the remaining life of the retired employee. The annuity may have different features, including a guaranteed minimum term, survivorship options or guarantees of the payout of employee contributions in the event of early death.

You should take great care in choosing your RPP annuity. If you choose a simple life annuity, with no guaranteed minimum term and no survivorship options, your survivors will receive nothing from the annuity after your death, even if you die shortly after its purchase. This is not a prudent way to invest the retirement benefits you have worked so hard to earn, unless you are leaving your dependants other substantial assets.

If you choose a guaranteed minimum term of say, ten years, the annuity payments will continue for the greater of ten years and the number of years you live after retirement. If you choose a joint-and-last survivor option, the annuity will continue to pay throughout your lifetime and that of your spouse, should he or she live longer. These options will reduce somewhat the amount of your monthly pension benefit (because the life insurance company expects to have to pay benefits for a longer time) but will give you much more certainty in planning for your retirement and for those you may leave behind.

Under the revised federal *Pension Benefits Standards Act* and under several existing and proposed provincial acts, RPP annuities must provide benefits for surviving spouses (for example, 60 or 66 2/3 percent of accrued benefits at the time of death of the first spouse). However, the spouse can waive this benefit.

The benefits paid by the various life insurance companies for otherwise similar life annuities can vary substantially. You should take the time and trouble to get several quotes from different suppliers, and if possible, consult an independent advisor (one who does not sell only one or two companies' products!) who can evaluate the different products available without bias.

Funds accumulated in a DPSP can be used on retirement to purchase an annuity (with or without a guaranteed minimum term, which cannot exceed fifteen years, or survivorship options), but may also be received in installments payable not less frequently than annually for a period of not more than ten years. As well, although lump sum payments are generally not allowed from RPPs, they can usually be made from DPSPs.

Flexibility in timing of retirement payments will be discussed more fully under *Taxation of Retirement Payments*.

Taxation of RPP and DPSP Payments

Because payments from RPPs and DPSPs are taxed in essentially the same manner as payments from Registered Retirement Savings Plans (RRSPs), taxation of these payments will be discussed together after the following general description of RRSPs.

REGISTERED RETIREMENT SAVINGS PLANS

Registered Retirement Savings Plans (RRSPs) are very flexible vehicles which can be used to build up retirement funds for those who are self-employed, as well as providing employees covered by company pension plans an opportunity to augment their retirement income. In essence, your RRSP is your own individual pension plan account. Unlike an RPP or a DPSP, there is no employer to fund the plan — all contributions must come from you.

RRSPs are allowed generous tax treatment, similar in many ways to that provided to RPPs. Up to specified limits, contributions to an RRSP are deductible from the contributor's taxable income. (These limits are discussed in Chapter 6.) As well, income earned in the RRSP on these contributions accumulates tax-free as long as it remains in the plan. This tax-free compounding of tax-deductible contributions allows the RRSP contributor to accumulate a significantly higher retirement fund by using an RRSP instead of another savings plan. (See the "Joe and Fred" example discussed earlier in this chapter under *Company Retirement Plans* for more details.) Examples of possible accumulations within an RRSP are outlined in Table 6-1 in Chapter 6.

Table 6-1 clearly demonstrates the advantage of starting your retirement savings as early as possible. The benefits of tax-free compounding of income within an RRSP are not earned evenly over time. Instead, the benefits are much greater in later years because income is earned not just on the initial contribution but on the continually growing pool of previously-earned income. You may need to be a mathematician to understand exactly how this happens, but a quick look at Table 6-1 indicates the potential benefits. For example, after ten years of contributing $7,500 each year, assuming a ten percent rate of return, your RRSP will contain $119,510. If you continue the same contributions for another ten years, earning the same rate of return, your RRSP will have grown to $429,560. After another ten years of the same contributions at the same rate of return, your RRSP will have grown to $1,233,710. These are very impressive numbers!

There are RRSPs which should suit any kind of investor, although the types of investments that can be made in an RRSP are limited by the *Income Tax Act*. For example, before 1990, you could not invest more than ten percent of your contributions in foreign investments. Starting in 1990, this foreign property limit will rise by two percentage points a year and will be capped at twenty percent after 1993.

RRSPs are offered by banks, trust companies, life insurance companies, most stock brokerage firms, credit unions, *caisses populaires* and mutual funds. For more conservative investors, there are RRSPs which invest in low-risk investments such as guaranteed investment certificates, money market funds and savings accounts. More speculative investments such as Canadian corporate bonds and equities are also available. And for those who like to make their own investment decisions, self-administered RRSPs are also available. In deciding the appropriate type of investments for your RRSP, consider the discussion of *Investment Objectives* in Chapter 10. As well, before choosing a plan offered by a particular bank, trust company, etc., compare the features of the plan to similar ones offered by other companies. For example, you should compare fees charged to purchase, transfer and withdraw funds from the plan, administration fees, expected rates of return, frequency of compounding, length of time the rate of return is guaranteed and portability (the ability to transfer funds from one plan to another).

You may also make contributions to an RRSP for the benefit of your spouse. The tax advantages of this have already been discussed in Chapter 6.

Taxation of Retirement Payments

Let's assume now that you have accumulated substantial retirement funds in your company's RPP or DPSP, or in your own RRSP. How can these funds be received and what are the tax consequences on receipt?

Retirement benefits from an RPP will generally start as regular monthly receipts as soon as you retire, although they may be delayed until you reach age sixty-five in the case of early retirement. The amount of your monthly benefit will be affected by the various options you choose — guaranteed periods of payment, survivorship options, etc.

Retirement benefits from a DPSP can be paid to you on retirement as an annuity payable monthly, although you can choose instead to receive your benefits in installments (paid no less frequently than annually) for a period of not more than ten years or in a lump sum payment. Receipt of retirement benefits from your DPSP can also be delayed until age seventy-one if desired, to prolong the advantage of tax-free compounding of income in the DPSP.

Your choice in timing the receipt of your retirement funds accumulated in an RRSP is even more flexible. As with RPPs and DPSPs, you can choose to receive monthly payments for life, with or without a guaranteed term or survivorship options. You can also choose to receive your funds as a fixed term annuity. You may also elect to receive your RRSP funds in a lump sum or use them to invest in a Registered Retirement Income Fund (RRIF). Prior to 1992 a RRIF was essentially a term annuity to age ninety which had minimum payout requirements. This meant that the RRIF would be fully paid out by the time you reached age 90. The payments increased every year until the fund was exhausted. Starting in 1992 the rules have changed to allow payments to continue throughout your lifetime. There is still a schedule of minimum annual withdrawals; however, they are significantly lower in later years than the previous schedule. For age 94 and subsequent years, the minimum payments will be twenty percent of the value of the RRIF funds at the beginning of the year. This ensures that RRIF payments may continue for the life of the taxpayer.

Since 1986, individuals have been allowed even more flexibility in timing the receipt of RRSP and RRIF retirement funds. It is possible to cancel and withdraw a lump sum payment (i.e. commute) from a term of life annuity under an RRSP.

If you can't decide which is the single best choice for your RRSP funds, you can invest your funds in a combination of the options available.

No matter how you choose to time the payments of your retirement benefits from an RPP, RRSP, or DPSP, these payments will be included in your taxable income in the year received as pension income, and will therefore be subject to tax at that time. (There are certain exceptions to this general rule. For example, the repayment from a DPSP of an employee's contributions to the plan are not taxed when received, as these contributions are not deductible for tax purposes by the employee when originally made.)

There are some opportunities to delay the tax bite. Up until 1989, if you did not need all the retirement benefits you received in the year for current living expenses, you could delay the payment of tax on this excess by contributing it to your RRSP (although such RRSP contributions are not allowed after the year in which you turn seventy-one). Old Age Security and Canada or Quebec Pension Plan benefits plus RPP benefits and certain DPSP payments could be "rolled over" to an RRSP, over and above your annual RRSP contribution limit. These funds could then continue to accumulate tax-free. Such contributions could only be made to an RRSP for your own benefit, and could not be contributed to a spousal RRSP.

Beginning in 1990, the transfer of pension benefits to an RRSP is no longer available. However, for 1990 to 1994, up to $6,000 a year of periodic DPSP and RPP payments can be rolled into a spousal RRSP.

We should make one other comment on deferring receipt of all or part of your retirement income. The longer you can delay payment of funds from your RRSP, the longer they can accumulate tax-free and the more retirement benefits you will ultimately have. But it may not be a good idea to delay until the last possible moment converting your RRSP into an annuity or RRIF (assuming you will not want to receive all of it in a lump sum cash payment). The amount of benefits you will receive in the future from your RRIF or annuity will depend, among other things, on the interest rates prevailing at the time of your RRSP conversion. If they are temporarily low in the year in which you turn seventy-one, some of the benefit of delaying receipt of your retirement benefits will be offset by unnecessarily low annuity or RRIF payments. So watch the interest rates during your retirement years and if you believe they are higher in a year than you expect in the future, that may be the best time to convert your RRSP (or at least a portion of it) even though it accelerates, to some extent, receipt and taxation of your RRSP funds. And if you don't feel competent to make this kind of decision, consult investment advisors you trust for their views.

As you can see, there are several opportunities to delay taxation of retirement benefits and earn tax-free income in the meantime by deferring their receipt. But although your retirement benefits will be taxable when eventually received, the tax cost may not be high. When you retire, your primary source of income usually ceases, and is replaced with pension and investment income. This replacement income is generally lower than your preretirement employment or business earnings, and therefore you should be paying tax at a lower marginal rate. You have an additional personal tax credit when you turn sixty-five and may be able to claim the pension income tax credit to further reduce your tax bill. Many kinds of investment income are taxed in a favoured way as already discussed in Chapter 6. All this should help to keep the tax costs down in your retirement years.

You can receive a tax credit of up to $1,000 on certain types of pension income each year. (The types of pension income which are eligible are described in Chapter 6.) Where only one spouse will be entitled to pension benefits from an RPP or DPSP, both spouses may still be able to take advantage of the annual pension income tax credit by doing some advance planning. Annuity payments from an RRSP received by a person sixty-five or older are eligible for this $1,000 tax credit. Therefore, the spouse who will be receiving other eligible pension income should contribute, if possible, to a spousal RRSP on behalf of the spouse who will not otherwise receive eligible pension income. Enough contributions should be made so that there are sufficient funds to purchase an annuity when that spouse turns sixty-five which will pay at least $1,000 annually. Then both spouses can take advantage of the pension income tax credit.

Home Buyers Plan

The February 1992 federal budget announced the RRSP home buyers plan which allows you to use some of your RRSP funds to buy a home. Between February 25, 1992 and March 1, 1994, a Canadian resident individual can withdraw up to $20,000 from an RRSP to use as a downpayment on a home. A husband and wife who both have RRSPs can take a total of up to $40,000 ($20,000 each) to buy a home that they jointly own.

The money you take out is not taxable as long as you pay it back to your RRSP in annual installments over 15 years. It's just an interest free loan. The house can be new or used, detached, semi-detached, townhouse or a condominium. It doesn't have to be your first home, but you must have an agreement to buy or build the house in Canada, acquire the home within a certain time period, and occupy it within one year of getting it. The money must be repaid starting December 31, 1995 in at least 15 equal, annual installments. It's interest free and you don't have to repay the same RRSP plan that you took the money from. For example, if you took out $15,000, you should repay $1,000 a year.

If you don't repay at least the minimum annual amount, you'll pay tax on the difference. If you repaid more than you had to in any one year, the balance to be repaid will be lower and the annual repayments lower.

This is a complicated plan so you should check with your tax advisor, financial advisor or Revenue Canada.

PERSONAL RESIDENCE

For many people, retirement signals a major change in lifestyle, with a corresponding change in housing needs. If you have considerable equity in your home, a change in your personal residence may create a substantial pool of capital that will generate additional retirement income.

As a general rule, gains realized on the disposition of your principal residence will be exempt from tax and will not affect the cumulative amount of your lifetime capital gains exemption.

The principal residence exemption is based on a formula, under which the tax-free portion of the gain is calculated as the number of years (plus one) for which the property qualified and was designated as a principal residence over the number of years it was owned after 1971.

If the property did not qualify as a principal residence for two or more years during the period of ownership, part of the resulting gain may be subject to tax.

Before 1982, it was possible for a family to obtain an exemption from capital gains tax for more than one residential property by designating each property as the principal residence of a different member of the family. For example, if one spouse owned the family home, the other owned the summer vacation property.

Now, each family unit, consisting of a taxpayer, his or her spouse (unless legally separated and living apart throughout the year) and any unmarried children under eighteen years of age, is collectively entitled to designate only one property as a principal residence. Where a second property was also designated as a principal residence before 1982, only gains accruing after 1981 will be taxed when that property is eventually disposed of.

Although it is not necessary to designate which property is the principal residence (and for how many years) until one of the previously eligible properties is sold, it may be prudent to determine (and record for future reference) the values of each of the properties at the end of 1981, so that you will be in a position to make the appropriate decision when a disposal occurs sometime in the future.

To the extent that the principal residence exemption does not apply, any gain you realize on disposal of your residential or vacation property is generally subject to the normal capital gains rules. Three-quarters of the gain must be included in income, and taxed at regular rates unless you choose to exclude all or part of it from taxable income by applying any available portion of your capital gains exemption for this purpose. Accordingly, the decision as to which property to designate as your principal residence is still relevant and will likely depend on which property reflects the greater increase in market value — particularly after 1981.

Another important factor to consider is the phasing-out of the $100,000 lifetime capital gains exemption for gains realised on the disposition of real estate after February 1992. If you own a house and a second property, it would be a good idea for you to analyse your tax situation to determine whether you should take advantage of the $100,000 exemption before it is lost. The tax rules are quite complicated, so you should consider getting professional advice.

Reverse Mortgage

In some provinces there is another vehicle available to provide income in retirement years — a reverse mortgage. Generally, a substantial portion of a senior's net worth is tied up in his or her home. A reverse mortgage allows you to tap into this resource to provide a tax-free income in the form of a lump sum payment or a series of payments over time.

How it works is that the homeowner obtains a loan based on the current value of his or her home (usually up to thirty-five percent of the property value). The loan is secured by a first mortgage on the property. The proceeds of the loan can be used to finance anything such as home renovations or a vacation, or to subsidize your income so that you can afford to live at home longer. No payments are required to be made over the term of the loan. Interest accumulates and must be paid at the end of the term, usually by using the proceeds from the sale of the property. If the lifetime term is chosen, the loan will be repaid out of the proceeds when the senior dies. If the home appreciated in value, any remaining proceeds after the property is sold go to the person's beneficiaries. If, however, the loan value exceeds the mortgage value, the lender has no recourse against the borrower's other assets.

INVESTMENT ASSETS

As mentioned earlier, retirement planning should include the build-up of your investments during the ten to fifteen years before you retire. Investment assets can be used to provide income during your retirement. To build up your investment funds prior to retirement, you need to manage your present investment assets effectively (see Form 21, *Review of Present Investments*). Try to boost the return on your investments. That generally means sacrificing some safety in order to be more aggressive. But you can go from a long-term yield of six percent to eight or perhaps even ten percent without unreasonably endangering your capital.

Another way to increase your investment assets at retirement is to put aside each year more income for investment. Maximize your RRSP contributions and take advantage of any other tax-deferred programmes available to you.

As you approach retirement, you will probably have current income as your primary investment objective. Such an objective can be achieved through quality bonds, dividend-paying stock, and income-producing real estate. You should still keep up to forty percent of your investments at retirement in something with growth potential, such as growth stocks or real estate.

Another way of getting retirement income is to sell those investments that have increased in value. Consider, for example, two retirement funds of $250,000 each. If one fund consisted of bonds yielding ten percent and maturing in ten years, the annual income would be $25,000 — all fully taxed — and the $250,000 capital amount would not increase in value if the bonds were bought at face value and held to maturity; thus, no inflation protection. If the other fund consisted of growth stocks paying no dividends but appreciating at an average rate of twelve percent per year over the ten years, you could sell $25,000 of the stocks the first year. The fund would have grown to $252,500 at the end of the first year and to $254,200 at the end of the second year, after you sold another $25,000. Thus, even though you were deriving current income from it, your retirement fund would be appreciating and providing some hedge against inflation, and on top of that, your income from it would be taxed as capital gain (only three-quarters taxed, or tax-free to the extent of any unused capital gains exemption limit).

OLD AGE INCOME SECURITY

The Canadian and provincial governments provide some financial assistance to retired persons through the Old Age Security programme, the Canada or Quebec Pension Plans, the Guaranteed Income Supplement programme and provincial supplementary programmes in many provinces.

Old Age Security benefits are paid to all persons sixty-five years or older who satisfy certain Canadian residency requirements, regardless of their income level. These payments are taxable. In 1992, the maximum benefits available were $4,509.

Since 1989, higher-income individuals have been required to repay Old Age Security benefits to the extent of fifteen percent of their net income over $50,000, partially indexed over time ($53,215 in 1993). Repayments are calculated on the individual's income tax return. This measure was phased in over three years: for 1989, the repayment was limited to one-third of the amount calculated using the fifteen percent formula. The repayment increased to two-thirds of the formula amount in 1990 and was fully phased-in in 1991. Any amount repaid is not taxable.

Benefits paid by the Canada or Quebec Pension Plans are funded by both employer and employee contributions. Your benefits after retirement at age sixty-five are determined by the amount of contributions you and your employer made during your working life. In 1993, the maximum benefit available was $8,008 ($7,633 in 1992). These benefits are included in your taxable income.

Since 1987, retired persons can choose to start to receive Canada Pension Plan benefits at any time between age sixty and seventy. Their retirement benefits will be increased by six percent for each year receipt is delayed beyond sixty-five (to a maximum of 130 percent) and will be reduced by six percent for each year receipt is accelerated (to a minimum of seventy percent).

Also since 1987, spouses can choose to share their CPP (but not their QPP) retirement pension payments. Both spouses must be at least 60 years old and have applied for any CPP benefits to which they are entitled. Each spouse will receive a portion of the other's CPP retirement pension, if any. The shared portion is calculated based on the length of time the couple have lived together compared to the total CPP contributory period. The total CPP benefits received do not change, but this presents an opportunity to transfer some income to a lower-income spouse who will pay tax at a lower rate.

The Guaranteed Income Supplement is only paid to retired persons with limited income and is not subject to tax. The maximum benefit for a single person in 1993 was approximately $5,450. As well, the province you live in may pay a further supplement to those who qualify for the federal supplement.

Income security legislation may change from time to time and cost-of-living increases and indexing computations can make it difficult to calculate the exact amount of your government-provided retirement benefits. You should contact the local Health and Welfare Canada office and ask for specific information on benefit payments, eligibility and how to apply as you near retirement.

WILL YOUR RETIREMENT INCOME MATCH YOUR EXPENDITURES?

You began by setting the date at which you might like to retire. Then you estimated how much an enjoyable retirement and its less enjoyable taxes might cost you. But none of this has yet been measured against the financial resources you expect to have at retirement.

Now the moment has come to probe the feasibility of your various retirement objectives. Will the annual income from your retirement plans and present investments cover your anticipated expenditures? If not, will your retirement plans, your present investments, and the investments you will make before retirement give you an annual income that will cover your retirement expenditures? If not, there are some more questions to ask yourself. Could you step up your investment schedule by earning more or spending less? Were you too extravagant when you forecast your retirement expenditures? Should you retire later than you intended?

FORM 27 — RETIREMENT INCOME

On this form, you will relate your retirement needs to your retirement sources. We have provided an example of Form 27 in Figure 12-1. You might want to review it before you complete your own.

- On line 1, enter the annual amount you listed on line 5 of Form 26.

- On lines 2(a), 2(b), 2(c) and 2(d), enter the annual amounts you are likely to receive after retirement from sources that will distribute payments in forms other than a lump sum. You may have to get the required information from your company's personnel office, your local Health and Welfare Canada office, and other sources from which retirement funds will come. Do not include projected RRSP income in this section of Form 27. You will consider this source of retirement income further down on the form.

- Total the estimated annual income from all your retirement plans on line 3.

- Subtract the total annual income from your retirement plans (line 3) from your estimated annual retirement needs (line 1) and enter the result on line 4 of the worksheet. If the estimated income from your retirement plan exceeds your requirements, you could consider retiring earlier or look forward to a more comfortable retirement period. If you still need additional sources of retirement income, go on to the next step.

- Convert the annual income still needed on line 4 into a capital amount that will yield the annual income required. Perform these steps:

  - On line 5(a), enter the estimated pre-tax rate of return on your investment capital when you retire.

  - On line 5(b), enter the estimated capital required at retirement by dividing the amount on line 4 by the rate on line 5(a).

- The next step on Form 27 is probably more complicated because it involves making judgements about your present investment assets, RRSP funds, and any lump sum retirement plans. It also involves forecasting what the value of these assets might be at retirement.

  - Enter on line 6(a) the present value of your investment assets and RRSP funds. Most of this data will come from your net worth statement (Form 4).

  - Enter on line 6(b) the estimated rate of return you think you will get on your investment assets (after-tax) and RRSP funds (pre-tax) between now and your retirement. Refer to Form 22, Your Investment Strategy, for your estimates.

  - Enter on line 6(c) the number of years from now to retirement. Next, enter the approximate factor from Table 1 in Appendix I on line 6(d).

FIGURE 12-1

File under RETIREMENT PLANNING　　　　　　　　Date: _November 1_

FORM 27　RETIREMENT INCOME

Projected Retirement Age: _62_　　　　　　　Number of Years to Retirement: _7_

1.　Estimated Annual Retirement Needs　　　　　　　　　_$90,200_

2.　Estimated Annual Income from Retirement Plans
　　(other than lump-sum distributions)

　　a.　Old Age Security and Canada or
　　　　Quebec Pension Plan　　　　　　　_$11,000_

　　b.　Company Retirement Plan　　　　　_$37,200_

　　c.　Deferred Compensation　　　　　　——

　　d.　Other Retirement Plans　　　　　　——

3.　TOTAL Annual Income from Retirement Plans　　　　_$48,200_

4.　Annual Income Gap　　　　　　　　　　　　　　_$42,000_

5.　Retirement Capital Required to Fill Gap

　　a.　Estimated Pre-Tax Rate of Return　　　　　　_8%_

　　b.　Retirement Capital Required　　　　　　　　_$525,000_

6.　Sources of Retirement Capital

		INVESTMENT ASSETS	LUMP SUMS FROM RETIREMENT PLANS	RRSPs	TOTAL
a.	Value of Present Investment Assets and Retirement Accounts	_$165,000_		_$54,700_	_$219,700_
b.	Estimated Rate of Return from Now until Retirement	_10%_		_12%_	
c.	Years until Retirement	_7_		_7_	
d.	Compound Factor from Table 1 (in Appendix I)	_1.95_		_2.21_	
e.	Estimated Value of Your Investment Assets and Retirement Accounts at Retirement	_$321,800_	_0_	_$120,900_	_$442,700_

FIGURE 12-1 Cont'd

	INVESTMENT ASSETS	RRSPs	OTHER	TOTAL
7. Additional Capital from Annual Investments You Are Planning to Make				
a. Annual Amount to Be Invested Between Now and Retirement	$4,000	$3,500		$7,500
b. Estimated Rate of Return on Annual Investment	10%	12%		
c. Years until Retirement	7	7		
d. Compound Factor from Table 2 (in Appendix I)	9.49	10.09		
e. Estimated Value of Additional Capital from Your Annual Investments	$38,000	$35,300		$73,300
8. TOTAL Estimated Retirement Capital				$516,000
9. Additional Capital Needed, if Any, to Provide Retirement Income				$9,000
10. Additional Annual Investment Needed to Provide Capital on Line 9				
a. Estimated Rate of Return From Now until Retirement			10%	
b. Years until Retirement			7	
c. Compound Factor from Table 2 (in Appendix I)			9.49	
d. Annual Amount Required				$950

- On line 6(e), estimate the value of your investment assets and retirement capital at retirement by multiplying the amount on line 6(a) by the factor on line 6(d). You are getting really good at these calculations! Also enter on 6(e), under the "Lump Sum" column, the amount to be paid in a lump sum, at retirement, from retirement plans.

- Finally, add the totals across on line 6(e) to get the total estimated value of your capital at retirement.

- Compute the additional capital you will obtain by making annual additions to your investment funds and annual contributions to your RRSPs.

  - Enter on line 7(a) the annual amount to be invested between now and retirement.

- On line 7(b), enter the estimated rate of return on your annual investments.

- On line 7(c), enter the number of years from now until retirement.

- On line 7(d), enter the appropriate factor from Table 2 in Appendix I.

- On line 7(e), estimate the value of additional capital by multiplying the amount on line 7(a) by the factor on line 7(d).

- Finally, add the totals across on line 7(e) to get the total estimated value of your additional capital at retirement.

- On line 8, enter your total estimated retirement capital from lines 6(e) and 7(e).

- On line 9, enter the amount that results from subtracting the amount on line 8 from the amount on line 5(b). If the amount is negative — because your estimated retirement capital exceeds your requirements — consider early retirement or look forward to a much more comfortable retirement lifestyle, or plan a really big retirement party. If you need additional capital to meet your needs, go to the next and final step.

- If the result on line 9 of the worksheet suggests you will need additional investment capital at retirement, then you will need to start putting even more funds aside each year for investment. How much you need to set aside can be computed on the worksheet.

  - On line 10(a), enter the estimated rate of return on your investments from now until retirement.

  - On line 10(b), enter the number of years between now and retirement.

  - On line 10(c), enter the compound factor from Table 2 in Appendix I.

  - On line 10(d), compute the annual amount of additional funds required by dividing the amount of capital required on line 9 by the factor on line 10(c).

In our example in Figure 12-1, the individual would have to invest about $950 for seven years at ten percent to have the additional capital needed at retirement. Some clients with whom we have worked have a much greater investment requirement and say, "Are you kidding me?" If this is your case, you will need to reevaluate the variables in your plan and consider the choices you have.

YOUR RETIREMENT PLANNING CHOICES

What choices do you have between now and retirement that will help you meet your estimated retirement needs? Here are several you should consider:

- You can manage your investments and retirement funds more effectively to get a greater annual return.

- You can set aside more funds for annual investment by decreasing your current expenditures.

- You can plan to sell your personal residence at or before retirement and move into something less expensive to provide additional investment capital.

- You can plan to use some of your investment capital during retirement to handle your needs. Maybe the easiest estate planning is to spend your last dime as you take your last breath! Systematic use of investment capital during retirement may, in fact, be a very good choice for some people. If you have the option available, consider a reverse mortgage to increase your cash flow during retirement.

If, after considering the above choices, you still do not think it will be feasible to retire when you want to and still maintain a desired standard of living, you may have to hang in there and continue to work for your living.

THINKING OF EARLY RETIREMENT?

Many people think about retiring at an early age, such as fifty or fifty-five. It's an appealing idea, but one that should be considered carefully if you want to avoid frustration, anger and financial problems. The advice we would give to anyone who is not independently wealthy is the following:

- Do not retire early unless you are free of major financial obligations, such as putting your children through university or college or paying off your mortgage.

- Do not retire early unless you have a vested pension — meaning one that belongs to you — as well as substantial savings or investments.

- Be wary if your retirement benefits are heavily dependent on the stock market.

- Try to negotiate any extra benefits your employer may be willing to give you because you take early retirement.

- Make sure the terms of your retirement plan will not prevent you from working elsewhere if you so desire.

- Have a plan to use your time effectively.

A RETIREMENT PLANNING CHECKLIST

As you approach your retirement date, you should do the following:

- Call your local Health and Welfare Canada office to find out what you must do to apply for benefits.

- Make an appointment with the official in your company who is responsible for your pension and profit-sharing benefits. Find out what payment plans are available to you, and consider which of the payment options would be most beneficial to you.

- Discuss the tax consequences of your retirement payment options with your tax advisor.

- Review your life insurance coverage. In retirement you may need less than your present coverage. If you have and want to keep a company-paid or company-sponsored group policy, check the options available to you.

- Review your health care coverage. Find out what your provincial medical insurance plan provides. If you need supplemental coverage, shop around. If you have a company plan, find out whether you can convert it to an individual plan.

- Review your will and your estate plan. You may wish to meet with your lawyer and a chartered accountant to evaluate estate-planning ideas.

- Find out about senior citizens' programmes and discounts in the area you choose for your retirement.

13

RISK MANAGEMENT AND THE ROLE OF INSURANCE

Personal financial planning is a process which includes steps to help you minimize your income taxes and select the right tax shelter or mutual fund. But if you fail to properly evaluate and insure risks that create uncertainty or financial loss, you have not completed the financial planning process. Protecting your financial well-being is as important as the planning and implementation process you use to accumulate your wealth.

In this chapter, we discuss the concept of risk management and how the orderly approach to identifying and analysing the risks enables you to make more informed and financially sound decisions for meeting your insurance needs, whether for life, property-casualty, or health insurance.

RISK MANAGEMENT

Risk management includes all the efforts necessary to conserve assets by controlling the uncertainty of financial loss. This concept is readily applied to all forms of insurance whether it is homeowners, auto, personal and professional liability, life, disability, or medical insurance. In fact, the risk management approach can be applied in all personal and business circumstances where there is uncertainty about the risk of financial loss from the partial or complete decline in value in an unexpected or unpredictable manner. Risk of financial loss is the basis for the need for risk management evaluation and the purchase of the necessary insurance. Simply stated, insurance reduces or eliminates the uncertainty by transferring it to a large group of insured people who have uncertainties of loss, just as you do.

Deciding how much insurance you need is the end product of a decision-making process that includes objective analysis, characterization of possible losses and determination of the financial impact of financial loss based on a risk analysis.

Risk analysis is very important and involves the following three factors:

- Identification of risks (assets and activities risk analysis)

- Measurement and evaluation of potential losses

- Evaluation and implementation of alternative techniques for handling the various risks

Let's consider each of these elements more closely.

Identification. The risk of financial loss must be identified before any other steps in risk management can be taken. The following three questions should be asked:

- What could happen to your assets?

- What accidents could impair your assets or your earning power?

- What activities could create liabilities to others due to personal injury or damage to property?

The answers to these questions can provide broad guidelines on vulnerability to financial losses for both assets and activities.

Measurement and evaluation. After identifying the exposures to financial loss, it is crucial to evaluate the nature of possible losses and the degree of control you may exert over their occurrence. This is also known as risk-treatment planning. Methods for dealing with risk management fall within one of the following basic techniques:

- *Avoiding risk*. Simply put, risk avoidance minimizes the possibility of risks by removing their causes. For example, if one does not skydive, the possibility of an accident from that cause has been completely eliminated.

- *Risk reduction*. Beyond taking measures to prevent a calamity from happening, this technique involves recognizing the potential for damage and keeping it to a minimum. The installation of a smoke-and-fire alarm system in your home is a risk-reduction technique. If a fire breaks out, there should be less property damage or personal injury because you have this early warning system.

- *Risk retention*. Once a risk is properly evaluated and every effort is made to diminish it, then the question becomes one of how much risk you can afford to retain or assume yourself — also known as self-insurance. As we will see, the cost of sharing or transferring that risk (insurance) may be too expensive, or coverage may not even be available for a given calamity. Increasing or decreasing insurance deductibles is one form of risk retention. In other words, once you have evaluated an insurable risk and its possible economic consequences, you can then decide how much risk of loss you want to retain before acquiring insurance coverage.

- *Risk transference*. This is the best understood technique of personal risk management. Simply stated, you remove the risk of loss from yourself and transfer it to a third party, namely an insurance company. In exchange for relieving you of this risk of loss, the insurance company receives a premium from you to cover the costs of assuming that risk.

Evaluation and Implementation of Alternative Techniques. Ideally, you should retain as much risk as you yourself can handle financially and then acquire insurance to cover the risks of loss that are beyond your means. At this point, you should ask yourself:

- What risks am I willing to accept?

- What measures for controlling risks are available?

- Can the risk be eliminated or avoided?

You now decide how to deal with the risk and uncertainties of loss either by insuring or not insuring. The key is that you are making your insurance decision based on the results of the information you have gathered and evaluated. Your insurance will be systematic and organized, not merely a haphazard, inefficient patchwork of coverages. The result is that your personal financial management plan is comprehensive and has a much greater assurance of being completed as planned rather than being vulnerable to risks and uncertainties.

The following discussion is divided into these categories:

- Life insurance

- Property and liability

- Health insurance

- Selecting the insurance company and agent

LIFE INSURANCE

Most of our financial planning is based on the assumption that we will continue to live for a long time and thus can earn an income for as long as we choose. There is a possibility, though, that we won't live to a ripe old age and good planning must take this risk into account. If premature death would disrupt or dry up the income stream needed to maintain our dependants, then life insurance should be used to prevent such financial disruption.

In essence, all life insurance policies say the same thing: In return for premiums duly received, the insurance company will pay the *face amount* (the promised benefit) of the policy to the beneficiary upon receiving proof of the insured person's death. The death benefits are paid out very quickly and are generally not taxable to the beneficiary.

In order to assess whether your present life insurance coverage is adequate, inadequate, or excessive, you have to envisage the needs and resources of your dependants in the event of your or your spouse's unexpected death. Which dependants, if any, will require financial support? When will they need it, how much will they need, and for how long? What income will be available from other sources? How much income will the proceeds of the life insurance have to provide? What debts should be discharged by the insurance proceeds?

DO YOU REALLY NEED LIFE INSURANCE?

The major purpose of insuring your life is to provide income for your dependants after your death. Therefore, the first question to ask yourself is, "Do I have any dependants for whom I should provide after my death?"

There may be none, and therefore little or no need for life insurance, if you are single, or married but without children or mortgage and both of you are working. Similarly you may not need the safety net of life insurance once your children are independent and you have ample net worth. However, if your spouse, children, or parents depend on your earnings, you may have to insure your life quite heavily.

As your financial responsibilities and circumstances change, so will your need for life insurance.

Surprisingly, life insurance can be very useful for wealthy people because of the attractive Canadian tax treatment of life insurance policies. For example, life insurance can be used to provide liquidity in a person's estate to cover capital gains taxes arising on death. Another use of life insurance is to provide the funding for a shareholder "buy-sell" agreement.

FORM 28 — YOUR PRESENT LIFE INSURANCE COVERAGE

The obvious way to begin your insurance review is by listing the significant aspects of any insurance you presently carry on your life and the life of your spouse. You will be able to obtain the necessary information from the actual policy or policies or from your insurance agent.

Under *Type of Policy*, identify each policy as either whole life, individual term, group term, endowment, or whatever other description is appropriate. Under *Cash Surrender Value* and *Loan on Policy*, the total amounts should agree with those on your net worth statement (Form 4). Under *Owner of Policy*, indicate who owns the policy. Usually, the insured is the owner. Under *Beneficiary*, identify the person who is entitled to receive the face amount of the policy on your death.

HOW MUCH INSURANCE DO YOU NEED?

Before you can tell how much life insurance you should carry, you have to forecast the financial needs of your dependants and have a good idea of the amount and liquidity of your assets.

Your dependants' financial needs will normally fall into the following categories:

- Cash to pay immediate obligations, including potential taxes at the time of your death (see Chapter 14 for a discussion of these taxes)

- Money to pay the mortgage and other debts

- Money for education

- Cash to cover living expenses

It may be a good idea for the survivors to set up four separate funds in separate accounts to cover these four different needs.

Immediate Cash Requirements

Many of the expenses that come into existence at death are expenses that simply did not exist before. Cash is required for funeral expenses, for current bills (including medical bills and administrative expenses), for an emergency fund, and possibly for taxes. Funeral costs may vary depending on whether you want your ashes spread at sea or wish to be buried with your ship and other accessories for the life hereafter, as the Vikings were. The average cost of death is about $6,000, which includes the funeral and burial in a cemetery.

An emergency fund is required to cover living expenses during the period when the estate is being settled and the nature and amount of assets to be received by the survivors may be uncertain. Since most of us do not plan to die soon, there may not be enough liquid assets available to your survivors to take care of the cash requirements in the first months following your death, and life insurance could fill this gap.

Mortgages

In this age of buying expensive homes and financing the purchase with a large mortgage, many breadwinners die leaving their families indebted to a lending institution. From a purely financial perspective, it may not make much difference whether the mortgage is paid off immediately or is covered by a "living expenses fund" in the insurance; but for the peace of mind of the survivors, it may be important to have a mortgage insurance fund for clearing your home of debt.

Education Costs

Education, like a mortgage, can be paid from the living expenses fund; but your children may find it reassuring to have a specific fund set aside for educational purposes. The amount of the fund will depend on several factors: location of university or community college; length of education; the children's ability to generate money for their education; availability of scholarships; and your views on providing support for the children after you die.

Living Expenses

The calculation of living expenses raises the fundamental question of how well the family should be provided for. Most of us would like our dependants to maintain the standard of living to which they are accustomed. Maintaining this same standard of living may not, however, require the same level of expenditure. With one member of the family gone, some expenses may either be reduced or eliminated, since this person will no longer need any clothes, transportation, or food. Some life insurance premiums will also be eliminated. Income taxes will be lower, and mortgage payments will be eliminated if insurance proceeds have been used to pay off the balance. However, other costs could go up. For example, the death of a spouse who was good at fixing things around the house could require the survivor to hire people to do the work.

If the mortgage is paid off or is paid from a separate mortgage fund, the surviving spouse and children will need less gross income for living expenses (as a general rule of thumb, about sixty percent of the gross income that the family needed before the spouse's death). If the mortgage payments are still a part of the general living costs, then the family will need more gross income — perhaps seventy-five percent of the complete family's former gross income, as a rule of thumb. To more accurately estimate the expected reduction in living expenses after one spouse dies, Forms 7 and 8 can be redone to reflect anticipated changes in basic and discretionary expenditures, and Form 11 can be filled out to estimate the remaining family's tax burden.

Some families may be able to meet their expenses with the income from accumulated assets, government assistance (Canada or Quebec Pension Plan, Old Age Security), and the surviving spouse's income. A housewife who survives her husband may need to find a job outside the home after her husband's death. Some income may also be generated by teenage children. Consider also the reverse situation where the homemaker dies leaving small children. The surviving spouse may need substantial funds to hire a housekeeper or to make other child-care arrangements.

LIFE INSURANCE POLICIES

There are two basic types of life insurance policies: pure insurance, called *term insurance*, and "permanent" life insurance which has a savings or investment component. These two basic types can be further subdivided according to some of their special features.

Term Insurance

Term life insurance is like the automobile, fire and health insurance you have in that it protects you for a limited specified time. If, as you hope, you are still living at the end of the specified time, your protection ceases, just as a fire insurance policy expires, and there is no residual value in that policy. Term policies are ideal for providing a large amount of protection for a limited time at the lowest premium outlay.

By paying an additional premium, term insurance may be renewable or convertible or both. If the policy is renewed or another term policy is issued to replace it, a higher premium is charged because the policy holder is now older and has a greater chance of dying than in the previous period.

Renewable term policies include an option permitting you to renew the contract for a number of specified periods — five, ten, fifteen, or twenty years, or to a certain age, such as sixty, sixty-five, or seventy — without further medical examination. Term policies may allow you to convert the full amount of insurance to a *whole life or endowment policy* without medical reexamination at any time while your insurance is still in force.

Term policies have several advantages. Term offers the lowest cost for pure protection. The needs of a family tend to change over the years, so term insurance can be very useful for providing the funds for temporary needs, such as university education or mortgage payments. With the flexibility of its renewable policies and its low premiums, term insurance has a definite place in all well-planned life insurance programmes.

There are three basic kinds of term policies: *annual renewable term, decreasing term*, and *level term*.

Annual Renewable Term

With an annual renewable term policy, the face amount of your insurance remains the same, and the premium increases every year.

Decreasing Term

Your premium remains the same with a decreasing term policy, but the face amount of the insurance decreases.

Level Term

With a level term policy, the face amount of the policy remains the same for a chosen period — five, ten, fifteen, twenty, twenty-five, or thirty years, or until you reach the age of sixty-five. The premium remains level throughout the period, and it approximates the average of the annual renewable term rates for the specified number of years. If you chose a twenty-year level term policy, for example, the insurance company would essentially add up the renewable term rates for twenty years and divide the total by twenty, and you would pay the same annual rate for each of the twenty years.

Permanent Life Insurance (Whole Life)

With so-called "whole life" permanent insurance, you normally buy a level face amount of insurance — say, $100,000 — which remains in effect for your entire life. Part of the premium you pay covers the insurance risk and the other portion represents a "savings" or investment element of the policy. In reality, you are buying a form of decreasing term insurance, for as your investment account increases, your insurance protection goes down, but the combined value of your savings and your insurance protection remains the same.

You can obtain the cash from your investment account in two ways. You may be able to stop paying premiums after a period of time, take the cash surrender value (i.e. the current realizable value of the investment account) and terminate the policy. Alternatively, you can borrow from the cash surrender value. Then your insurance coverage will be reduced by the amount you borrowed until the loan is repaid. You can repay your policy loan at any time, but you are not required to do so.

When you hold a life insurance policy that has a cash surrender value, you may be able to do any of the following things with your cash surrender value:

- Convert the contract to paid-up life insurance for a lesser amount than the original face amount.

- Have the original face amount continued as term insurance for a specified period. The length of the period will depend on the amount of the cash surrender value and on the face amount of the original policy.

- Arrange for a minimum deposit plan that will allow you to take part of your annual dividend in the form of additional term insurance, instead of taking it all as cash. The additional term insurance is usually sold at a lower price than regular term insurance.

Other Types of Life Insurance Policies

Two other insurance products have been introduced in recent years and deserve some mention. One is universal life insurance, which is similar to conventional whole life insurance with one important exception. The investment portion of a universal life insurance policy earns income at a variable rate, which fluctuates with prevailing interest rates. There may be a minimum guaranteed rate of return, but otherwise your investment income will not be fixed, as is the case with most conventional whole life policies. Because you are bearing more of the investment risk with a universal life insurance policy, these policies usually provide cheaper insurance coverage than the other whole life policies.

Another relatively new product is variable whole life insurance. Here cash values are invested in either a money market fund or a common stock fund, and both the return on the cash value and the amount of the death benefit vary with investment performance.

Tax Considerations for Life Insurance Policies

Generally, there is no income tax and no capital gains taxation on life insurance proceeds received when an insured person dies. We have said "generally" because there are two types of life insurance policies — *exempt* and *non-exempt* policies. There is no tax payable on insurance proceeds received when a person insured under an exempt policy dies and there is no income tax payable on the "investment" element of an exempt policy during the life of the insured. Taxation of non-exempt policies is not so generous, however.

Insurance policies where there is a substantial degree of savings in addition to insurance protection may be non-exempt policies (unless they were issued before December 1982). Investment income earned on such policies is accrued for tax purposes and an individual must pay tax on this accrued income at least every three years. For policies acquired after 1989, annual accrual will be required. When the person insured under a non-exempt policy dies, any accrued investment income which has not yet been taxed must be brought into income. Only the pure insurance element of the policy will be tax-free.

Tax may also be payable if an insurance policy (exempt or non-exempt) is disposed of during your lifetime. A disposition would include such things as surrender of a policy, conversion of a policy to an annuity or a transfer of ownership. If a policy is disposed of, the policy owner must include in income the amount by which the proceeds of disposition exceed the adjusted cost basis of the policy. Proceeds of disposition will generally be the cash surrender value of the policy. The adjusted cost basis is generally the total of premiums paid less dividends and loans received by the owner and the cumulative insurance cost of the policy prior to surrender. Premiums paid after May 1, 1985 must exclude the insurance portion of the premium and will effectively represent only the portion of the premium designated for savings.

Dividends and loans also have tax consequences, in that they reduce the adjusted cost basis of your policy. However, tax will not be payable at the time the dividend or loan is received unless the adjusted cost basis of the policy becomes negative as a result.

This is a very brief summary of the more common tax issues involving insurance policies. The taxation of life insurance policies is extremely complex. You should usually ask for professional tax advice and consult with your life insurance agent before making any major change in your insurance coverage.

SHOULD YOU DISCONTINUE OR REPLACE OLD POLICIES?

Should you discontinue old policies? The answer depends on a number of factors, including your age, health, and insurability, and the nature of the particular policies that are currently in force. Your best approach is to review your life insurance coverage with an experienced life insurance agent. The agent will have the necessary expertise to be able to determine whether your existing coverage meets your needs.

PROPERTY AND LIABILITY INSURANCE

Even though you may have thoroughly planned all other aspects of your personal financial plan, you can still encounter ruinous setbacks if you suffer a catastrophic loss for which you are inadequately insured. Today, it is more important than ever to protect yourself against financial liability caused by your acts or those of your family.

Two Broad Property Coverage Types

There are two broad types of property coverage — *named-peril* and *all risks*. Peril coverage protects you against loss stemming from a named and specific calamity. Common named perils include fire, theft and collision.

The second type of property coverage is all risks. This insurance typically covers property against loss from *any* source of "peril." Be forewarned: Not all policies cover all perils; there are usually exclusions from coverage. It is important to review your current policies to identify the specific exclusions and decide whether you want to assume the risk of loss from the excluded events. When considering policies from different companies, you should compare the specific perils excluded from each policy and determine how those exclusions bear on your specific situation. Since coverage is generally broader under an all risks policy, the cost is generally more expensive.

Homeowner's Insurance

A homeowner's policy is actually a collection of coverages combined into one policy. This covers the dwelling and its contents, liability and medical payments for personal injury.

Perhaps one of the most important concepts of homeowners insurance is that of replacement cost riders. Without these you may recover only up to your original cost — and sometimes just the depreciated value. Thus, a replacement cost rider can be quite valuable since, with adequate coverage, you can recover the full replacement cost of an entire lost structure — or part of it — without any reduction for depreciation. You should be sure that your coverage will at least equal the replacement cost as values increase, and this can be achieved with an automatic escalator.

If you don't have adequate replacement cost coverage, you may not collect the full amount of the loss even if it is less than the policy's face amount. Recovery for a loss under an eighty percent co-insurance clause — the most common one used — is determined using this formula:

$$\frac{\text{Face amount of the insurance policy}}{80\% \times \text{full replacement cost}} \times \frac{\text{Cost of}}{\text{Replacement or repair}}$$

An example can best illustrate how a co-insurance clause works.

> *Example*: You bought a house in 1974 for $100,000, exclusive of the land. Over the years, you increased the coverage on the house from $100,000 to $160,000. However, the cost to replace the house in 1990 is $300,000. A kitchen fire resulted in a $30,000 repair cost and the formula determines how much you recover under your policy:
>
> $$\frac{\$160,000}{80\% \times \$300,000} \times \$30,000 = \$20,000$$

The $10,000 difference would come out of your pocket simply because you had failed to keep up with the required replacement-cost provision.

Had you suffered a total loss, the formula indicates that you would recover $200,000:

$$\frac{\$160,000}{80\% \times \$300,000} \times \$300,000 = \$200,000$$

but this is limited, of course, by the $160,000 face amount of your policy. By maintaining at least $240,000 coverage (80% of full replacement value), recovery would be the full $240,000 face value.

How do you maintain adequate coverage? First, by having your insurance agent recommend coverage based on construction costs and real estate values for your area. Then, you can add to your policy an inflation rider that automatically increases your coverage. This additional "endorsement," however, does not automatically guarantee adequate coverage, since it is based on a broad-based inflation factor and does not necessarily reflect the replacement-cost increases for your geographic area.

Furthermore, homeowners' policies contain built-in ceilings on the amount of personal property that can be covered under the basic policy. For example, you may have a rare stamp collection worth $50,000. If nothing is done to cover that item specifically, it will be insured with all other personal property, with a limit of perhaps $500. Therefore, it is very important to add specific floaters to the general policy that will cover more valuable items like jewellery, stamps, cameras, furs and artwork.

Since, under any policy, part of the problem in collecting after a loss is proving the existence of an item, it is highly advisable to maintain a current pictorial inventory of insured assets. More and more people, for example, are photographing or videotaping their home and its contents and writing detailed descriptions of jewellery, clothes, antiques, collections, artwork, furniture, silver, and so on. Photographs, accompanied by complete descriptions, are also a good form of identification. Of course, it goes without saying that this pictorial evidence should be kept in a safe location outside the home, preferably in a vault.

Your homeowner's insurance policy should also include adequate liability insurance to cover any losses or damage caused by your negligence. As an example, any homeowner with a pool should have insurance to protect against any injuries a visitor might suffer while using the pool. Coverage usually includes the amount stated in the policy as well as costs of defence. It is very important that you understand and comply with all the conditions in the policy. Liability coverage is relatively inexpensive and is one of the best bargains in the insurance industry. Most homeowners can have the comfort of carrying $1,000,000 or more in liability coverage at a very reasonable price.

Automobile Insurance

Generally speaking, automobile insurance covers liabilities stemming from accidents, medical payments, damage or destruction to vehicles, theft of vehicles, etc. Ancillary costs, such as renting a car if yours is stolen, towing charges, and glass coverage may also be covered. Depending on provincial law and your own needs, there are specified limits in the policy for each category. For instance, there may be a $350,000 liability limit or a $5,000 medical-payment ceiling for any person injured in an accident. These restrictions on liability are very important. Here, as with the homeowner's policy, it is very important to review the coverage exclusions specifically mentioned in the policy.

For your coverage to be more cost-effective, you should get the answers to certain questions to determine the cost of your automobile and homeowner's coverage. Since risk retention is one technique of risk management, by selecting a deductible on a policy, you are deciding how much of the risk you are willing to assume. The higher the deductible, the higher the risk retention and the lower the premiums.

It is possible to get better overall coverage on a policy for the same dollars if you are willing to pay a higher deductible. Then, too, the need for collision coverage decreases as your car gets older. For example, after four years, the value of a vehicle is so much less than you originally paid that collision insurance coverage may not be cost-effective.

In certain provinces, auto insurance is now provided under government-operated plans.

Excess Liability or "Umbrella" Coverage

It is frequently said that Canada is becoming a more litigious society, and the astonishing size of some awards in recent liability trials should make you think twice about your liability coverage.

Suppose you had done a painstaking job of financial planning for retirement, which is a month away. Unfortunately, however, you have an automobile accident and injure someone. You settle out of court for $500,000. The automobile insurance company pays its share up to the $350,000 liability limits of your policy. Where does the remaining $150,000 come from? You guessed right. It comes out of those assets you so diligently saved for a comfortable retirement.

This would be a financial disaster for most people. If you had an excess liability policy in place, you could have averted this financial calamity. Excess liability policies are sometimes referred to as "umbrella" policies. They are designed to provide you with coverage over and above the liability limits of your homeowner's and automobile policies.

The cost of these umbrella policies is minuscule compared with what you'd have to pay in a lawsuit. One of these policies belongs in everyone's insurance portfolio.

HEALTH INSURANCE

Under the broad category of health insurance there are two distinct and critical areas of coverage needs: disability income and medical expenses.

Without comprehensive coverage in each area, the best planning can be devastated due to financial losses from sickness or accidents.

Disability Income Insurance

Perhaps no other area of personal risk management is so often neglected. Part of this neglect — and sometimes confusion — may arise from uncertainty over the range of eligibility and adequacy of coverage, which varies greatly from insurer to insurer.

Scrupulous review of existing disability policies is in order before you can reach a conclusion on the proper choice of policy.

The following five definitions should help you decide on the coverage you need:

1. **Elimination period.** This is the period from the onset of the disability until the benefits begin under the policy. The shorter the elimination period, the more costly the premiums. It might be possible under a policy to extend the elimination period and increase the monthly disability benefits while keeping the cost of the policy (that is, the premiums) even. The question involving the elimination period is: How long can you live on your savings before the benefits start?

2. **Period of benefits.** This is the length of time over which the benefits may be payable. It can be expressed in terms of months, years, a specified age or a lifetime. The period of the benefit selected generally depends on, among other things, cost of premiums, other assets, and other income. The longer the period, the more benefits to be received and the higher the premium.

3. **Reason for disability.** Some policies cover disability only from accidents as opposed to disability from a prolonged illness. Coverage for accidents alone is somewhat limited, and coverage for both types of disability should be sought.

4. **Disability defined.** Perhaps nowhere else is there more confusion and potential for problems than in the definition of disability. The definition under which each insurance company will pay benefits differs greatly from policy to policy. If you are totally disabled, any company will pay benefits.

5. **Definition of occupation.** Will you be paid benefits if you are unable to carry on your normal occupation or only if you cannot carry on any occupation? This distinction could be critical in many circumstances.

The greatest differences come about in those circumstances when you are partially and permanently disabled, or disabled with symptoms that will ultimately go away. Some policies may say that an injured person able to work at "any occupation" is not disabled and thus no benefits should be payable. At the other end of the spectrum, some companies say that if you cannot work at "*your own* occupation," you are considered disabled.

For example, if a surgeon hurts his hands and cannot operate but can teach in a medical school, is he disabled? Under a strict interpretation of the word "disabled," the insurance company could answer no, since he can work at "any occupation." Under more liberal policies, the answer would be yes, since his specialty was surgery, which he can no longer perform. Read the definitions of "disability" and "occupation" very carefully when comparing policies from different carriers.

Be aware, too, that although your employer provides a long-term disability policy as part of your benefits programme, that does not necessarily mean that you are adequately covered. Study the coverage for elimination periods, benefit periods, causes of disability, and the definitions of disability and partial disability. You may need to buy additional disability income coverage from an outside insurance company.

Also consider the tax treatment of payments from your disability plan. Where you have paid premiums out of your own after-tax income, any benefits will be received tax-free. But if your employer has paid all or a portion of the disability insurance premiums, any benefits you receive will be taxed, so that only a portion of these benefits will be available to cover your living expenses.

Other forms of disability insurance can address other financial needs that may arise, such as the buy-out of a private business corporation or partnership triggered by a disability, or to finance a deferred tax liability.

Medical Expense Coverage
Many Canadians do not carry additional coverage for medical expenses because most basic medical procedures are provided under the various provincial health care plans.

Additional private coverage can be purchased to supplement this basic level of coverage. Typically, this coverage could include semi-private or private rooms for hospital stays, extended services such as eyeglasses and prescription drugs, and dental plans. Many employers provide additional private medical insurance on a group basis. Employees do not pay tax on the value of the extra coverage. If you are not covered at work, consider buying additional coverage on your own, although the cost will be considerably higher for an individual subscriber, compared to that for members of a group plan.

Health care costs outside Canada can be very expensive and may not be fully covered by provincial health care plans. If you have private health insurance through your employer, you may be adequately covered. If not, you can purchase additional protection for health care costs while you are travelling outside Canada at very reasonable rates. With some "gold" credit cards, out-of-country health care coverage for limited periods of time is automatically provided at no additional cost.

SELECTING THE INSURANCE COMPANY

There are generally two types of insurance companies: those that generate a profit and those that are "not for profit." Carriers owned by shareholder/investors are for-profit companies. They pay a portion of their profits to the shareholders as dividends. Because the policyholders do not share in the company's earnings, premiums on policies are generally level.

There are many life insurance companies in Canada. Carriers owned by the policyholders themselves are mutual insurance companies. The earnings of a mutual are returned to the policyholders. So it is not always easy to find out what the premiums on a policy will be, since the earnings for the year can only be projected.

Selecting the one that is right for you requires evaluation of three important factors:

- The financial strength and integrity of the company

- Service

- The cost of the policy

Financial Strength and Integrity

Insurance involves a long-term financial guarantee, so you should be concerned about the company's ability to fulfill its obligations to you whenever it is called upon to do so —tomorrow, or fifty years from now.

For information on the financial strength and integrity of insurance companies, we suggest that you look at a copy of *Best's Insurance Reports*. This hefty volume is available in the reference rooms of most metropolitan public libraries, and contains a report on many Canadian life insurance companies. It will give you detailed financial information about a company, an analysis of the company's investments, a brief history of the company and its growth, and a description of the company's method of operation.

Best's Insurance Reports also includes a policyholder's rating for most insurance companies. The classifications used are

A+ and A	Excellent
B+	Very Good
B	Good
C+	Fairly Good
D	Fair

As an alternative, ask for financial information about the insurance companies whose products you are considering. Look at their annual financial statements — is the company currently profitable? Does it have a history of profits, or is its performance record up and down? See if you can find any reports on the company in the financial press.

Service

Most people do not have the expertise to be able to determine their life insurance requirements. So it is important for you to seek the advice of an experienced life insurance agent who has competence and integrity. Ask your friends, associates, or trusted business advisors whether they can recommend any such person working for companies that you know have financial strength and stability. Talk to several agents and find out about their experience and approach to determining your needs. Obtain a proposal and a sample policy; then study their provisions thoroughly at your leisure. Make sure you understand what insurance policy you are buying, and why, before you sign the application.

Cost

Cost is an important factor in deciding from which company you will buy your insurance. In any company, the cost of a policy depends on such factors as the company's investment performance, its selection of policyholders, its efficiency of operation, and its costs of acquiring new policyholders. These factors have to be managed, and the net result of company management is the cost of the insurance policy. Since management performance differs from company to company, so do costs. As more than one consumer-oriented publication has suggested: Shop around for your insurance!

To help you compare the net costs of different insurers' policies, insurers provide interest-adjusted cost estimates, which apply an interest factor to the yearly premiums, dividends, and increases in cash value. When you are shopping for life insurance, ask the insurance agents to provide you with interested-adjusted cost estimates for any policy you are considering.

The interest-adjusted cost estimates given by different insurance companies can differ greatly for the same benefit and type of policy. A recent study published by the American Institute of Economic Research, *Life Insurance from the Buyer's Point of View*,* included a cost ranking of companies that had a Best's rating of A or A+ (excellent) and insurance contracts totalling $1 billion or more. To rank the companies, this study used the interest-adjusted annual cost of a $25,000 whole life policy for a man 35 years of age. The findings showed a difference of $4,505 between the least costly and the most costly company. This study only included those companies that were rated excellent. If all companies had been analysed, the cost difference would have been even greater.

Choosing the Agent

A competent insurance agent often makes the choice of a qualified insurance company much easier. When you select an agent, be sure that person has had extensive experience with the particular type of insurance you are shopping for. The agent should be involved not only in the original sale of coverage but also in monitoring and updating it. References from existing clients are an excellent way of checking the service and professionalism of a prospective broker.

Another factor involved in your selection should be a review of the professional designations they have earned. This is often a sign of the professionalism and commitment they have made to their careers. The designation important in the property-casualty field is the chartered property casualty underwriter (CPCU). In the life and health areas, the designations to look for are chartered life underwriter (CLU), or chartered financial planner (CFP). Each of these designations demonstrates a willingness to provide competent service. Obviously, this does not imply that individuals without these designations are not competent.

Remember, you should purchase insurance only after you have completed the risk management process. This offers the assurance that you are making informed, knowledgeable and sound decisions about your insurance coverages.

---

*Available from the American Institute of Economic Research, Great Barrington, Massachusetts 01230.

CLOSING OBSERVATIONS

Knowing that there really is a logical and comprehensive way to tackle the task of risk management in your complete personal financial management strategy should assure you that your insurance needs can be met in an understandable, straightforward fashion. The primary purpose of this chapter has been to give you the insight necessary to take action rather than just react in determining where insurance in its myriad forms may be used to your best benefit.

No personal financial management process would be complete without a thorough application of the risk-management process described here. Simply stated, we cannot plan with assurance unless we adequately protect ourselves from financial loss due to risks we overlook, neglect, or cannot escape.

14

ESTATE PLANNING

"You can't take it with you" — so goes the adage on worldly wealth that we've all heard. But you may not have heard the punchline, "The reason you can't take it with you is that *it* goes before *you* go." Assume though, that with the help of this book, yours won't go before you go — you will want your heirs to receive the maximum of your estate with a minimum of aggravation.

Since a smooth transfer of your property is by no means automatic, you should plan and organize your estate now in order to prevent needless delays and losses later on. The preparation of your Financial Planner should be very helpful in estate planning.

WHAT IS ESTATE PLANNING?

Estate planning is the process of providing for the orderly transfer of all your assets at death to your chosen beneficiaries in the time frame you select. For example, you may wish to leave all of your assets to your minor son on the condition that he obtain full control of these assets only when he reaches twenty-five years of age.

WHY DO IT?

One of the major reasons people plan their estates is to reduce taxes payable on death. This is certainly an important motive but appropriate estate planning can also minimize some of the problems and disruptions that often arise when a family member dies. Cash flow problems between the time of death and the settlement of the estate can be prevented. The length of time necessary to settle the estate can be minimized.

Planning your estate will also ensure that your assets are distributed according to your wishes, based on your intimate knowledge of your family situation, rather than being distributed as dictated by provincial statute. As well, both the emotional and monetary cost of administering your estate can be reduced by pre-planning, lessening some of the burden on your executors and beneficiaries who must deal with the consequences of your death, and get on with their own lives.

TAX CONSEQUENCES ON DEATH

Before we discuss the process of estate planning, let's first consider the potential tax consequences of your death.

You will, of course, be subject to tax on any salary, wages, investment income, etc., received in the year before you die. These will be reported in your final tax return. Income such as interest or dividends which have accrued up to the date of death are included in taxable income, even though they are not received until after death. For example, any accrued interest on compound savings bonds will be included in taxable income. But you may have income in addition to this to be reported on your final return.

At the time of writing, there are no estate or gift taxes payable in Canada. There are, however, additional income taxes that may be payable just as a result of your death. When you die, the *Income Tax Act* deems you to have disposed of all your non-depreciable capital assets (stocks, bonds, etc.) at their fair market value immediately before your death. Therefore, if you own investments or other non-depreciable capital property with gains accrued since you acquired them, these gains will become taxable on your death. These gains are determined in the same manner as ordinary capital gains, as discussed in Chapter 6. To the extent you have accrued losses on non-depreciable capital properties, you will be able to offset these losses against any gains in the year of death to reduce the amount of the net capital gain reported in your final return.

There are additional special rules to govern the taxation on death of depreciable property, eligible capital property, resource properties and other special business assets. If you have significant holdings in these types of property, you probably need some expert tax advice to formulate an appropriate estate plan.

The tax payable on accrued gains at death can be deferred by leaving these assets unconditionally to your surviving spouse or to a trust which cannot benefit anyone other than your spouse during the remainder of his or her lifetime (spousal trust). Tax on the accrued gains will be deferred until the subsequent death of your spouse or until the property is sold by your spouse. This deferral can allow time for an orderly disposal of assets to minimize tax or to spread its payment over several years.

Capital gains triggered on death may also be offset by any unused capital gains exemption, as previously described in Chapter 6. Since each spouse has his or her own lifetime capital gains exemption, total taxes may be reduced if you leave some assets with accrued gains directly to your children in order to trigger sufficient gains to use up your remaining exemption limit, rather than deferring these gains by leaving the assets to your spouse. Your unused exemption limit cannot be transferred to your spouse or anyone else — it expires on your death.

Additional income taxes may also be triggered if you have unmatured RRSPs at the time of death. (An unmatured RRSP is one which you have not yet converted to an annuity, RRIF or cash.) In general, the current value of investments and funds held in any unmatured RRSPs will be included in the taxable income reported in your final return. If you designate your spouse as the beneficiary of your RRSP, however, tax will only be payable when funds are actually received from the RRSP by your spouse. Your spouse may also be able to transfer tax-free your RRSP funds to his or her own RRSP. All or part of the tax payable on your unmatured RRSPs can also be deferred if you designate as beneficiaries financially dependent children or grandchildren. You can also choose, in certain conditions, to have all or part of an unmatured RRSP taxed in the hands of your spouse or a dependent child or grandchild, rather than in your final return.

An estate plan (or any other plan, for that matter) should not just be considered from a tax viewpoint. If, in order to save tax, you inadvertently deprive your spouse of a reasonable income after your death, it cannot be considered a successful plan. Tax savings are often the reason for choosing a particular method of estate planning, but they should never be the single determining factor.

The above discussion of the potential tax consequences on death is very simplified and general, and it does not include details relating to the filing of special returns, certain elections available, etc. An in-depth discussion of all these items could fill many chapters of this book and would probably not be of much interest to many readers. This discussion, along with the completion of Form 29 (discussed below), should allow you to come up with a fairly accurate estimate of potential taxes on death and you can use this as a first step in formulating your estate plan. A more detailed analysis of your potential tax situation should be done with the help of a qualified tax advisor.

FORM 29 — POTENTIAL INCOME TAX LIABILITY ON ASSETS OWNED AT DEATH

Form 29 can be used to estimate your potential tax liability at death on non-depreciable capital assets and unmatured RRSPs. Form 13B will supply you with most of the information required to determine accrued gains or losses on the non-depreciable capital properties you currently hold. Information on the current value of your unmatured RRSPs can be obtained from the financial institution that administers your plans.

FORM 30 — AFTER-TAX VALUE OF ESTATE

Form 30 is provided to help you determine the after-tax value of your estate, drawing from information contained in other forms in this book.

Start with Form 5, *Analysis of Net Worth.* If this has been recently updated, it will provide you with an accurate estimate of the pre-tax value of your estate excluding insurance. Put the amount of your total net worth, excluding insurance, as determined on line 10 of Form 5, onto line 1 of Form 30. Add to this the amount of insurance that will be paid to your estate on your death as indicated on Form 28. The after-tax value of your estate can then be obtained by deducting the estimated potential tax on death determined on Form 29, as well as estimated funeral expenses and administration costs for your estate.

STEPS TO IMPLEMENT YOUR ESTATE PLAN

All the steps which follow apply equally to both husband and wife. For simplicity, the completion of each step has been described only for one spouse. Obviously, it is important to consider an estate plan for both spouses, particularly when each own significant assets independent of one another.

Decide How You Would Like the After-tax Value of Your Estate Divided

Think carefully about how you would like to divide your assets. If your spouse is still alive and will not have sufficient income of his or her own to live comfortably after your death, estimate how much of your estate will be needed to make up this income gap. If your estate cannot provide sufficient assets to fund this income gap, you should consider additional life insurance (discussed in Chapter 13). If there is any excess, consider how you would like this divided among your children, other family members, friends, and charitable organizations. If you have changed your original allocation of assets to your spouse and others, reflect this by adjusting the potential taxes payable you estimated on Form 29 and recalculating the after-tax value of your estate. Remember that, in general, tax can be deferred on assets left to your spouse, while there is usually no deferral on assets left to others.

In some circumstances, you may not be able to divide your estate exactly as you wish. All provinces have family law legislation that deals with the division of assets acquired during the marriage between spouses in the event of marriage breakdown. The legislation may also extend to the division of assets on death of a spouse. For example, in Ontario, the surviving spouse is entitled to one-half the assets accumulated during the marriage (with some exceptions). If the deceased spouse's will bequeaths less than this amount to the surviving spouse, he or she has a legal right to demand an equalizing payment from the estate. Therefore, if you live in Ontario and wish to leave the bulk of your estate to someone other than your spouse, your will may not be followed, unless you and your spouse have previously agreed in a valid domestic contract to forego your rights under the *Family Law Act* to vary the division of assets on death. The lawyer you consult to draft or revise your will should be able to explain your rights and obligations to your spouse under the applicable provincial legislation. It may be that you need not only an updated will, but a marriage contract as well.

Consider Reviewing your Situation with a Tax Specialist

Particularly with the introduction of the lifetime capital gains exemption and the minimum tax, estate tax planning can be complex. If you have a substantial estate or investments with large accrued gains, investments in private companies, partnerships or other business interests, or investments in foreign properties such as U.S. real estate, it is almost certainly worth your while to invest several hundred dollars or more in the services of a tax specialist. There may be legitimate opportunities for you to reduce tax, opportunities which you might otherwise be unaware of. For example, a business owner who intended to eventually transfer ownership of his company to his children could reduce further taxes on death (or retirement) by "freezing" the value of his company at its current value, with future growth accruing to shares held by his children. In the meantime, the business owner could retain control of the company, if he wishes. The lawyer you consult to draft your will may have this specialized tax knowledge, or you may wish to consult a CA with expertise in estate planning to work along with your lawyer.

Consult a Lawyer to Draft or Review Your Will

This is such an important step that it's hard not to put it before the previous two steps. (It's only placed here because you really need to decide on the division of your estate and consult a tax specialist before you can provide your lawyer with the information needed to draft or revise your will.)

Should everyone have a will? Maybe not. But anyone with a spouse or children, or some interest in the disposition of their property after death, should definitely make a will. It is *essential* unless you want your assets distributed according to the intestacy law of the province in which you live, and your minor children placed under a guardianship determined by the courts. A will allows you to consider the special needs of your family members. For example, you may wish to delay the time at which your children unconditionally receive their inheritance until they turn twenty-five. Without a will, they would automatically receive their share of your estate at the age of majority (generally eighteen).

Without a will, you cannot choose the executors (administrators) of your estate — they will be selected by the court. If you die intestate, there will be a period immediately after your death (until the court appoints the executors of your estate) when no one has the legal authority to administer your estate. This can be inconvenient for your survivors, and cause them cash flow problems. Failure to draft a will almost certainly will delay the distribution of your estate and will result in higher administration costs. As well, most opportunities to defer or reduce taxes on death will be lost if you do not have a will.

In some cases, you can control the transfer of your assets without a will. For example, property owned in joint tenancy with the right of survivorship will pass automatically on death to the surviving joint owner. As well, you can name a beneficiary under an insurance policy or an RRSP, so that on your death the property passes to that beneficiary.

However, even if you can structure all your assets to pass automatically to specified beneficiaries on your death, it is still prudent to have a will to provide alternative beneficiaries should you and your specified beneficiaries die in a common disaster.

TERMS OF YOUR WILL

For people of modest wealth with relatively straightforward estate plans, their needs can be met by a simple will. The following points should be remembered in drawing up a will:

- your (testator's) identity and address.

- revocation of prior wills and codicils (revisions to prior wills).

- burial instructions or other disposition of your body (such as donating it for medical purposes).

- specific bequests (gifts) of identifiable real or personal property, sums of money or shares of stock to a specified beneficiary, such as your spouse, your children, or charities.

- bequests of tangible personal property, such as personal and household effects, jewellery and cars, to family members, friends or charities.

- establishment of trusts to hold specific or residuary bequests for certain beneficiaries who may need ongoing assistance in handling their bequests. Trusts are particularly common for minor children, and for spouses not experienced in financial matters.

- residuary bequests of assets that have not been specifically bequeathed. In small estates, such assets are usually left outright to the surviving spouse or children. In large estates, the residual assets are more important and their disposition is more complicated, often involving trusts and other matters requiring legal advice. When there is no close family or surviving spouse, the residual assets are often left to charities.

- survivorship provisions that establish a presumed order of death in case you and your spouse or other beneficiary die in the same accident and there is no proof of which one died first. This component in the will should also include provisions that will serve to avoid the expense of double administration in case two parties, one inheriting from the other, die within a short time of each other.

- appointment of a guardian for your minor children in the event you and your spouse die at the same time.

- appointment of executor(s).

- appointment of trustee(s) when the will contains a trust.

- payment of funeral expenses, administration costs of the estate and debts of the estate, including income taxes payable as a result of your death.

- provision for contingencies. For example, you should select alternate beneficiaries in the event the expected beneficiaries die before you.

CHANGING YOUR WILL

Keep your will in a safe place where your executor, spouse or closest beneficiary can get to it quickly and easily. The original will might best be kept by your lawyer. Another copy can be kept in your safety deposit box but, if you plan to do so, find out first what procedures would have to be followed to open the box after your death. Keep another copy with your financial records at home for easy reference. It might be a good idea also to summarize and discuss the important provisions of your will with the persons affected by it.

Once you have a will, you should review it every few years to make sure it still fits your situation and have it adjusted, if necessary. Substantial changes in your financial situation, such as a large inheritance, may necessitate changes in the provisions of your will. There may also be changes in the tax law that affect your will and if you marry or divorce, you will almost certainly wish to make changes in your will. (Your existing will may be automatically revoked if your marital status changes.)

WHO WILL BE YOUR EXECUTOR?

What could be better than to have your spouse or other close relative serve as the executor of your estate? After all, he or she is most likely to know exactly what you would have done if you were still alive. However, you might be better off having a professional take on the job of executor.

The job of executor is complicated because of tax laws, inheritance rules and probate regulations, although much of the paperwork involved (including the filing of tax returns) can be dealt with by a family member executor with the help of a lawyer and a chartered accountant. This is particularly true when the estate is left outright to a spouse or other family member. But make sure any executor you select is willing to take on the responsibility.

When more complex estates are involved, for example, or when your will establishes trusts to invest funds bequeathed to minor children or other family members, it may be prudent to choose someone other than a family member as executor. One solution is to name a trust company and have your spouse or a relative as co-executor.

CLOSING OBSERVATIONS

You work hard — maybe a total of 80,000 hours during your lifetime — to earn your money and invest it wisely. It would be a shame if, at your death, your nearest and dearest were to suffer financially because you did not give sufficient consideration to the transfer of your estate. We hope you have taken time to estimate the existing value of your family's estate, to forecast how the estate will be divided on your death, and to estimate the potential tax consequences of your death (as well as consider ways to reduce this potential tax, where possible).

We know that estate planning can sometimes become quite complicated. If that's how it seems in your case, we suggest that you seek some good professional advice to help you conserve the maximum amount of your estate.

15

TAKE ACTION

This book has given you a structure for analysing your personal finances, for forecasting your financial future, and for identifying the financial steps that can bring you closer to your various objectives in life. This, in itself, may well prevent you from taking some ill-considered step you might have taken without it; but to reap major benefits from the knowledge and insight you have acquired, you must apply it by taking the appropriate positive action.

The first thing to do is ask and answer questions such as:

- How much do you want or can you afford to put aside for your long-term objectives of education, retirement, extended travel, remodelling, and so forth?

- Do your current and projected budgets permit you to set aside for your long-term objectives?

- What are the trade-offs to make between your current lifestyle and future objectives?

Before you answer such questions and prepare a projection for next year, here are some general guidelines for people of varying ages.

IN YOUR THIRTIES

Take care of the four firsts: an annual income, normally secured by a job; a place to live; a reserve fund that can be used in an emergency; and low-cost life insurance — a source of future income for your dependants should you die.

The first two, an annual income and place to live, have far-reaching implications for long-term financial planning. Income obviously is a big factor in providing sufficient resources for accumulating assets and establishing a comfortable standard of living. However, it is not necessarily true that the larger the income, the larger the resources accumulated or the estate developed. Maintaining an income level sets in motion complicated problems of living up to one's career position. Many people of significant income have lifestyle expenses as great, if not greater, than their income, and they never seem to accumulate assets for future needs.

So during your thirties, concentrate on your income and basic lifestyle expenditures — housing, transportation, food and clothing. Resist the instant gratification craze and get in the habit of saving something for investment. Consider starting an education fund if you have children.

Remember that the cash reserve fund should be kept in liquid, low-risk investments such as Canada Savings Bonds. Try to attain a level of three months' take-home pay for this reserve. Life insurance is usually an easy goal to achieve at this age because most employers offer group term insurance at little or no cost. If this is the case in your situation, you won't have to purchase additional coverage from an independent agent. Make sure that you have adequate disability coverage, as this is the most important aspect of insurance planning at this time in your life.

IN YOUR FORTIES

Control the increase in lifestyle expenditures. Look for investments, other than your personal residence, that the family can use and enjoy — vacation property, a boat, a computer. Concentrate on education funds and try to shift income to your children to pay for their education. Start a retirement programme. Focus on growth and tax savings in selecting your investments.

IN YOUR FIFTIES

The children, you hope, are educated and on their own. You might even be able to decrease your basic lifestyle expenditures at this stage. Focus on new personal growth activities, such as travel, photography, or art collecting. Concentrate on retirement planning and increasing your investment assets and retirement funds to make your retirement years golden. Pay off your home mortgage. Concentrate your savings and investment dollars in instruments of moderate to low risk.

IN YOUR SIXTIES

Pare your basic lifestyle costs. Get those retirement activities lined up and going. Concentrate on being active and continue your zest for life. Get out of debt and manage your investment assets to stay even with inflation. Get your estate in order and keep your financial affairs simple.

FORM 31 — INCOME AND EXPENDITURE PROJECTION

To complete this form, you need to refer to forms you previously completed about your objectives and to follow the steps below:

- Enter in the *Last Year* column your actual income and expenditures from Forms 6, 7, 8 and 9.

- Enter on lines 1, 2, 3 and 4 in the *Next Year* column your estimates of next year's expenditures for long-term objectives.

- On line 1, enter the amount for each of your children from line 15(c) of Form 23, *University, Graduate School and College Costs*. Using the example shown in Figure 11-1 for Form 23, you would enter $20,886 on line 1 of Form 31.

- On line 2, enter the amounts from lines 7(a) and 10(d) of Form 27, *Retirement Income.* Using the example in Figure 12-1 for Form 27, you would enter $8,450 on line 2 of Form 31.

- On line 3, enter your answer to question 5 from Form 22, *Your Investment Strategy.* Using the example shown in Figure 10-5 for Form 22, you would enter $10,000 on line 3 of Form 31.

- On line 4, enter the amounts for the next year of the major discretionary expenditures you listed on Form 17, *Income and Expenditure Objectives.*

- On line 5, enter the totals of lines 1 through 4 to get the amount you would like to set aside next year for long-term objectives.

- On line 6(a) in the *Next Year* column, enter your estimate of employment income for next year. Review lines 1 and 2 of Form 17 for the estimate you previously prepared.

- On line 6(b), enter your estimate of investment income for next year. Review information on Form 11, *Tax-Planning Worksheet,* as a starting point here. Total your estimated income for next year on line 6(c).

- On line 7, enter your estimate of basic lifestyle expenditures for next year. Review Form 7, *Basic Lifestyle Expenditures,* as a starting point; remember that some very significant basic expenditures may not increase — for example, your mortgage payment. Remember also that whether these expenditures increase is up to you — the quality of your future lifestyle is not necessarily dependent on more quantity, more expenditures.

- On line 8, enter your estimate of discretionary expenditures. Review Form 8, *Discretionary Expenditures,* as a starting point.

- On line 9(a), enter your estimate of income taxes for next year. Use your estimate of taxable income from Form 11, *Income Tax-Planning Worksheet,* and refer to Appendix III for the taxes payable on this amount.

- On line 9(b), enter your estimate of other payroll deductions, including Canada or Quebec Pension Plan contributions, Unemployment Insurance premiums, and any provincial health insurance payments. Total your estimated income taxes and other deductions on line 9(c).

- On line 10, enter the totals from lines 7, 8 and 9(c).

- On line 11, enter the amount that results from subtracting line 10 from line 6(c).

At this point, compare the amount on line 5 to the amount on line 11. If the amount on line 11 is less than the amount on line 5, determine what changes you need to make in your financial situation to achieve your long-term objectives. Can you increase your income? Can you reduce your discretionary expenditures? Can you manage your taxes more effectively? These are choices you can make to increase the amount available for long-term objectives. If you are unwilling or unable to increase the amount on line 11, then you will have to revise the amounts you can set aside next year for long-term goals.

Once you have evaluated your choices and trade-offs, get the amounts on line 5 and line 11 in balance. Then commit yourself to making your projections a reality. The income and expenditure projection then becomes a blueprint for the first year of your financial future.

FORM 32 — YOUR ACTION STEPS

Have you been noting your potential action steps for next year as you were working on various other forms? If not, let us remind you of the planning areas into which they might fall.

- Net worth planning

- Controlling or reducing expenditures

- Increased earned income

- Reducing taxes

- Increasing investments and return on investments

- Financing your children's education

- Retirement planning

- Life insurance

- Estate planning

In listing steps on Form 32, try to be as specific as you can. Decide on the type of action to take, on the amount of money involved, and on the date by which the action should be accomplished. Something vague like "My wife and I want to set aside some funds for retirement this year" is less likely to be translated into action than "My wife and I want to contribute $4,000 to an RRSP by May 31 this year," which sets you a specific and presumably well-considered target.

As has been mentioned earlier, it is unrealistic to assume that you can accomplish more than ten such action steps in one year. Therefore, select the most feasible of your proposed action steps and make a commitment to complete them.

To keep to your timetable, and to make sure that nothing is left undone because it just slipped your mind, take a look at this form once a month, and transfer the appropriate action step(s) onto your everyday list of things you must remember to do. The timely accomplishment of these goals is imperative to a successful financial management programme.

PROFESSIONAL ADVICE

As you face the increasing complexity of our tax laws and a multitude of investment opportunities, you may feel a need for professional guidance or confirmation before you make some weighty financial decision. Depending on your particular concerns — income tax planning, retirement or estate planning, investments, or life insurance — you might want to consult a professional advisor in an accounting firm, a bank, a brokerage firm, a *caisse populaire*, a credit union, a financial counselling firm, an insurance company or a law firm.

The institution or organization you consult should be experienced in the particular field of your inquiry, and you should ask how clients with problems similar to your own have been counselled. Get references on the quality of the organization's work in this field, and find out what professional training your prospective counsellor has had.

The majority of these counselling services will charge you a fee. Certain accounting firms, banks, trust companies, brokerage firms, insurance companies, credit unions and *caisses populaires* may provide some financial counselling. Some of these organizations may be primarily in the business of selling products and they may offer free counselling services in order to make their products more attractive or to promote their sale.

Any professional advisor you choose will find the analyses you have made of your financial holdings, needs, objectives, and expectations enormously helpful; and wherever the advisor's fee is determined by the time spent on your behalf, the work you have done on your forms will reduce such a fee, perhaps by forty to fifty percent. If there is going to be a fee, agree on the terms of it beforehand and make sure you will get an itemized bill.

Except in matters of law, rules, and regulations, which the advisor should know insofar as they relate to the advisor's specialty, the professional guidance you receive will not be based on certainties but on estimates of probabilities. On the whole, the professional's estimates should be correct more often than your own. Even so, any professional advice that is based on an estimate of probabilities should not be followed blindly, nor should you ever take financial action on the basis of rationales that you do not understand. A good advisor will be ready to explain the reasons for any advice or recommendation.

For those who might want to consult an advisor, the following paragraphs give a brief description of the organizations that provide various types of financial advice.

Accounting Firms

Personal financial planning services are offered by some medium-sized accounting firms and by all of the large ones. As well as helping you to formulate financial plans and goals, they can advise you on particular concerns like tax planning, tax shelters, investment planning and performance, educational financing, and retirement and estate planning. Their unique expertise lies in the field of taxation, and this is quite crucial, since tax considerations enter into just about every phase of financial planning and management. To determine which combination of variables will be the most advantageous to you, they make extensive use of computer analysis, in addition to their knowledge of the tax laws.

The advice you get from an accounting firm will not be coloured by self-interest. Accounting firms don't act as brokers or sell insurance on the side. If they suggest that you buy or sell some product, it will not be because they receive a commission on it. They don't. They work for a fee based on hourly rates, and before entering into an engagement with you, they should give you an estimate of their fee. They will also be able to put you in touch with competent and reliable firms of stockbrokers, insurers, or whatever else you may need to put your financial plans in action.

Banks, Credit Unions, and Trust Companies

Some banks, credit unions and trust companies provide a variety of financial planning services. These services may include tailor-made loans, estate planning, asset management, trust services, stock purchases and financial counselling.

Investment Counsellors

Most investment counsellors provide investment management of a portfolio of securities. Many firms will not handle portfolios below some minimum size — from $100,000 to $250,000. Investment counsellors charge a fee for their financial advice based on some percentage of the value of the portfolio. This percentage may run from one or two percent of the minimum portfolio to one-half a percent of larger portfolios.

In using an investment counselling firm, it normally makes sense to give the professional manager the power to buy and sell investments without your consent. Remember, the professional counselling firm is being paid for its judgement. If you do not want the firm to exercise its judgement, you should probably not pay for investment management. If you do choose to let an investment counselling firm handle your investments, you should review its performance quarterly or semi-annually and either retain or dismiss the firm, based on its performance.

Since there are many investment counselling firms available, one of the biggest problems is to select the right firm for you. One approach is to check the banks and trust companies in your area to see if they provide an investment counselling service. Often they do. If they do not, they might be able to give you a list of investment advisors who may help you. In addition, your CA and lawyer should know of investment counselling firms they can recommend to you. Usually stock brokerage firms know of investment firms, since investment counselling firms have to work through a stock broker in order to buy and sell securities for their clients. And many stock brokerage firms have their own affiliated investment advisory services.

Mutual Funds

For those who do not have sufficient investments to interest a personal investment counsellor, consider mutual funds. A mutual fund is an enterprise that obtains money from institutional and individual investors and invests the money in securities selected to achieve certain financial objectives. By pooling the funds of many investors, the mutual fund provides diversification, professional management, and continuous supervision of investments.

There are hundreds of mutual funds from which to choose, varying in size, purpose and policy. Refer back to Chapter 10 for a general description of mutual funds.

Brokerage Houses

In recent years, some brokerage houses have established financial planning departments staffed with investment counsellors, CAs, lawyers and insurance specialists. They provide comprehensive services and charge a fee for the services. Some of them arrange that if the client buys investment products from the brokerage house, the brokerage commissions are deducted from the financial planning fees.

Of course, brokerage houses are organized primarily to provide investment products, ranging from money market funds, stocks and bonds to real estate or oil and gas tax shelters. A good broker should first perform an analysis of your investment needs, including your present assets and your investment objectives. The broker should know whether you wish to emphasize capital gains or income, short-term or long-term investments, safety or speculation, and so forth. In essence, the broker attempts to find out what types of investments you feel comfortable with. After reviewing your personal data, present financial situation, and investment objectives, the stock broker should develop an appropriate investment plan based on what you consider to be a desirable or acceptable rate of risk and return.

Full-service brokerage houses provide research reports on specific securities, reference libraries, and safekeeping services for your securities. Of course, they buy and sell securities, for which they charge a commission. A full-service brokerage house charges a higher commission than a discount brokerage house because of the extensive services it offers. Discount brokers do nothing more than buy and sell securities.

Financial Planners

People with the designation of Chartered Financial Planner (CFP) have completed a comprehensive educational programme in areas of financial planning. Typically, a CFP has experience in a specific financial field such as selling stocks, mutual funds or insurance. Some financial planners are independent and objective in their analyses and recommendations and charge a fee for their services; others do not charge a fee and hence will tend to recommend the products that they sell on commission.

Insurance Advisors

Primarily, insurance advisors provide professional assistance in the broad area of insurance — health, disability, casualty and life insurance. Such an advisor often acts as a catalyst in the financial planning process, bringing the client together with other experts — a CA, a lawyer or an investment broker.

A good insurance advisor will review the client's financial affairs and will call in these other financial advisors when appropriate. If the client's business transactions are too complex for the insurance agent to handle, the agent should consult the proper specialist — a CA about possible tax advantages, a trust company or lawyer about changing a client's will or the setting up of a trust.

The role of the life insurance agent as a financial advisor is a difficult one because of the obvious conflict of interest. The insurance agent is expected to make an objective analysis of the client's needs and to recommend the appropriate insurance coverage, but the agent is compensated on a commission basis: The more insurance the agent sells, the greater the agent's income.

KEEPING UP WITH CURRENT FINANCIAL INFORMATION

Periodicals

There are several sources of financial information and analyses.

Canadian Sources:

1. *The Globe & Mail*, Report on Business Section (daily)
   Canadian Newspapers Company Limited
   444 Front Street West
   Toronto, Ontario
   M5V 2S9
   (a good source of general business information, along with recent developments in taxation and personal finance)

2. *The Financial Post* (daily)
   333 King St. E.
   Toronto, Ontario
   M5A 4N2
   (concentrates on reporting developments in the business world, including stock market information, but has regular features on personal tax and financial planning matters. Also has regular reviews of mutual fund performance)

3. *Financial Times of Canada* (weekly)
   440 Front St. W.
   Toronto, Ontario
   M5V 2S9
   (also concentrates on general business and investment information but with regular personal financial management features and monthly reviews of mutual fund performance)

4. *Canadian Business* (monthly)
   CB Media Limited
   70 The Esplanade
   2nd Floor
   Toronto, Ontario
   M5E 1R2
   (reports on many business topics, including personal tax and financial planning)

U.S. Sources

5. *The Wall Street Journal* (daily)
   200 Burnett Road
   Chicopee, Massachusetts 01020
   (in every Monday issue is a column entitled "Your Money Matters")

6. *Business Week* (weekly)
   McGraw-Hill Inc.
   1221 Avenue of the Americas
   New York, New York 10020
   (has a "Personal Business" column, in addition to articles covering many economic areas)

7. *Forbes* (bi-weekly)
   60 Fifth Avenue
   New York, New York 10011
   (includes a "Personal Affairs" column as well as several money and investment columns in each issue. Also has an annual mutual fund analysis in August or September issue)

8. *Fortune* (bi-weekly)
   Time Life Building
   Rockefeller Center
   New York, New York 10020
   (has a "Personal Investing" column, in addition to comprehensive business articles)

9. *Money* (monthly)
   Time Life Building
   Rockefeller Center
   New York, New York 10020
   (includes articles on many personal financial matters with a how-to-do-it approach; it includes a regular article on "one family's finances" that discusses specific financial recommendations)

Newsletters

There are many newsletters available. Many brokerage houses and banks provide letters to their clients, as do investment counselling firms. Some specialize in certain kinds of investments. Many of these newsletters are advertised by direct mail. If you are interested in one that seems to fit your objectives, we suggest you write and ask for a sample copy.

Television

There are television news programmes and talk shows that stress money matters. Global TV has a weekly programme, "Everybody's Business," that covers current issues. Canadian public television also has programmes dealing with personal finances, including business programmes on the CBC "NewsWorld" channel. "Wall Street Week" is a half-hour U.S. Public Broadcasting System production that covers a variety of current investment ideas and products primarily in the U.S. market.

Seminars

There are a variety of financial planning seminars — some free, some expensive — offered by universities, community colleges, banks, investment firms, trust companies and accounting firms.

16

YOUR ANNUAL FINANCIAL CHECKUP

Congratulations to all of you who have worked your way through this book and filled in all its forms. At this point, you know what you own, what you need, what you want, what you can reasonably expect, and what you can do. You have made some choices, evaluated the consequences, committed yourself to some action, and are in control of your financial affairs. In addition, you have saved $2,000 to $3,000 in professional fees by putting your Financial Planner together. You have earned the laurels and might like to wear them around the house for a month or so.

Beware of resting on your laurels, though. Time marches on, and some of your current records and plans will inevitably become out-of-date. So you should periodically update everything that has some bearing on your financial plans and decisions.

Some of the forms you have completed may merely need to be reviewed and amended where necessary. Others should be completed anew.

Because few people can or want to update their affairs in one sitting, we suggest that you do your updating systematically and do it over the course of the year. In our experience, the following timetable is the best and most convenient.

JANUARY — FEBRUARY

In these first months of the year, make some inroads on the tax returns due on April 30 by assembling all data pertinent to your financial transactions in the last calendar year.

When you have finished with that, review and update the following forms:

- *Form 1*, *Personal and Family Data* (Chapter 2), filed under *Personal Data* in your Financial Planner. The information listed here will not change greatly from year to year, so merely check your completed form and amend it as necessary.

- **Form 2**, *Financial Documents* (Chapter 2), filed under *Financial Documents* in your Financial Planner. Use your completed form. Make sure the listings are complete and that the documents are in their stated locations. Go over this list with your spouse and also let someone else in your family know that this list exists and where to find it.

- **Form 3**, *Financial Advisors* (Chapter 2), filed under *Financial Documents* in your Financial Planner. Use your filled-in form. Evaluate your original choices and amend them if that seems advisable.

- **Form 4**, *Statement of Net Worth*, and Form 5, *Analysis of Net Worth* (Chapter 3), filed under *Financial Profile* in your Financial Planner. Here your filled-in forms are out-of-date by up to one year. Since you can now take some of the required data from your original form and the rest from the data collected for your tax return, this second time around will be much easier than the first.

- **Form 6**, *Income Sources* (Chapter 4), filed under *Financial Profile* in your Financial Planner. Take a copy of this form and complete it with the information you have collected for your tax return. Compare it with your original form and set some goals for the current year.

- **Form 7**, *Basic Lifestyle Expenditures*, and Form 8, *Discretionary Expenditures* (Chapter 4), filed under *Financial Profile* in your Financial Planner. Update these forms with data for the last calendar year. Then challenge your expenditure patterns and set some goals for the current year.

MARCH

Focus on completing your tax return for last year by the end of March. If you want a tax accountant to review or prepare your return, stay away from the April 30 scramble. You are likely to get much better service before April, and to obtain that, you must give your accountant the necessary data by early to mid-March. Be sure to keep a copy of your tax return.

When you have mailed your tax return to Revenue Canada, update the following forms:

- **Form 9**, *Income Taxes and Other Deductions* (Chapter 4), filed under *Financial Profile* in your Financial Planner. Use a duplicate of this form, and take your figures from your newly completed tax return. Find your top tax rate from the appropriate schedule in Appendix II. Find your average tax rate by adding lines 2 and 3 and then dividing the result by line 1.

- **Form 10**, *Analysis of Earned Income and Expenditures* (Chapter 4), filed under *Financial Profile* in your Financial Planner. Use a copy of this form, and take your figures from your newly completed Form 6, Form 7, Form 8 and Form 9.

Now, after either updating or completing anew Forms 1 through 10, you have an updated financial profile and are again in a position to do some planning for the future.

APRIL — MAY

Now that you have completed and mailed your last year's tax return, prepare a tax plan for this year on Form 11, *Income Tax Planning Worksheet*. You may wish to use a tax professional to help you prepare your plan and to identify tax-saving ideas (Form 12).

Finally, you should prepare an estimate of this year's tax liability. Make sure you understand how much tax will be withheld from your paycheques and the estimated tax payments, if any, you will need to make on March 15, June 15, September 15, and December 15 of this year.

Before the summer rolls around, you can do a little more reviewing and updating of the following forms:

- *Form 16*, *Financial Security* (Chapter 9), filed under *Financial Objectives* in your Financial Planner.

- *Form 17*, *Income and Expenditure Objectives* (Chapter 9), filed under *Financial Objectives* in your Financial Planner.

- *Form 20*, *Investment Objectives* (Chapter 9), filed under *Investment Strategy* in your Financial Planner. Review your completed form and amend it as necessary.

- *Form 21*, *Review of Your Present Investments* (Chapter 10), filed under *Investment Strategy* in your Financial Planner. Review your completed form and amend it as necessary.

- *Form 22*, *Your Investment Strategy* (Chapter 10), filed under *Investment Strategy* in your Financial Planner. Review your completed form and amend it as necessary.

- *Form 31*, *Income and Expenditure Projection* (Chapter 15), filed under *Action* in your Financial Planner. Use the copy of this form and update your projections for this year.

JUNE — AUGUST

Even the most conscientious financial planners must take time off to recharge their batteries. Try to relax during these months and temper your financial planning with lots of sunshine, hikes, vacation trips, sailing, or whatever gives you a break from work and gets you closer to your family and friends.

SEPTEMBER — OCTOBER

Imagine how boring fall would be if you had no financial planning to do — nothing but falling leaves, apples, pumpkins and football games! As a change from all that, you will want to update the following forms:

- *Form 28*, *Your Present Life Insurance Coverage* (Chapter 13), filed under *Insurance* in your Financial Planner. Review your completed form and amend it as necessary.

- *Form 13*, *Capital Gains and Losses* (Chapter 8), filed under *Tax Planning* in your Financial Planner. Use a copy of this form and complete it with your data for the current year.

- *Form 14*, *Year-End Tax Plan* (Chapter 8), filed under *Tax Planning* in your Financial Planner. Use a copy of this form and complete it with your data for the current year.

- *Form 15*, *Year-End Tax Action* (Chapter 8), filed under *Tax Planning* in your Financial Planner. Use a copy of this form, and try to render as little as possible unto Caesar — legally, of course.

NOVEMBER — DECEMBER

Continue to implement your year-end tax action steps through December.

If you have had any second thoughts about your financial retirement needs, make the appropriate changes in your completed Form 24, *Estimated Basic Lifestyle Expenditures at Retirement* or Form 25, *Estimated Discretionary Expenditures at Retirement* (Chapter 12), filed under *Retirement Planning* in your Financial Planner. If there is any change in your expected retirement income, amend your completed Form 27, *Retirement Income* (Chapter 12), filed under *Retirement Planning* in your Financial Planner.

Unless the secret of immortality has been discovered and is available to you by the time you read this, review the following forms, and use copies to complete them anew if there are any changes.

- *Form 29*, *Potential Income Tax Liability on Assets owned at Death* (Chapter 14), filed under *Estate Planning* in your Financial Planner.

- *Form 30*, *After-Tax Value of Estate* (Chapter 14), filed under *Estate Planning* in your Financial Planner.

And finally, now that you have finished updating all the forms, review your Financial Planner and complete Form 32, *Action Steps* (Chapter 15), filed under *Action* in your Financial Planner.

CONCLUDING OBSERVATIONS

You have prepared your Financial Planner and are well on your way to financial control and financial security. Spend according to your plan and invest in those assets that are tailored to your objectives. Evaluate your plan at least once a year and update it for changes in your objectives, the economic situation, and other events that affect you financially. But, by all means, remember to have a good life. May you grow old gracefully and with a good deal of prosperity.

COMPOUND
INTEREST TABLES

TABLE 1
FUTURE WORTH OF ONE DOLLAR WITH AMOUNT OF RETURN COMPOUNDED ANNUALLY

Year	1%	2%	3%	4%	5%	6%	7%	8%	9%	10%	13%	15%
1	1.01	1.02	1.03	1.04	1.05	1.06	1.07	1.08	1.09	1.10	1.13	1.15
2	1.02	1.04	1.06	1.08	1.10	1.12	1.15	1.17	1.19	1.21	1.28	1.32
3	1.03	1.06	1.09	1.12	1.16	1.19	1.23	1.26	1.30	1.33	1.44	1.52
4	1.04	1.08	1.13	1.17	1.22	1.26	1.31	1.36	1.41	1.46	1.63	1.75
5	1.05	1.10	1.16	1.22	1.28	1.34	1.40	1.47	1.54	1.61	1.84	2.01
6	1.06	1.13	1.19	1.27	1.34	1.42	1.50	1.59	1.68	1.77	2.08	2.31
7	1.07	1.15	1.23	1.32	1.41	1.50	1.61	1.71	1.83	1.95	2.35	2.66
8	1.08	1.17	1.27	1.37	1.48	1.59	1.72	1.85	1.99	2.14	2.66	3.06
9	1.09	1.20	1.30	1.42	1.55	1.69	1.84	2.00	2.17	2.36	3.00	3.52
10	1.10	1.22	1.34	1.48	1.63	1.79	1.97	2.16	2.37	2.59	3.40	4.05
11	1.12	1.24	1.38	1.54	1.71	1.90	2.11	2.33	2.58	2.85	3.84	4.65
12	1.13	1.27	1.43	1.60	1.80	2.01	2.25	2.52	2.81	3.14	4.34	5.35
13	1.14	1.29	1.47	1.67	1.89	2.13	2.41	2.72	3.07	3.45	4.90	6.15
14	1.15	1.32	1.51	1.73	1.98	2.26	2.58	2.94	3.34	3.80	5.54	7.08
15	1.16	1.35	1.56	1.80	2.08	2.40	2.76	3.17	3.64	4.18	6.25	8.14
16	1.17	1.37	1.60	1.87	2.18	2.54	2.95	3.43	3.97	4.60	7.07	9.36
17	1.18	1.40	1.65	1.95	2.29	2.69	3.16	3.70	4.33	5.05	7.99	10.76
18	1.20	1.43	1.70	2.03	2.41	2.85	3.38	4.00	4.72	5.56	9.02	12.38
19	1.21	1.46	1.75	2.11	2.53	3.03	3.62	4.32	5.14	6.12	10.20	14.23
20	1.22	1.49	1.81	2.19	2.65	3.21	3.87	4.67	5.60	6.73	11.52	16.37
21	1.23	1.52	1.86	2.28	2.79	3.40	4.14	5.03	6.11	7.40	13.02	18.82
22	1.24	1.55	1.92	2.37	2.93	3.60	4.43	5.44	6.66	8.14	14.71	21.65
23	1.26	1.58	1.97	2.46	3.07	3.82	4.74	5.87	7.26	8.95	16.63	24.89
24	1.27	1.61	2.03	2.56	3.23	4.05	5.07	6.34	7.91	9.85	18.79	28.63
25	1.28	1.64	2.09	2.67	3.39	4.29	5.43	6.86	8.62	10.83	21.23	32.92
26	1.30	1.67	2.16	2.77	3.56	4.55	5.81	7.40	9.40	11.92	23.99	37.86
27	1.31	1.71	2.22	2.88	3.73	4.82	6.21	7.99	10.25	13.11	27.11	43.54
28	1.32	1.74	2.29	3.00	3.92	5.11	6.65	8.63	11.17	14.42	30.63	50.07
29	1.33	1.78	2.36	3.12	4.12	5.42	7.11	9.32	12.17	15.86	34.62	57.58
30	1.35	1.81	2.43	3.24	4.32	5.74	7.61	10.06	13.27	17.45	39.12	66.21
31	1.36	1.85	2.50	3.37	4.54	6.09	8.15	10.87	14.46	19.19	44.20	76.14
32	1.37	1.88	2.58	3.51	4.76	6.45	8.72	11.74	15.76	21.11	49.95	87.57
33	1.39	1.92	2.65	3.65	5.00	6.84	9.33	12.68	17.18	23.23	56.44	100.70
34	1.40	1.96	2.73	3.79	5.25	7.25	9.98	13.69	18.73	25.55	63.78	115.81
35	1.42	2.00	2.81	3.95	5.52	7.69	10.68	14.79	20.41	28.10	72.07	133.18
36	1.43	2.04	2.90	4.10	5.79	8.15	11.42	15.97	22.25	30.91	81.44	153.15
37	1.45	2.08	2.99	4.27	6.08	8.64	12.22	17.25	24.25	34.00	92.02	176.13
38	1.46	2.12	3.07	4.44	6.39	9.15	13.08	18.63	26.44	37.40	103.99	202.54
39	1.47	2.16	3.17	4.62	6.70	9.70	14.00	20.12	28.82	41.15	117.51	232.93
40	1.49	2.21	3.26	4.80	7.04	10.29	14.97	21.73	31.41	45.26	132.78	267.86

TABLE 2
FUTURE WORTH OF ONE DOLLAR INVESTED EACH YEAR WITH INTEREST (RETURN) PAYABLE AND REINVESTED AT END OF EACH YEAR

Year	Annual Rate of Return											
	1%	2%	3%	4%	5%	6%	7%	8%	9%	10%	13%	15%
1	1.00	1.00	1.00	1.00	1.00	1.00	1.00	1.00	1.00	1.00	1.00	1.00
2	2.01	2.02	2.03	2.04	2.05	2.06	2.07	2.08	2.09	2.10	2.13	2.15
3	3.03	3.06	3.09	3.12	3.15	3.18	3.22	3.25	3.28	3.31	3.41	3.47
4	4.06	4.12	4.18	4.25	4.31	4.37	4.44	4.50	4.57	4.64	4.85	4.99
5	5.10	5.20	5.31	5.42	5.53	5.64	5.75	5.87	5.99	6.10	6.48	6.74
6	6.15	6.31	6.47	6.63	6.80	6.98	7.15	7.33	7.52	7.71	8.32	8.75
7	7.21	7.43	7.66	7.90	8.14	8.39	8.65	8.92	9.20	9.49	10.41	11.07
8	8.29	8.58	8.89	9.21	9.55	9.90	10.26	10.64	11.03	11.43	12.76	13.73
9	9.37	9.75	10.16	10.58	11.03	11.49	11.98	12.49	13.02	13.58	15.42	16.78
10	10.46	10.95	11.46	12.01	12.58	13.18	13.82	14.49	15.19	15.94	18.42	20.30
11	11.57	12.17	12.81	13.49	14.21	14.97	15.78	16.65	17.56	18.53	21.81	24.35
12	12.68	13.41	14.19	15.03	15.92	16.87	17.89	18.98	20.14	21.38	25.65	29.00
13	13.81	14.68	15.62	16.63	17.71	18.88	20.14	21.50	22.95	24.52	29.99	34.35
14	14.95	15.97	17.09	18.29	19.60	21.02	22.55	24.22	26.02	27.98	34.88	40.51
15	16.10	17.29	18.60	20.02	21.58	23.27	25.13	27.15	29.36	31.77	40.42	47.58
16	17.26	18.64	20.16	21.82	23.66	25.67	27.89	30.32	33.00	35.95	46.67	55.72
17	18.43	20.01	21.76	23.70	25.84	28.21	30.84	33.75	36.97	40.55	53.74	65.08
18	19.61	21.41	23.41	25.65	28.13	30.91	34.00	37.45	41.30	45.60	61.73	75.84
19	20.81	22.84	25.12	27.67	30.54	33.76	37.38	41.45	46.02	51.16	70.75	88.21
20	22.02	24.30	26.87	29.78	33.07	36.78	41.00	45.76	51.16	57.27	80.95	102.44
21	23.24	25.78	28.68	31.97	35.72	39.99	44.87	50.42	56.77	64.00	92.47	118.81
22	24.47	27.30	30.54	34.25	38.51	43.39	49.01	55.46	62.87	71.40	105.49	137.63
23	25.72	28.84	32.45	36.62	41.43	47.00	53.44	60.89	69.53	79.54	120.21	159.28
24	26.97	30.42	34.43	39.08	44.50	50.82	58.18	66.77	76.79	88.50	136.83	184.17
25	28.24	32.03	36.46	41.65	47.73	54.86	63.25	73.10	84.70	98.35	155.62	212.79
26	29.53	33.67	38.55	44.31	51.11	59.16	68.88	79.95	93.32	109.18	176.85	245.71
27	30.82	35.34	40.71	47.08	54.67	63.71	74.48	87.35	102.72	121.10	200.84	283.57
28	32.13	37.05	42.93	49.97	58.40	68.53	80.70	95.34	112.97	134.21	227.95	327.10
29	33.45	38.79	45.22	52.97	62.32	73.64	87.35	103.97	124.14	148.63	258.58	377.17
30	34.78	40.57	47.58	56.08	66.44	79.06	94.46	113.28	136.31	164.49	293.20	434.75
31	36.13	42.38	50.00	59.33	70.76	84.80	102.07	123.35	149.58	181.94	332.32	500.96
32	37.49	44.23	52.50	62.70	75.30	90.89	110.22	134.21	164.04	201.14	376.52	577.10
33	38.87	46.11	55.08	66.21	80.06	97.34	118.93	145.95	179.80	222.25	426.46	664.67
34	40.26	48.03	57.73	69.86	85.07	104.18	128.26	158.63	196.98	245.48	482.90	765.37
35	41.66	49.99	60.46	73.65	90.32	111.44	138.24	172.32	215.71	271.02	546.68	881.17
36	43.08	51.99	63.28	77.60	95.84	119.12	148.91	187.10	236.13	299.13	618.75	1,014.35
37	44.51	54.03	66.17	81.70	101.63	127.27	160.34	203.07	258.38	330.04	700.19	1,167.50
38	45.95	56.11	69.16	85.97	107.71	135.90	172.56	220.32	282.63	364.04	792.21	1,343.62
39	47.41	58.24	72.23	90.41	114.10	145.06	185.64	238.94	309.07	401.45	896.20	1,546.17
40	48.89	60.40	75.40	95.03	120.80	154.76	199.64	259.06	337.88	442.59	1,013.70	1,779.09

TABLE 3
$10,000 LUMP-SUM INVESTMENT COMPOUNDED ANNUALLY END-OF-YEAR VALUES

Year	5%	6%	7%	8%	9%	10%	11%	12%	13%	14%	15%
1	10,500	10,600	10,700	10,800	10,900	11,000	11,100	11,200	11,300	11,400	11,500
2	11,025	11,236	11,449	11,664	11,881	12,100	12,321	12,544	12,769	12,996	13,225
3	11,576	11,910	12,250	12,597	12,950	13,310	13,676	14,049	14,428	14,815	15,208
4	12,155	12,624	13,107	13,604	14,155	14,641	15,180	15,735	16,304	16,899	17,490
5	12,763	13,382	14,025	14,693	15,386	16,105	16,850	17,623	18,424	19,254	20,113
6	13,401	14,185	15,007	15,868	16,771	17,715	18,704	19,738	20,819	21,949	23,130
7	14,071	15,036	16,057	17,138	18,280	19,487	20,761	22,106	23,526	25,022	26,600
8	14,775	15,938	17,181	18,509	19,925	21,435	23,045	24,759	26,584	28,525	30,590
9	15,513	16,894	18,384	19,990	21,718	23,579	25,580	27,730	30,040	32,519	35,178
10	16,289	17,908	19,671	21,589	23,673	25,937	28,394	31,058	33,945	37,072	40,455
11	17,103	18,982	21,048	23,316	25,804	28,531	31,517	34,785	38,358	42,262	46,523
12	17,959	20,121	22,521	25,181	28,126	31,384	34,984	38,959	43,345	48,179	53,502
13	18,856	21,329	24,098	27,196	30,658	34,522	38,832	43,634	48,980	54,924	61,527
14	19,799	22,609	25,785	29,371	33,417	37,974	43,104	48,871	55,347	62,613	70,757
15	20,789	23,965	27,590	31,721	36,424	41,772	47,845	54,735	62,542	71,379	81,370
16	21,829	25,403	29,521	34,259	39,703	45,949	53,108	61,303	70,673	81,372	93,576
17	22,920	26,927	31,588	37,000	43,276	50,544	58,590	68,660	79,860	92,764	107,612
18	24,066	28,543	33,799	39,960	47,171	55,599	65,435	76,899	90,242	105,751	123,754
19	25,270	30,255	36,165	43,157	51,416	61,159	72,633	86,127	101,974	120,556	142,317
20	26,533	32,071	38,696	46,609	56,044	67,274	80,623	96,462	115,230	137,434	163,665
21	27,860	33,995	41,405	50,338	61,088	74,002	89,491	108,038	130,210	156,675	188,215
22	29,253	36,035	44,304	54,365	66,586	81,402	99,335	121,003	147,138	178,610	216,447
23	30,715	38,197	47,405	58,714	72,578	89,543	110,262	135,523	166,266	203,615	248,914
24	32,251	40,489	50,723	63,411	79,110	98,497	122,391	151,786	187,880	232,122	286,251
25	33,864	42,918	54,274	68,484	86,230	108,347	135,854	170,000	212,305	264,619	329,189
26	35,557	45,493	58,073	73,963	93,991	119,181	150,798	190,400	239,905	301,665	378,567
27	37,335	48,223	62,138	79,880	102,450	131,099	167,386	213,248	271,092	343,899	435,353
28	39,201	51,116	66,488	86,271	111,671	144,209	185,799	238,838	306,334	392,044	500,656
29	41,161	54,183	71,142	93,172	121,721	158,630	206,236	267,499	346,158	446,931	575,754
30	43,219	57,434	76,122	100,626	132,676	174,494	228,922	299,599	391,158	509,501	662,117
31	45,380	60,881	81,451	108,676	144,617	191,943	254,104	335,551	442,009	580,831	761,435
32	47,649	64,533	87,152	117,370	157,633	211,137	282,055	375,817	499,470	622,148	865,650
33	50,032	68,405	93,253	126,760	171,820	232,251	313,082	420,915	564,402	754,849	1,006,998
34	52,533	72,510	99,781	136,901	187,284	255,476	347,521	471,425	637,774	860,527	1,158,048
35	55,160	76,860	106,765	147,853	204,139	281,024	385,748	527,996	720,685	981,001	1,331,775
40	70,399	102,857	149,744	217,245	314,094	452,592	650,008	930,509	1,327,815	1,888,835	2,678,635

TABLE 4

FUTURE WORTH OF $1,200 INVESTED EACH YEAR AT VARYING RATES COMPOUNDED EACH YEAR

Rate of Return	End of Year							
	5	**10**	**15**	**20**	**25**	**30**	**35**	**40**
5%	6,631	15,903	25,894	39,679	57,272	79,727	108,384	144,960
6%	6,764	15,817	27,931	44,143	65,836	94,870	133,722	185,714
7%	6,901	16,580	30,155	49,194	75,891	113,353	165,884	239,562
8%	7,040	17,384	32,583	54,914	87,727	135,940	206,780	310,868
9%	7,182	18,231	35,233	61,392	101,641	163,569	258,853	405,459
10%	7,326	19,125	38,127	68,730	118,016	197,393	325,229	531,111
11%	7,473	20,066	41,286	77,043	137,296	238,825	409,907	698,191
12%	7,623	21,058	44,736	86,463	160,001	289,599	517,996	920,510
13%	7,776	22,104	48,501	97,136	186,743	351,839	656,017	1,216,445
14%	7,932	23,205	52,611	109,230	218,245	428,144	832,287	1,610,430
15%	8,091	24,364	57,096	122,932	255,352	521,694	1,057,404	2,134,908

TABLE 5

RATES OF RETURN AND THE INVESTMENT AMOUNTS REQUIRED TO HAVE $100,000 AVAILABLE AT END OF SPECIFIED PERIOD

Rate of Return	End of Year							
	5	**10**	**15**	**20**	**25**	**30**	**35**	**40**
5%	78,353	61,391	48,102	37,689	29,530	23,138	18,129	14,205
6%	74,726	55,839	41,727	31,180	23,300	17,411	13,011	9,722
7%	71,299	50,835	36,245	25,842	18,425	13,137	9,367	6,678
8%	68,058	46,319	31,524	21,455	14,602	9,938	6,763	4,603
9%	64,993	42,241	27,454	17,843	11,597	7,537	4,899	3,184
10%	62,092	38,554	23,940	14,864	9,230	5,731	3,558	2,209
11%	59,345	35,218	20,900	12,403	7,361	4,368	2,592	1,538
12%	56,743	32,197	18,270	10,367	5,882	3,340	1,894	1,075
13%	54,276	29,460	15,989	8,678	4,710	2,557	1,388	753.12
14%	51,937	26,974	14,010	7,276	3,780	1,963	1,019	529.43
15%	49,718	24,718	12,289	6,110	3,040	1,510	750.89	373.32
16%	47,611	22,683	10,792	5,139	2,447	1,165	554.59	264.05
17%	45,611	20,804	9,489	4,329	1,974	900.38	410.67	187.31
18%	43,711	19,107	8,352	3,651	1,596	697.49	304.88	133.27
19%	41,905	17,560	7,359	3,084	1,292	541.49	226.91	95.10
20%	40,188	16,151	6,491	2,610	1,048	421.27	169.30	68.04
21%	38,554	14,864	5,731	2,209	851.85	328.43	126.62	48.82
22%	37,000	13,690	5,065	1,874	693.43	256.57	94.93	35.12
23%	35,520	12,617	4,482	1,592	565.42	200.84	71.34	25.34
24%	34,112	11,635	3,969	1,354	461.80	157.52	53.72	18.33

TABLE 6
APPROXIMATE ANNUAL INVESTMENT REQUIRED TO EQUAL $100,000 AT VARYING RATES

Rate of Return	End of Year							
	5	10	15	20	25	30	35	40
5%	17,236	7,572	4,414	2,880	1,966	1,433	1,054	788
6%	16,736	7,157	4,053	2,565	1,720	1,193	847	610
7%	16,254	6,764	3,719	2,280	1,478	989	656	468
8%	15,783	6,392	3,410	2,024	1,267	817	537	357
9%	15,332	6,039	3,125	1,793	1,083	673	425	272
10%	14,890	5,704	2,861	1,587	924	552	335	205
11%	14,467	5,388	2,618	1,403	787	453	263	155
12%	14,055	5,088	2,395	1,239	670	370	206	116
13%	13,658	4,805	2,190	1,070	569	302	168	87
14%	13,270	4,536	2,001	964	482	246	126	65
15%	12,898	4,283	1,828	849	409	200	99	49

APPENDIX II

TAX RATE
SCHEDULES

1993 Federal Tax Rates for Individuals

Taxable Income	Tax Rate	Tax Rate Including Federal Surtax
$29,590 or less	17%	17.5%
$29,591 to $59,180	26%	26.8%
$59,181 to $62,195*	29%	30.0%
$62,196 and above	29%	31.3%

* This is the point at which federal tax reaches $12,500, and the federal surtax increases from 3.0% to 8.0%.

1993 Provincial Tax Rates for Individuals

	Provincial Tax				Maximum Combined Fed/Prov Rate
	Basic Rate	Surtax	Flat Tax	Maximum Rate*	
Newfoundland	69.0%			69.0%	51.3%
Nova Scotia (1)	59.5%	10.0%		65.5%	50.3%
Prince Edward Island (2)	59.5%	10.0%		65.5%	50.3%
New Brunswick (3)	62.0%	8.0%		67.0%	50.7%
Quebec (4)		10.0%		26.4%	52.9%
Ontario (5)	58.0%	17.0%		72.5%	52.3%
Manitoba (6)	52.0%	2.0%	2.0%	65.8%	50.4%
Saskatchewan (7)	50.0%	15.0%	2.0%	71.0%	51.9%
Alberta (8)	45.5%	8.0%	0.5%	51.0%	46.1%
British Columbia (9)	52.5%	20.0%		68.3%	51.1%
Northwest Territories	45.0%			45.0%	44.4%
Yukon (10)	50.0%	5.0%		52.5%	46.5%

* Expressed as a percentage of the basic federal tax except for Quebec.

Notes to Provincial Personal Tax Rate Table:

1) The 10% surtax applies on provincial tax in excess of $10,000. At the time of printing, Nova Scotia has not yet tabled a budget.

2) A 10% provincial surtax applies on provincial tax in excess of $12,500.

3) New Brunswick imposes an 8% surtax on provincial tax in excess of $13,500.

4) The full Quebec rate table is provided below. Note that residents of Quebec receive an abatement of 16.5% of basic federal tax. The maximum rate applies to Quebec taxable income.

5) The surtax on Ontario tax between $5,500 and $8,000 is 17% and the surtax on Ontario tax in excess of $8,000 is 25%.

6) In Manitoba, the 2% flat tax is calculated on net income. The 2% surtax is calculated on net income in excess of $30,000.

7) Saskatchewan levies a 2% flat rate tax on net income. A 15% provincial surtax applies to Saskatchewan tax (including the flat tax) in excess of $4,000. An additional "deficit" surtax of 10% applies to Saskatchewan basic tax plus the flat tax.

8) Alberta's 0.5% flat tax is applied to taxable income. The 8% surtax is calculated on Alberta tax (excluding the flat tax) in excess of $3,500.

9) A 20% surtax applies to B.C. tax in excess of $5,300. An additional 10% surtax applies on tax in excess of $9,000. Thus tax in excess of $9,000 is subject to surtax at 30% in 1993.

10) For 1993 and subsequent years a surtax of 5% applies to Yukon tax in excess of $6,000.

1993 Quebec Marginal Tax Rates for Individuals

Quebec Taxable Income	Tax Rate (1)
$0 to $7,000	16.0%
$7,001 to $14,000	19.0%
$14,001 to $23,000	21.0%
$23,001 to $50,000	23.0%
over $50,000	24.0%

(1) Quebec has introduced a surtax of 5.0% on Quebec tax in excess of $5,000. This surtax increases to 10% when Quebec tax exceeds $10,000.

1993 Federal Marginal Tax Rates for Individuals Resident in Quebec

Taxable Income	Tax Rate Including Federal Surtax*
$29,590 or less	14.7%
$29,591 to $59,180	22.5%
$59,181 to $62,195	25.1%
$62,196 and above	26.5%

* These rates take into account the 16.5% federal abatement for Quebec residents.

APPENDIX III

CALCULATION OF NET TAX PAYABLE

CALCULATION OF NET TAX PAYABLE

Taxable Income (per Form 11 or 14) $ _____

Federal Tax

     17% on first $29,590* $ _____

     26% on next $29,590   _____

     29% on balance   _____

     Total $ _____

Tax Credits (federal portion only)

     UI/CPP contributions credit   _____

     Tuition credit   _____

     Education credit   _____

     Dividend tax credit (13 1/3% of the taxable amount of
       Canadian dividend income received)   _____

     Medical expenses credit   _____

     Charitable donations credit   _____

     Pension income credit   _____

     Basic credit   _____

     Married credit   _____

     Equivalent-to-married credit   _____

     Dependant credit   _____

     Age 65 and older credit   _____

     Disability credit   _____

     Credits transferred from spouse   _____

     Credits transferred from other dependants   _____

     Total federal tax credits $ _____

Total Federal Tax Before Surtax
     (total federal tax previously calculated
     minus total federal tax credits)   _____

Add 3.0% federal surtax   _____

Add high income federal surtax (8.0% of federal tax
     over $12,500)   _____

Less federal GST credit   _____

Total Federal Tax $ _____

Provincial Tax — see Appendix II for rate   _____

Total Taxes Payable $ _____

* These are the 1993 tax brackets. Tax brackets for 1994 and future years will be increased to reflect the annual increase in the Consumers Price Index at September 30 of the previous year less a 3% threshold.

Note: This worksheet does not include a calculation of alternative minimum tax. If this tax applies, your total taxes payable will be higher than the amount calculated here.

YOUR PERSONAL FINANCIAL PLANNER

Your Personal Financial Planner

Contents

INSURANCE

ESTATE PLANNING

ACTION

File under PERSONAL DATA

Date: _____

FORM 1   PERSONAL AND FAMILY DATA

1. **YOU**
   Name: _____   Birth Date: _____

   Social Insurance Number: _____

2. **YOUR SPOUSE**
   Name: _____   Birth Date: _____

   Social Insurance Number: _____

3. **YOUR PRESENT HOME**
   Address: _____

   _____

4. **YOUR OCCUPATION**
   Business Address: _____

   Employer's Name: _____

   Address: _____

   Phone: _____

   Your Job Title: _____

5. **SPOUSE'S OCCUPATION**
   Business Address: _____

   Employer's Name: _____

   Address: _____

   Phone: _____

   Spouse's Job Title: _____

6. CHILDREN

Name	Birth Date	Social Insurance Number
_____	_____	_____
_____	_____	_____
_____	_____	_____
_____	_____	_____
_____	_____	_____
_____	_____	_____
_____	_____	_____
_____	_____	_____
_____	_____	_____
_____	_____	_____
_____	_____	_____
_____	_____	_____

7. GRANDCHILDREN

Name	Birth Date	Social Insurance Number
_____	_____	_____
_____	_____	_____
_____	_____	_____
_____	_____	_____
_____	_____	_____
_____	_____	_____
_____	_____	_____
_____	_____	_____

8. OTHERS DEPENDENT ON YOU

Name	Relationship	Social Insurance Number	Amount of Annual Support
_____	_____	_____	_____
_____	_____	_____	_____
_____	_____	_____	_____
_____	_____	_____	_____
_____	_____	_____	_____
_____	_____	_____	_____
_____	_____	_____	_____
_____	_____	_____	_____
_____	_____	_____	_____
_____	_____	_____	_____

File under FINANCIAL DOCUMENTS

Date: _____

FORM 2   FINANCIAL DOCUMENTS

USE THE FOLLOWING LOCATION CODE:

SD	Safe deposit box located at _____
HF	At home in fireproof file cabinet
HD	At home in desk
HS	At home in safe
LA	Lawyer's office
BR	Broker's office
	Other (describe below)

_____   _____

_____   _____

_____   _____

	DESCRIPTION	LOCATION
Your Will	_____	_____
Spouse's Will	_____	_____
Trust Agreements	_____	_____
Mortgages	_____	_____
	_____	_____
	_____	_____
Loans	_____	_____
	_____	_____
	_____	_____
Property Deeds	_____	_____
	_____	_____
	_____	_____
	_____	_____
Car and other Vehicle Titles	_____	_____
	_____	_____
	_____	_____

Stock Certificates

_____   _____

_____   _____

Stock Options

_____   _____

Stock Purchase Plan

_____   _____

Bonds

_____   _____

_____   _____

Canada Savings Bonds

_____   _____

Term deposit
Certificates

_____   _____

_____   _____

Real Estate Contracts

_____   _____

_____   _____

_____   _____

Chequing Accounts

_____   _____

_____   _____

Savings Passbooks

_____   _____

_____   _____

Life Insurance
Policies

_____   _____

_____   _____

_____   _____

Insurance Policies

_____   _____

RRSP Agreements

_____   _____

Employer Pension Plans

_____   _____

DPSP Agreements

_____   _____

Birth Certificates

_____   _____

_____   _____

_____   _____

Deloitte & Touche Canadian Guide to Personal Financial Management © 1993 Deloitte & Touche

Marriage Contracts

Marriage Licences

Divorce Papers

Notes Receivable

Notes Payable

Employment Contracts

Income Tax Returns

Financial Surveys

Insurance Surveys

Safe Deposit Keys

Who has access to your safe deposit box? _____

In whose name is the safe deposit box registered? _____

Other Records and
Valuables

File under FINANCIAL DOCUMENTS   Date: _____

FORM 3   FINANCIAL ADVISORS

List advisors who currently assist you in your financial affairs.

LAWYER

Name: _____   Street: _____

Firm: _____   City, Province: _____

                                           Phone: _____

Name: _____   Street: _____

Firm: _____   City, Province: _____

                                           Phone: _____

BANKING OFFICER

Name: _____   Street: _____

Firm: _____   City, Province: _____

                                           Phone: _____

Name: _____   Street: _____

Firm: _____   City, Province: _____

                                           Phone: _____

BROKER

Name: _____   Street: _____

Firm: _____   City, Province: _____

                                           Phone: _____

Name: _____   Street: _____

Firm: _____   City, Province: _____

                                           Phone: _____

CHARTERED ACCOUNTANT

Name: _____   Street: _____

Firm: _____   City, Province: _____

Phone: _____

Name: _____   Street: _____

Firm: _____   City, Province: _____

Phone: _____

INSURANCE AGENT

Name: _____   Street: _____

Firm: _____   City, Province: _____

Phone: _____

Name: _____   Street: _____

Firm: _____   City, Province: _____

Phone: _____

INVESTMENT ADVISOR

Name: _____   Street: _____

Firm: _____   City, Province: _____

Phone: _____

Name: _____   Street: _____

Firm: _____   City, Province: _____

Phone: _____

OTHERS

Name _____   Street: _____

Firm: _____   City, Province: _____

                                   Phone: _____

Name: _____   Street: _____

Firm: _____   City, Province: _____

                                   Phone: _____

To which of these would you turn to discuss a serious business problem or an important financial decision?

_____

_____

_____

_____

File under FINANCIAL PROFILE

Date: _____

FORM 4   STATEMENT OF NET WORTH

WHAT YOU OWN	ESTIMATED CURRENT VALUE	% OF TOTAL ASSET VALUE

1.   LIQUID ASSETS

Cash (chequing, savings accounts):

_____   _____

Short-term Investments
  Treasury Bills:

_____   _____

  Short-term Deposits:

_____   _____

  Money Market Funds:

_____   _____

Cash Surrender Value of Life Insurance

_____   _____

  TOTAL Liquid Assets

_____   _____

2.   INVESTMENT ASSETS

Canada Savings Bonds

_____   _____

Term Deposits

_____   _____

Marketable Securities
  Stocks:

_____   _____

  Bonds:

_____   _____

  Mutual Funds:

_____   _____

Real Estate (investment)

_____   _____

Tax Incentive Investments

_____   _____

Other Investment Assets (describe below)

_____   _____

  a. _____

_____   _____

  b. _____

_____   _____

  c. _____

_____   _____

  d. _____

_____   _____

Retirement Funds
  RRSPs

_____   _____

  Employer Pension Plan

_____   _____

Deloitte & Touche Canadian Guide to Personal Financial Management © 1993 Deloitte & Touche

	ESTIMATED CURRENT VALUE	% OF TOTAL ASSET VALUE
DPSPs		
Other		
TOTAL Investment Assets		

3. PERSONAL ASSETS

Residence		
Vacation Property		
Art, Antiques		
Furnishings		
Vehicles		
Boats		
Other		
TOTAL Personal Assets		
TOTAL ASSETS		

WHAT YOU OWE

	ESTIMATED CURRENT VALUE	INTEREST RATE	INTEREST DEDUCTIBLE
4. SHORT-TERM OBLIGATIONS			
Consumer Credit Obligations			
Personal Loans			
Installment Loans			
Borrowings on Life Insurance			
Accrued Income Taxes			
Other Obligations (describe below)			
a.			
b.			
c.			
d.			
TOTAL Short-term Obligations			

5. **LONG-TERM OBLIGATIONS**

	ESTIMATED CURRENT VALUE	INTEREST RATE	INTEREST DEDUCTIBLE
Mortgage on personal residences	_____	_____	_____
Loans to purchase investment assets	_____	_____	_____
Loans to purchase personal assets	_____	_____	_____
TOTAL Long-term Obligations	_____	_____	_____
TOTAL LIABILITIES	_____	_____	_____

TOTAL ASSETS	_____
− TOTAL LIABILITIES	_____
= NET WORTH	_____

Deloitte & Touche Canadian Guide to Personal Financial Management © 1993 Deloitte & Touche

Date: _____

FORM 5   ANALYSIS OF NET WORTH

		AMOUNT	PERCENT
LIQUIDITY			
1. Total Liquid Assets	_____		
2. Total Short-term Obligations	(_____)		
3. Excess (Deficiency) of Liquid Assets		_____	_____
INVESTMENT ASSETS			
4. Total Investment Assets	_____		
5. Total Long-term Investment Loans	(_____)		
6. Total Equity in Investment Assets		_____	_____
PERSONAL ASSETS			
7. Total Personal Assets	_____		
8. Total Long-term Personal Loans	(_____)		
9. Total Equity in Personal Assets		_____	_____
10. **TOTAL NET WORTH**	_____		

Deloitte & Touche Canadian Guide to Personal Financial Management © 1993 Deloitte & Touche

File under FINANCIAL PROFILE   Date: _____

FORM 6   INCOME SOURCES

	YOU	SPOUSE	TOTAL
1. INCOME FROM EMPLOYMENT			
Gross Salary	_____	_____	_____
Commissions	_____	_____	_____
Self-employment	_____	_____	_____
Other	_____	_____	_____
TOTAL Employment Income	_____	_____	_____
2. INVESTMENT INCOME			
Interest	_____	_____	_____
Dividends	_____	_____	_____
Rents (net of cash expenses)	_____	_____	_____
Annuities	_____	_____	_____
Old Age Security	_____	_____	_____
Canada/Quebec Pension Plan Benefits	_____	_____	_____
Other Pension Income	_____	_____	_____
Trust Fund	_____	_____	_____
Other	_____	_____	_____
TOTAL Income from Investments	_____	_____	_____
TOTAL Income from All Sources	_____	_____	_____
Investment Income as Percentage of Total Income			_____

Date: _____

FORM 7   BASIC LIFESTYLE EXPENDITURES

	AMOUNT	**PERCENT**
1. HOUSING		
Mortgage or Rent	_____	_____
Property Taxes	_____	_____
Insurance	_____	_____
Utilities	_____	_____
Other Housing Costs	_____	_____
TOTAL Housing Costs	_____	_____
2. FOOD	_____	_____
3. CLOTHING	_____	_____
4. TRANSPORTATION		
Loan Payments	_____	_____
Insurance	_____	_____
Fuel	_____	_____
Maintenance	_____	_____
Other Transportation	_____	_____
TOTAL Transportation Expenditures	_____	_____
5. PHONE	_____	_____
6. HOUSEHOLD PURCHASES AND SUPPLIES	_____	_____
7. HOUSE CLEANING AND HOUSEHOLD HELP	_____	_____
8. EDUCATION (not private secondary and university)	_____	_____
9. RECREATION AND CLUB MEMBERSHIP	_____	_____
10. PERSONAL CARE AND IMPROVEMENTS	_____	_____

Deloitte & Touche Canadian Guide to Personal Financial Management © 1993 Deloitte & Touche

	AMOUNT	PERCENT
11. **INSURANCE**		
Medical and Dental, Health and Disability Insurance	_____	_____
Life Insurance	_____	_____
Liability Insurance	_____	_____
Other Insurance	_____	_____
TOTAL Insurance Expenditures	_____	_____
12. **YARD MAINTENANCE**	_____	_____
13. **DEBT REDUCTION (exclude home and autos)**	_____	_____
14. **CHARITABLE CONTRIBUTIONS**	_____	_____
15. **OTHER BASIC LIFESTYLE COSTS**	_____	_____
TOTAL Basic Lifestyle Expenditures	_____	_____
Average Monthly Amount	_____	_____

Date: _____

FORM 8   DISCRETIONARY EXPENDITURES

	AMOUNT	PERCENT
1. EDUCATION (private secondary schools and university)	_____	_____
2. ENTERTAINMENT AND EATING OUT	_____	_____
3. REGULAR VACATIONS	_____	_____
4. EXTRAORDINARY CHARITABLE EXPENDITURES	_____	_____
5. HOBBIES	_____	_____
6. PERSONAL GIFTS	_____	_____
7. SUPPORT OF RELATIVES AND OTHERS		
Name _____	_____	_____
Name _____	_____	_____
Name _____	_____	_____
8. HOME IMPROVEMENTS	_____	_____
9. PURCHASE OF AUTOMOBILES, BOATS, ETC.	_____	_____
10. RETIREMENT PLANS		
Type _____	_____	_____
Type _____	_____	_____
Type _____	_____	_____
11. DEBT REDUCTIONS	_____	_____
12. OTHER		
_____	_____	_____
_____	_____	_____
_____	_____	_____
TOTAL Discretionary Expenditures	_____	_____
AVERAGE Monthly Amount	_____	_____

Deloitte & Touche Canadian Guide to Personal Financial Management © 1993 Deloitte & Touche

File under FINANCIAL PROFILE   Date: _____

FORM 9   INCOME TAXES AND OTHER DEDUCTIONS

1. **TAXABLE INCOME**   _____

2. **FEDERAL INCOME TAX**   _____

3. **PROVINCIAL INCOME TAX**   _____

4. **OTHER DEDUCTIONS**

    Canada/Quebec Pension Plan   _____

    Unemployment Insurance   _____

    Provincial Hospital Insurance
    (if applicable)   _____   _____

5. **TOTAL INCOME TAXES AND OTHER DEDUCTIONS**   _____

Date: _____

FORM 10   ANALYSIS OF EARNED INCOME AND EXPENDITURES

		AMOUNT	PERCENT OF TOTAL INCOME
1.	**TOTAL INCOME FROM EMPLOYMENT**	_____	_100%_
2.	**EXPENDITURES**		
	Basic Lifestyle	_____	_____
	Discretionary	_____	_____
	Income Tax and Other Deductions	_____	_____
3.	**TOTAL EXPENDITURES**	_____	_____
4.	**EXCESS (Deficiency)**	_____	_____

File under TAX PLANNING

Date: _____

FORM 11   INCOME TAX PLANNING WORKSHEET

	LAST YEAR	CURRENT YEAR
1. TOTAL INCOME		
(a) (i) Income from employment	_____	_____
(ii) Less allowable expenses	_____	_____
(iii) Net employment earnings	_____	_____
(b) Pension Income		
(i) Old Age Security and Canada or Quebec Pension Plan benefits	_____	_____
(ii) Other pension income	_____	_____
(c) Income from other sources		
(i) Unemployment Insurance benefits	_____	_____
(ii) Taxable amount of dividends from Canadian companies	_____	_____
(iii) Interest and other investment income	_____	_____
(iv) Rental income (loss)	_____	_____
(v) Taxable capital gains	_____	_____
(d) Self-employed income	_____	_____
(i) Business income		
(ii) Professional income	_____	_____
(iii) Commission income	_____	_____
(iv) Farming or fishing income	_____	_____
(e) Total income	_____	_____
2. DEDUCTIONS FROM TOTAL INCOME	_____	_____
(a) Registered pension plan contributions		
(b) Registered Retirement Savings Plan contributions	_____	_____
(c) Union and professional dues	_____	_____

	LAST YEAR	CURRENT YEAR
(d) Child care expenses		
(e) Allowable business investment losses		
(f) Other deductions		
(g) Total deductions		
3. NET INCOME		
4. OTHER DEDUCTIONS FROM NET INCOME		
(a) Non-capital losses of other years		
(b) Net Capital losses of other years (1972 - 1985)		
(c) Taxable capital gains exemption		
(d) Total other deductions		
5. (a) TAXABLE INCOME		
(b) Tax bracket		
6. (a) TARGETED TAXABLE INCOME		
(b) Targeted Tax Bracket		

File under TAX PLANNING   Date: _____

FORM 12   TAX-SAVING IDEAS

TAX-SAVING IDEA

Tax-Free Income: _____

_____

Tax-Favoured Income: _____

_____

Tax-Deferred Income: _____

_____

Tax-Sheltered Income: _____

_____

Shifting Income to Dependants: _____

_____

Tax-Deductible Expenditures: _____

_____

Action	Action Date	Funds Needed	Reduction of Taxable Income
Tax-Free Income	_____	_____	_____
	_____	_____	_____
Tax-Favoured Income	_____	_____	_____
	_____	_____	_____
Tax-Deferred Income	_____	_____	_____
	_____	_____	_____
Tax-Sheltered Investments	_____	_____	_____
	_____	_____	_____

Deloitte & Touche Canadian Guide to Personal Financial Management © 1993 Deloitte & Touche

Action	Action Date	Funds Needed	Reduction of Taxable Income
Shift Income to Dependants	_____	_____	_____
	_____	_____	_____
Tax Deductible Expenditures	_____	_____	_____
	_____	_____	_____
TOTALS	_____	_____	_____

File under TAX PLANNING

Date: _____

FORM 13A   CAPITAL GAINS AND LOSSES REALIZED TO DATE

Number of Units	Investment Type	Date Acquired	Adjusted Cost Base	Date Sold	Net Proceeds	Gain (Loss)
_____	_____	_____	_____	_____	_____	_____
_____	_____	_____	_____	_____	_____	_____
_____	_____	_____	_____	_____	_____	_____
_____	_____	_____	_____	_____	_____	_____
_____	_____	_____	_____	_____	_____	_____
_____	_____	_____	_____	_____	_____	_____
_____	_____	_____	_____	_____	_____	_____
_____	_____	_____	_____	_____	_____	_____
_____	_____	_____	_____	_____	_____	_____
_____	_____	_____	_____	_____	_____	_____

Capital Gains Dividends
    (received from mutual funds)   _____

Capital Loss Carry-overs*
    (full amount of loss)   (_____)

Total   _____

Taxable Capital Gains
    (Allowable Capital Losses)
    three-quarters × Total   _____

Cumulative Taxable Capital Gains
    exemption available (three-quarters of Cumulative
    Capital Gains exemption available)   _____

Taxable Capital Gains
    (Allowable Capital Losses)
    to be included in Taxable income   _____

* Up to $2,000.00 of allowable capital losses realized before May 23, 1985 can be claimed to reduce taxable income from any source. Capital losses realized after May 22, 1985 cannot be used to reduce taxable income other than capital gains.

File under TAX PLANNING

Date: _____

FORM 13B   UNREALIZED CAPITAL GAINS OR LOSSES IN CURRENT INVESTMENTS

Number of Units	Investment Type	Date Acquired	Adjusted Cost Base	Current Market Value	Unrealized Gain (Loss)
_____	_____	_____	_____	_____	_____
_____	_____	_____	_____	_____	_____
_____	_____	_____	_____	_____	_____
_____	_____	_____	_____	_____	_____
_____	_____	_____	_____	_____	_____
_____	_____	_____	_____	_____	_____
_____	_____	_____	_____	_____	_____
_____	_____	_____	_____	_____	_____
_____	_____	_____	_____	_____	_____
_____	_____	_____	_____	_____	_____

**Total Unrealized
Capital
Gains and Losses**   _____

Deloitte & Touche Canadian Guide to Personal Financial Management © 1993 Deloitte & Touche

File under TAX PLANNING

Date: _____

FORM 14   YEAR-END TAX PLAN

	ACTUAL TO DATE	ESTIMATES TO YEAR END	ESTIMATES TOTAL
1. TOTAL INCOME			
(a) (i) Income from employment	_____	_____	_____
(ii) Less allowable expenses	_____	_____	_____
(iii) Net employment earnings	_____	_____	_____
(b) Pension income			
(i) Old Age Security and Canada or Quebec Pension Plan benefits	_____	_____	_____
(ii) Other pension income	_____	_____	_____
(c) Income from other sources			
(i) Unemployment Insurance benefits	_____	_____	_____
(ii) Taxable amount of dividends from Canadian companies	_____	_____	_____
(iii) Interest and other investment income	_____	_____	_____
(iv) Rental income (loss)	_____	_____	_____
(v) Taxable capital gains	_____	_____	_____
(d) Self-employed income	_____	_____	_____
(i) Business income	_____	_____	_____
(ii) Professional income	_____	_____	
(iii) Commission income	_____	_____	_____
(iv) Farming or fishing income	_____	_____	_____
(e) Total income	_____	_____	_____

	ACTUAL TO DATE	ESTIMATES TO YEAR END	ESTIMATES TOTAL
2. DEDUCTIONS FROM TOTAL INCOME			
(a) Registered pension plan contributions	_____	_____	_____
(b) Registered Retirement Savings Plan contributions	_____	_____	_____
(c) Union and professional dues	_____	_____	_____
(d) Child care expenses	_____	_____	_____
(e) Allowable business investment losses	_____	_____	_____
(f) Other deductions	_____	_____	_____
(g) Total deductions	_____	_____	_____
3. NET INCOME	_____	_____	_____
4. OTHER DEDUCTIONS FROM NET INCOME	_____	_____	_____
(a) Non-capital losses of other years	_____	_____	_____
(b) Net capital losses of other years (1972 - 1985)	_____	_____	_____
(c) Taxable capital gains exemption	_____	_____	_____
(d) Total other deductions	_____	_____	_____
5. (a) TAXABLE INCOME	_____	_____	_____
(b) Tax bracket	_____	_____	_____
6. (a) TARGETED TAXABLE INCOME			_____
(b) Targeted Tax Bracket			_____

Deloitte & Touche Canadian Guide to Personal Financial Management © 1993 Deloitte & Touche

File under TAX PLANNING   Date: _____

FORM 15   YEAR-END TAX ACTION

Estimated Taxable Income Current Year
   (from Form 14, line 6(a))   _____

Targeted Taxable Income Current Year
   (from Form 14, line 7(a))   _____

Reduction in Taxable Income Required   _____

YEAR-END TAX-PLANNING ACTIONS	CASH REQUIRED	REDUCTION IN TAXABLE INCOME CURRENT YEAR
_____	_____	_____
_____	_____	_____
_____	_____	_____
_____	_____	_____
_____	_____	_____
_____	_____	_____
_____	_____	_____
_____	_____	_____
_____	_____	_____
TOTALS	_____	_____

Date: _____

FORM 16   FINANCIAL SECURITY

1. **What does financial security mean to you?**

_____

_____

_____

AMOUNT

Annual Income (today's dollars) _____   _____

Investment Assets_____   _____

Net Worth _____   _____

Debt Level_____   _____

Other

_____   _____

_____   _____

_____   _____

2. **When (how many years from now) would you like to achieve financial security?**

_____

3. **List the three greatest obstacles to your achieving financial security (as you defined it in Question 1):**

_____

_____

_____

Deloitte & Touche Canadian Guide to Personal Financial Management © 1993 Deloitte & Touche

File under FINANCIAL OBJECTIVES   Date: _____

FORM 17   INCOME AND EXPENDITURE OBJECTIVES

1.   Estimate employment income for each year:

	CURRENT YEAR	NEXT YEAR	THIRD YEAR
Your Income	_____	_____	_____
Spouse's Income	_____	_____	_____

2.   By what percentage could you reduce your basic lifestyle expenditures if you really wanted to?

_____

3.   By what percentage could you reduce your discretionary expenditures if you really wanted to?

_____

4.   What major discretionary expenditures other than education do you plan to incur in the next three years?

_____

	AMOUNT	YEAR
Cars	_____	_____
Boat	_____	_____
Extended Travel	_____	_____
Major Home Improvements	_____	_____
Major Charitable Contributions	_____	_____
Other		
_____	_____	_____
_____	_____	_____
_____	_____	_____

File under FINANCIAL OBJECTIVES   Date: _____

FORM 18   EDUCATION AND OTHER SUPPORT OF CHILDREN

1.   PRIVATE ELEMENTARY AND SECONDARY SCHOOLS

CHILD	AGE	YEARS OF SCHOOLING	YEAR BEGINNING	YEARLY COST	TOTAL COST
_____	_____	_____	_____	_____	_____
_____	_____	_____	_____	_____	_____
_____	_____	_____	_____	_____	_____
_____	_____	_____	_____	_____	_____
_____	_____	_____	_____	_____	_____
_____	_____	_____	_____	_____	_____
_____	_____	_____	_____	_____	_____

TOTAL Estimated Cost   _____

2.   COLLEGE AND UNIVERSITY EDUCATION

CHILD	AGE	YEARS OF SCHOOLING	YEAR BEGINNING	YEARLY COST	TOTAL COST
_____	_____	_____	_____	_____	_____
_____	_____	_____	_____	_____	_____
_____	_____	_____	_____	_____	_____
_____	_____	_____	_____	_____	_____
_____	_____	_____	_____	_____	_____
_____	_____	_____	_____	_____	_____
_____	_____	_____	_____	_____	_____

TOTAL Estimated Cost   _____

Deloitte & Touche Canadian Guide to Personal Financial Management © 1993 Deloitte & Touche

3. **ASSETS SET ASIDE FOR EDUCATION**

CHILD	TYPE OF ASSET	AMOUNT	HOW HELD

4. **OTHER SUPPORT OF CHILDREN**

CHILD	REASON FOR SUPPORT	NUMBER OF YEARS	YEARLY COST	TOTAL COST
	TOTAL Estimated Cost			

Deloitte & Touche Canadian Guide to Personal Financial Management © 1993 Deloitte & Touche

File under FINANCIAL OBJECTIVES   Date: _____

FORM 19   RETIREMENT PLANNING

1. When do you plan to retire? _____

    Your age at retirement? _____

    Number of years from now? _____

2. Do you or your spouse have any health problems that might make you retire at an earlier date?

    Explain: _____

    _____

    _____

3. If you retired tomorrow, with all educational expenditures behind you, and no one depended on you financially, how much spendable after-tax income would you and your spouse need for one year at today's prices? _____

4. Estimate your retirement income from various sources.

SOURCE	ESTIMATED ANNUAL AMOUNT AT RETIREMENT AGE
Retirement plan from company	_____
Retirement benefits from previous employer(s)	_____
Old Age Security	_____
Canada/Quebec Pension Plan	_____
Registered Retirement Savings Plan(s)	_____
Spouse's Retirement Plan	_____
Deferred Compensation	_____
Investment Assets	_____
Other Sources	_____
_____	_____
TOTAL	_____

Deloitte & Touche Canadian Guide to Personal Financial Management © 1993 Deloitte & Touche

5. What do you estimate your investment assets will be worth at retirement age?

    _____

6. When you retire, will you sell your house? _____
    If yes, will you

    Buy another?   _____

    Rent?   _____

    Relocate?   _____

    Based on your anticipated retirement age and housing arrangements, would your housing expenditures, at present prices, be higher or lower in retirement than they are today?

    _____ % higher   _____ % lower

    Why? _____

File under INVESTMENT STRATEGY   Date: ___95-0210___

FORM 20   INVESTMENT OBJECTIVES

Indicate the relative importance you attribute to the following considerations by placing the appropriate number after each statement.

NOT IMPORTANT	1
MARGINALLY IMPORTANT	2
REASONABLY IMPORTANT	3
DEFINITELY IMPORTANT	4
MOST IMPORTANT	5

Diversification	How important is it for you to hedge against big losses by spreading your risks?	4
Liquidity	How important is it that you have cash available for emergencies or investment opportunities?	5
Safety	If we went into a deep economic depression, how important would it be for you to sell your investments at about the price you paid for them?	5
Current Income	How important is it that you get maximum income from your investments this year and next?	3
Future Appreciation	How important is it that your investment dollars keep pace with inflation or do better than inflation?	4
Tax Advantage	How important is it that you get all the tax relief that may be available to you?	5
Leverage	How important is it for you to use borrowed money in hopes of reaping a higher return on your investment?	3
Ease of Management	How important is it for you to have investments you do not have to watch or worry about?	2

Deloitte & Touche Canadian Guide to Personal Financial Management © 1993 Deloitte & Touche

File under INVESTMENT STRATEGY   Date: _____95-02-10_____

FORM 21   REVIEW OF YOUR PRESENT INVESTMENTS

TYPE OF ASSET	CURRENT VALUE	% OF TOTAL	INVESTMENT OBJECTIVES	CURRENT INCOME	APPR'N (LOSS)	ANNUAL RATE OF RETURN
Cash	13,000	10.5%	Liquidity & safety	4%		4%
Condo	60,000	48.5%	Growth	loss		( )
RRSP's	50,500	41.0%	Tax deferred growth	6%		6%
		1%				
	3,000	1.0%				
		4.45%				
TOTAL	123,500	100%				

File under INVESTMENT STRATEGY

Date: _____

FORM 22   YOUR INVESTMENT STRATEGY

1. What investment objectives (see Form 20) will be most important for you during the next three years?

    Tax Shelter, Growth
    _____

    _____

2. What do you assume the inflation rate will be during the next three years?

    _3%_
    _____

3. What overall annual pre-tax return on your investments do you want to achieve in the next three years?

    _8%_
    _____

4. What specific changes do you have to make in your present investments to achieve your objectives and overall rate of return in the next three years?

    Decrease real estate investments
    _____

    _____

5. What annual amount do you believe you can set aside for investment during the next three years?

    Very little — $5,000 to $10,000 —
    _____

6. What investments will you make with your additional investment dollars?

    _____

    _____

    _____

Deloitte & Touche Canadian Guide to Personal Financial Management © 1993 Deloitte & Touche

File under EDUCATIONAL FINANCING   Date: _____

FORM 23   UNIVERSITY, GRADUATE SCHOOL AND COLLEGE COSTS

1. Children's Names   _____   _____   _____

2. Ages of Children   ___/_____   _____   _____

3. Number of Years until University   _____   _____   _____

4. Estimated Number of Years in
    University and Graduate School   _____   _____   _____

5. Number of Years for
    Inflation Adjustment   _____   _____   _____

6. Estimated Annual Inflation Rate
    between Now and End
    of Education   _____   _____   _____

7. Inflation Factor   _____   _____   _____

8. Estimated Annual University Costs
    in Today's Dollars   _____   _____   _____

9. Estimated Annual Costs Adjusted   _____   _____   _____

10. Estimated TOTAL Costs Adjusted   _____   _____   _____

11. Estimated After-tax Rate of Return
    on Educational Funds   _____   _____   _____

12. Compound Factor for Rate of
    Return on Line 11   _____   _____   _____

13. Present Value of Funds Set Aside
    for Education   _____   _____   _____

14. Future Value of Funds Set Aside   _____   _____   _____

15. Annual Amount to be Invested
    for Education   _____   _____   _____

File under RETIREMENT PLANNING   Date: _____

FORM 24   ESTIMATED BASIC LIFESTYLE EXPENDITURES AT RETIREMENT

	CURRENT YEAR	AT RETIREMENT
1. Housing		
Mortgage or Rent	_____	_____
Property Taxes	_____	_____
Insurance	_____	_____
Utilities	_____	_____
Other Housing Costs	_____	_____
TOTAL Housing Costs	_____	_____
2. Food	_____	_____
3. Clothing	_____	_____
4. Transportation		
Loan Payments	_____	_____
Insurance	_____	_____
Fuel	_____	_____
Maintenance	_____	_____
Other Transportation	_____	_____
TOTAL Transportation Expenditures	_____	_____
5. Phone	_____	_____
6. Household Purchases and Supplies	_____	_____
7. House Cleaning and Household Help	_____	_____
8. Education (not secondary or university)	_____	_____
9. Recreation and Club Membership	_____	_____
10. Personal Care and Improvements	_____	_____
11. Medical and Dental, Health and Disability	_____	_____
12. Life Insurance	_____	_____

	CURRENT YEAR	AT RETIREMENT
13. Liability Insurance	_____	_____
14. Other Insurance	_____	_____
15. Yard Maintenance	_____	_____
16. Debt Reduction (exclude home and autos)	_____	_____
17. Charitable Contributions	_____	_____
18. Other Basic Lifestyle Costs	_____	_____
19. TOTAL Basic Lifestyle Expenditures	_____	_____

20. Number of Years to Retirement   _____

21. Average Annual Rate of Inflation   _____

22. Inflation Factor
    (from Table 1 in Appendix I)   _____

23. TOTAL of Projected Annual Basic Lifestyle
    Expenditures Adjusted for Inflation   _____

File under RETIREMENT PLANNING   Date: _____

FORM 25   ESTIMATED DISCRETIONARY EXPENDITURES AT RETIREMENT

	CURRENT YEAR	AT RETIREMENT
1. Education (Private Secondary Schools and University)	_____	_____
2. Entertainment and Eating Out	_____	_____
3. Regular Vacations	_____	_____
4. Extraordinary Charitable Expenditures	_____	_____
5. Hobbies	_____	_____
6. Personal Gifts	_____	_____
7. Support of Relatives and Others:		
_____	_____	_____
_____	_____	_____
_____	_____	_____
8. Home Improvements	_____	_____
9. Purchase of Automobiles, Boat, etc.	_____	_____
10. Retirement Plans	_____	_____
11. Debt Reductions	_____	_____
12. Other:		
_____	_____	_____
_____	_____	_____
_____	_____	_____
13. TOTAL	_____	_____
14. Inflation Factor _____		
15. TOTAL Projected Annual Discretionary Expenditures Adjusted for Inflation		_____

File under RETIREMENT PLANNING

Date: _____

FORM   26 ESTIMATED RETIREMENT NEEDS, INCLUDING TAXES

ANNUAL AMOUNT

1.   Estimated Basic Lifestyle Expenditures   _____

2.   Estimated Discretionary Expenditures   _____

3.   TOTAL   _____

4.   Tax Factor (Percentage)   _____

5.   TOTAL Retirement Expenditures
     Including Taxes   _____

File under RETIREMENT PLANNING   Date: _____

FORM 27   RETIREMENT INCOME

Projected Retirement Age: _____   Number of Years to Retirement:_____

1. Estimated Annual Retirement Needs   _____

2. Estimated Annual Income from Retirement
       Plans (other than lump-sum distributions)

    a. Old Age Security and Canada or
        Quebec Pension Plan   _____

    b. Company Retirement Plan   _____

    c. Deferred Compensation   _____

    d. Other Retirement Plans   _____

3. TOTAL Annual Income from Retirement Plans   _____

4. Annual Income Gap   _____

5. Retirement Capital Required to Fill Gap

    a. Estimated Pre-tax Rate of Return   _____

    b. Retirement Capital Required   _____

    6. Sources of Retirement Capital

	INVESTMENT ASSETS	LUMP SUMS FROM RETIREMENT PLANS	RRSPs	TOTAL
a. Value of Present Investment Assets and Retirement Accounts	_____		_____	_____
b. Estimated Rate of Return from now until Retirement	_____		_____	
c. Years until Retirement	_____		_____	
d. Compound Factor from Table 1 (in Appendix I)	_____		_____	
e. Estimated Value of Your Investment Assets and Retirement Accounts at Retirement	_____	_____	_____	_____

Deloitte & Touche Canadian Guide to Personal Financial Management © 1993 Deloitte & Touche

	INVESTMENT ASSETS	RRSPs	OTHER	TOTAL
7. Additional Capital from Annual Investments You Are Planning to Make	_____	_____	_____	_____
a. Annual Amount to be Invested Between Now and Retirement	_____	_____	_____	_____
b. Estimated Rate of Return on Annual Investment	_____	_____	_____	_____
c. Years until Retirement	_____	_____	_____	_____
d. Compound Factor from Table 2 (in Appendix I)	_____	_____	_____	_____
e. Estimated Value of Additional Capital from Your Annual Investments	_____	_____	_____	_____
8. TOTAL Estimated Retirement Capital				_____
9. Additional Capital Needed, if any, to Provide Retirement Income				_____
10. Additional Annual Investment Needed to Provide Capital on Line 9				
a. Estimated Rate of Return from Now until Retirement			_____	
b. Years until Retirement			_____	
c. Compound Factor from Table 2 (in Appendix I)			_____	
d. Annual Amount Required				_____

File under INSURANCE

Date: _____

FORM 28   YOUR PRESENT LIFE INSURANCE COVERAGE

INSURANCE ON YOUR LIFE

Name of Insurance Company	Policy Number	Beneficiary	Type of Policy	Face Value	Cash Surrender Value	Loan on Policy	Owner of Policy
				TOTAL			

INSURANCE ON SPOUSE'S LIFE

Name of Insurance Company	Policy Number	Beneficiary	Type of Policy	Face Value	Cash Surrender Value	Loan on Policy	Owner of Policy
				TOTAL			

File under ESTATE PLANNING   Date: _____

FORM 29   POTENTIAL INCOME TAX LIABILITY ON ASSETS OWNED AT DEATH

NON-DEPRECIABLE CAPITAL ASSETS (UNLESS LEFT TO SPOUSE OR SPOUSAL TRUST)

Number of Units	Description of asset	Adjusted cost base	Current market value	Accrued gain (loss)
_____	_____	$ _____	$ _____	$ _____
_____	_____	$ _____	$ _____	$ _____
_____	_____	$ _____	$ _____	$ _____
_____	_____	$ _____	$ _____	$ _____
_____	_____	$ _____	$ _____	$ _____
_____	_____	$ _____	$ _____	$ _____
_____	_____	$ _____	$ _____	$ _____

Sum of accrued gains (losses) $ _____

Less unused lifetime capital
gains exemptions   (_____)

TOTAL   _____

Three-quarters of Total   _____ 1

Current value of funds and investments held in unmatured RRSPs (unless
spouse or financially dependent children or grandchildren are designated beneficiaries)   _____ 2

Potential income to be added to final tax return (Line 1 + 2) $ _____ 3

Estimated marginal tax rate in year of death   _____ 4

Estimated tax liability on assets owned at death (Line 3 x 4) $ _____ 5

Note: This form does not include income that may result on death from ownership of
other types of assets such as depreciable property, eligible capital property,
resource properties, etc. You should consult a tax expert to estimate your potential tax liability on death, if you own significant amounts of such properties.

File under ESTATE PLANNING   Date: _____

FORM 30   AFTER-TAX VALUE OF ESTATE

1. Total net worth excluding insurance $ _____

2. Present life insurance coverage   _____

3. Potential income tax liability on assets owned at death   (_____)

4. Funeral expenses   (_____)

5. Administrative expenses   (_____)

6. After-tax value of your estate   _____

    (Line 1 + Line 2 - Line 3 - Line 4 - Line 5) $ _____

File under ACTION

Date: _____

FORM 31 INCOME AND EXPENDITURE PROJECTION

Amount desired for long-term objectives:	LAST YEAR	NEXT YEAR
1. Education and Support of Children	_____	_____
2. Retirement	_____	_____
3. Investments	_____	_____
4. Other	_____	_____
5. TOTAL	_____	_____

What's available for long-term objectives:

	LAST YEAR	NEXT YEAR
6. Income		
a. From Employment	_____	_____
b. From Investments and Other Sources	_____	_____
c. TOTAL	_____	_____
7. Basic Expenditures	_____	_____
8. Discretionary Expenditures	_____	_____
9. Income Taxes and Other Deductions		
a. Income Tax	_____	_____
b. Other Deductions	_____	_____
c. TOTAL	_____	_____
10. TOTAL Expenditures and Taxes	_____	_____
11. Amount Available for Long-term Goals	_____	_____

File under ACTION

Date:_____

FORM 32   ACTION STEPS

List 10 specific steps you will take during the next year to implement your personal financial plan.

_____

_____

_____

_____

_____

_____

_____

_____

_____

_____

Glossary of Terms

adjusted cost base — your cost of acquiring an asset plus the cost of any capital additions or improvements in the case of real estate.

advisors — people you use to help you make investment decisions who have experience and expertise greater than your own. These could include a lawyer, chartered accountant, banker, or stockbroker.

assets — things you own that have value in financial terms, such as your house, car, or investments.

buying on margin — the purchase of investments such as stocks and bonds, where a portion of the cost is borrowed from the investment dealer or stockbroker, using investments as collateral.

capital cost allowance — the deduction of the capital cost of equipment or a building over a time period which may be shorter than its estimated useful life.

capital gain — a capital gain is realized to the extent that the selling price of capital property is greater than the sum of its adjusted cost base plus any costs of dispositions. If the selling price is less than this sum, then you have realized a capital loss.

capital property — assets such as shares, bonds and real estate that you hold as an investment.

collateral — assets pledged by a borrower as security for repayment of a loan or other debt.

compound interest — interest paid on interest. This occurs when interest is paid on an investment at periodic intervals which is then added to the amount of the investment. As a result, future interest payments are based on the original investment plus an increasing amount of interest added to it.

consumer price index — a measure of the annual increase in the cost of certain consumer goods and services, which is used as a common indication of the inflation rate.

current return — the annual return on an investment expressed in dollars.

current yield — the annual rate of return on an investment expressed as a percentage.

dividend — an amount paid to a common or preferred shareholder from the earnings of the company.

DPSP — A Deferred Profit Sharing Plan is a vehicle for saving for retirement on a tax-assisted basis. Employer contributions within certain limits are deductible for tax purposes and income earned in the plan accumulates tax-free as long as the funds remain in the plan. When funds are withdrawn from the plan, the amounts received (both capital and income) are generally fully taxable at that time.

estate planning — the process of providing for the orderly transfer of all your assets at death to your chosen beneficiaries in the time frame you select.

fair market value — the value of an asset assuming it is sold to a willing purchaser under normal conditions.

flow through shares — a share that entitles its owner to claim certain deductions or credits that would otherwise only be available to the company. These deductions or credits are "flowed through" to the investors, as if the investor had directly been involved in specific company activities. These shares make sense where the investor will realize a larger benefit from the deductions and credits than the company would.

income deferral — postponement of the taxation of income until a future year.

leverage — the use of borrowed money to acquire investment assets.

liabilities — amounts you owe to various creditors, including bank loans, mortgages, and credit card balances.

liquidity — refers to your ability to respond quickly to an immediate need for cash. This is usually accomplished by holding liquid assets which can be very quickly turned into cash, such as Canada Savings Bonds, Treasury bills, and savings accounts.

margin — the difference between the market value of the investment bought and the loan which the broker will make against it.

money market — short term debt, including Treasury bills, commercial paper, bankers' acceptances, and guaranteed investment certificates from trust companies, which mature in three years or less.

mutual funds — professionally managed pools of investments which provide an individual investor with an opportunity to invest in the stock market or other areas without the responsibility of making specific investments.

net investment loss — is essentially the amount by which your investment losses and expenses in 1987 and later years have exceeded investment income in the same period. This amount will limit your ability to use the capital gains exemption to realize tax-free capital gains.

net worth — the difference between your total assets less your total liabilities.

non-recourse debt — debt secured only by the property purchased with the particular borrowed funds. Therefore if you default on non-recourse debt, the lender can seize the property purchased with the debt but none of your other assets.

QSSP — Quebec residents can claim a deduction for Quebec income tax purposes for the cost of eligible shares contributed to a Quebec Stock Savings Plan. A QSSP is established and administered by a registered broker or other financial institution that retains custody of share certificates contributed to the plan. Only newly issued shares of public corporations are eligible for inclusion in a QSSP.

return — income earned and/or capital gain realized on an investment.

risk — the probability of loss in the future.

RPP — A Registered Pension Plan is a pension plan sponsored by your employer, which is subject to specific government regulations to qualify for registration and the special tax status that confers. Contributions by employees and their employer are deductible for tax purposes within certain limits, and income earned in the plan accumulates tax-free as long as the funds remain in the plan. When funds are withdrawn from the plan, the amounts received (both capital and income) are fully taxable at that time.

RRIF — A Registered Retirement Income Fund can be established with funds from a maturing RRSP to provide retirement income. A minimum amount must be withdrawn each year until the fund ends at age 90, although payments can be increased above this required annual minimum amount.

RRSP — A Registered Retirement Savings Plan allows you to save on a tax-deferred basis for retirement. Up to specified limits, amounts contributed to an RRSP are deductible for tax purposes, and income earned in the plan accumulates free of tax as long as the funds remain in the plan. When funds are withdrawn from the plan, the amounts received (both capital and income) are fully taxable at that time.

surtax — An additional income tax over and above the regular income tax amount. Usually used as a temporary measure to raise funds for short-term needs.

tax bracket — the rate of income tax you pay generally increases as your income exceeds certain limits or brackets. All income within a given tax bracket is taxed at the same rate.

tax credit — tax credits reduce taxes payable to the same extent for all taxpayers, regardless of their income level and marginal tax rate, as opposed to deductions from taxable income which are more valuable as your income and tax rate increases.

tax shelter — a tax shelter is an investment which features significant tax savings, such as immediate deductions or credits or income deferral.

term insurance — term insurance provides protection against risk (such as death) for a specific term or time period, with no investment component.

Treasury bills — short-term government debt which do not pay interest but are sold at discount and mature at par. The difference between the purchase price and par at maturity is your income in lieu of interest.

umbrella coverage — insurance coverage over and above the liability limits of other specific insurance policies.

Index

Deloitte & Touche Offices

National Offices

Toronto (Sun Life Tower)	(416) 599-5399
Toronto (Wellington St W.)	(416) 601-5650
Montréal (Place Ville-Marie)	(514) 393-7115
Montréal (Lloyd's)	(514) 861-8361

British Columbia

Langley	(604) 534-7477
New Westminster	(604) 664-6200
Prince George	(604) 564-1111
Vancouver	(604) 669-4466
Victoria	(604) 360-5000

Alberta

Calgary	(403) 267-1700
Edmonton	(403) 421-3611

Saskatchewan

Prince Albert	(306) 763-7411
Regina	(306) 525-1600
Saskatoon (Midtown Plaza)	(306) 343-4200
Saskatoon (PCS Tower)	(306) 343-4400

Manitoba

Winnipeg	(204) 942-0051

Ontario

Cornwall	(613) 932-5421
Guelph	(519) 822-2000
Hamilton	(905) 523-6770
Hawkesbury	(613) 632-4178
Kitchener	(519) 576-0880
London	(519) 679-1880
Markham	(905) 475-4100
Mississauga	(905) 275-4000
North York	(416) 229-2100
Oshawa	(905) 579-8202
Ottawa	(613) 236-2442
Sarnia	(519) 336-6133
St. Catharines	(416) 688-1841
Toronto (BCE Place)	(416) 601-6150
Toronto (Insolvency - 390 Bay)	(416) 365-0665
Toronto (Braxton Associates)	(416) 601-5683
Waterloo	(519) 747-3207
Windsor	(519) 258-8833

Québec (Samson Bélair/ Deloitte & Touche)

Alma	(418) 668-8325
Amos	(819) 732-8273

Québec (continued)

Baie-Comeau	(418) 589-5761
Chicoutimi	(418) 549-6650
Dolbeau	(418) 276-0133
Farnham	(514) 293-5327
Granby	(514) 372-3347
Grand-Mère	(819) 538-1721
Hull	(819) 770-3221
Jonquière	(418) 542-9523
La Baie (Ville de)	(418) 544-7313
La Malbaie	(418) 665-3965
Lac-Etchemin	(418) 625-5921
Laval	(514) 668-8910
Longueuil	(514) 670-4270
Matagami	(819) 739-2589
Matane	(418) 566-2637
Montréal	(514) 393-7115
Québec	(418) 624-3333
Rimouski	(418) 724-4136
Roberval	(418) 275-2111
Rouyn-Noranda	(819) 762-0958
Saint-Hyacinthe	(514) 774-4000
Senneterre	(819) 737-2614
Sept-Îles	(418) 968-1311
Shawinigan	(819) 537-7281
Sherbrooke	(819) 564-0384
St-Félicien	(418) 679-4711
St-Georges (Ville)	(418) 228-6676
Trois-Pistoles	(418) 851-2232
Trois-Rivières (rue Royale)	(819) 691-1212
Trois Rivières (Insolvency)	(819) 691-1313

New Brunswick

Fredericton	(506) 458-8105
Moncton	(506) 857-8400
Saint John	(506) 632-1080

Nova Scotia

Halifax	(902) 422-8541
Sydney	(902) 564-4517

Prince Edward Island

Charlottetown	(902) 566-2566

Newfoundland

St. John's	(709) 576-8480

NOTES

NOTES